MASTERING COMMAND LEVEL CODING USING COBOL

W. BRUNO   L. BOSLAND

A SPECTRUM BOOK

PRENTICE-HALL, INC.
Englewood Cliffs, New Jersey 07632

Library of Congress Cataloging in Publication Data

Bruno, William.
   CICS: mastering command level coding using COBOL.

   "A Spectrum Book."
   Includes index.
   1. CICS/VS (Computer system) 2. COBOL (Computer
program language) I. Bosland, Lois. II. Title.
III. Title: C.I.C.S.
QA76.6.B7774 1984   001.64'2   84-15091
ISBN 0-13-134040-9

This book is available at a special discount when ordered
in bulk quantities. Contact Prentice-Hall, Inc., General
Publishing Division, Special Sales, Englewood Cliffs, N. J. 07632.

10 9 8 7 6 5 4 3 2

Printed in the United States of America

Editorial/production supervision by Cyndy Lyle Rymer
Editorial assistance by Lori Baronian
Manufacturing buyer: Joyce Levatino
Cover design by Hal Siegel

ISBN 0-13-134040-9 {PBK.}

Prentice-Hall International, Inc., *London*
Prentice-Hall of Australia Pty. Limited, *Sydney*
Prentice-Hall Canada Inc., *Toronto*
Prentice-Hall of India Private Limited, *New Delhi*
Prentice-Hall of Japan, Inc., *Tokyo*
Prentice-Hall of Southeast Asia Pte. Ltd., *Singapore*
Whitehall Books Limited, *Wellington, New Zealand*
Editora Prentice-Hall do Brasil Ltda., *Rio de Janeiro*

CONTENTS

Preface

The purpose of this book is to serve as a primer and a tutorial in the Command Level feature of the Customer Information Control System (CICS). This is accomplished by the use of transactions and programs. Each chapter leads the reader through a presentation of a particular facility, and at the end of the chapter there is a question-and-answer session to help reinforce the ideas previously presented. Diagrams, along with programs, are also used to aid in the presentation. Common Business Oriented Language (COBOL) is the program language used in all programming examples because it is the most widely used. The reader who is versed in Assembler, PL/1, or RPG II will encounter no difficulties with this text because CICS commands work in virtually the same way regardless of the language.

Although this book contains all the elements available within Command Level and explains their use, the intent is that it be used in conjunction with a formal training program in which personalized assistance and guidance can be obtained.

The text is organized in such a manner as to be ideally suited for use as a primer before formal training. Using this approach, the student will feel comfortable and have a grasp of the basics when he or she enters the formal classroom environment.

The book can also serve as a handy reference guide for the newly trained, as well as the experienced, CICS Command Level programmer. So let's proceed to our first topic!

Foreword

Some time ago, I was approached by Bill Bruno with the idea of his writing a CICS textbook for application programmers. Together we decided the book would be based on On-line Software International's highly popular CICS command-level programming class. It could serve as a tool for use either before or after a course and possibly as a reference during a class. It could also be used as a self-teaching guide for those unable to attend a class. So began the odyssey that has resulted in this book.

It had often puzzled me as to why, with the popularity of CICS as a teleprocessing monitor, there were no really good textbooks to help the novice CICS programmer. There are some books around, but these seemed to me to be either technically inferior or geared toward the system programmer—or at least a programmer familiar with programming in Assembler (BAL). Neither of these types would be of much use to the COBOL programmer who wants to find out about CICS Command Level. Why was there no text for such a person?

In working with Lois Bosland and Bill over the past few months, I have come to find out why a book like this did not exist previously. It is far more difficult to produce a text like this than it would at first appear. It took more than just the technical data to write the text.

Those of us who have stood in front of a classroom of students are used to being able to gauge the level of the students and the required pace to follow from the students' visual reaction. That just does not work in a textbook. One must judge the level of the audience and proceed accordingly—and consistently. When questions arise, it is impossible to ask the book!

This difficulty helps explain why there were no good texts on the market. To produce this kind of a book requires not only the technical ability and experience that one can only gain from years of hands-on experience with CICS, but also the communication experience of the stand-up instructor and the experience gained from years of working with people in the applications and systems areas. Lois and Bill have the ideal backgrounds. Their 21 years of combined CICS experience, the past four years as OSI instructors, have given them a keen insight into the needs of the application person. They have written in a manner which endeavors to address those questions usually asked in classroom environments.

There is one additional factor that cannot be forgotten. Many of the other CICS books were written by one or two people working in a "test tube" environment. This tends to result in a one-sided view—either too system-oriented or too application/batch-oriented. The avoidance of this slanting was one of the major efforts in the production of this book. Both authors are employed by On-Line Software International, the most respected firm of its type in the industry today. As such, there were a significant number of people to whom the authors could turn for technical review and evaluation. This helped to produce a high-quality, unbiased book.

People may wonder why OSI would want to see the introduction of a book of this nature. After all, OSI does teach CICS Command Level programming. On reflection, though, one comes to the realization that books of this type are going to be on the market, so it is in the best interests of all concerned if they are books of a technically sound nature. Although no textbooks can totally replace an experienced instructor regardless of any claims made, textbooks are excellent tools in the learning process. It is fully in line with this desire for excellence that OSI has given full support to the development of this textbook. I hope this will benefit both current and future CICS application programmers.

We at OSI would like to commend Bill and Lois for the efforts made in the production of this textbook and we hope that the data processing industry finds it as beneficial as we feel it can be.

Ira W. David
Executive Vice President
On-Line Software International
Fort Lee, New Jersey 07024

On-Line Software International provides software products and software development aids, as well as consulting and educational services, to the rapidly growing market of intermediate and large-scale IBM computer users. OSI has been awarded special membership in both SHARE and GUIDE for its contributions to the industry.

1 Introduction

WHAT IS CICS?

The Customer Information Control System (CICS), which is comprised of many management modules/programs, is a data base/data communication system developed by IBM to run on IBM and IBM-compatible mainframes. The system allows data to be transmitted from a terminal to a computer, have the data processed, access files (another term could be data bases) and then have data transmitted back to the requesting terminal. To do this processing, the system must use a telecommunications package (i.e., VTAM, TCAM, or BTAM) and one or more of the following file access methods: VSAM, BDAM, ISAM, or DL/I. Thus it can be stated that CICS is a data base/data communication (DB/DC) system. CICS will support the following program languages: COBOL, Assembler, PL/I, RPG II. Also, there are two coding levels of CICS. Macro is similar to Assembler, and Command is similar to COBOL. Keep in mind that CICS runs under the control of the operating system.

WHAT IS ON-LINE PROCESSING?

On-line processing as known to CICS is accepting information (data) from a terminal, manipulating that information, and then sending a message back to the user. All this usually can be done in a matter of seconds in a

Figure 1-1.

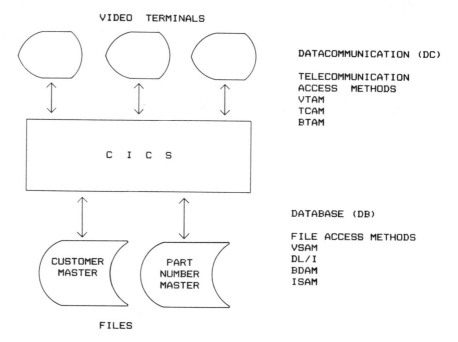

Figure 1-1 clearly illustrates that CICS is truly a DB/DC system.

well-designed CICS system. In many companies, a quick response is very important. Let's examine the following example, which will be used throughout this book to illustrate how CICS functions.

An individual decides to order some seeds for the garden from the Happy Seed Company. The individual (now a customer) takes the order form from the Happy Seed Company catalog and writes down the seeds (products) desired along with the quantity and price. In effect, the product has now become a line item consisting of a quantity, price and product description. The entire order, along with a check, is mailed to the company. The company receives the order two days later and begins to process it. The order is received by the data entry department, which enters the information onto disk storage. The information, along with other orders, is sent to the data processing department. The DP department will now run a job to process the information and produce a paper report along with shipping invoices. The invoices must now be sent to the shipping department. When shipping gets the invoices, it can then assemble the order and mail it. The customer would probably receive the order two days after mailing. As one can see, the entire process could take between 5 and 7 days. Well, the Happy Seed Co. decided that this process is too long because of customer complaints and competition. Some other seed companies are placing and delivering orders much faster. So the company decides to install CICS because they have been told it can cut the entire time in half. Let's see how this is possible.

The company established a toll free number for customer orders and will accept credit cards as a form of payment. Now a customer simply has to dial a number to place an order. This alone has removed at least two days from the order process. The company has also employed individuals (operators) to answer the phones. When a customer calls to order, the operator must have a tool to log the order information. The tool used will be a cathode ray tube (CRT). When the operator has collected all the necessary information, the order is immediately sent to the host CPU for processing. After the processing has been completed, an order accepted message is sent back to the operator's CRT along with an order number. The operator can inform the customer of the order number and complete the order. The operator is now finished and can await a call from another customer and repeat the process.

When the order-accepted message was sent to the operator, a message was also sent to the shipping department to ship the order. This entire process could be accomplished within an extremely short period of time. Thus, the order is in the mail the same day as it was placed. With this process, we have removed at least 3 to 4 days.

The benefits are obvious: a satisfied customer, rapid order processing within the company, faster customer billing, and a sharper competitive edge. This is a very typical on-line system and will be referred to throughout the course of this book to illustrate the concepts of CICS.

So we could summarize on-line processing as follows: the process of accepting information from a device (in our example the CRT), processing the information, and sending a message to the appropriate areas (again in our example to the operator and the shipping department) in a matter of seconds.

Thus, a very key element to on-line processing is response time. In our example, there are two levels of response. From the operator's point of view, response can be measured from the time data was sent to CICS to the time a message was sent back. From the customer's point of view, response can be measured from the moment the operator answered the phone until the time the conversation ends. Fortunately, operator response time can be controlled through proper application design and proper programming techniques. In this book, we cover the best programming techniques to use to optimize response time.

Obviously, if response time is very slow it can cause tremendous user dissatisfaction because the user must be kept waiting. In addition, the company must pay for additional phone time in our example, and if there is an increase in order volume, more operators may be required.

2 Transaction Flow

CICS SYSTEM INITIALIZATION

The following will be a somewhat detailed explanation of the internal workings of CICS. Although it is possible to write programs in CICS without this knowledge, an understanding of the internals will result in more efficient code and better application designs. More efficient programs and better designs will give better response time, thus keeping the customer satisfied!

The CICS system normally runs in its own partition, region, or address space (whatever the current terminology is). From that standpoint, CICS and batch are similar because both run in their own regions. In fact, if one were to look at the job control of CICS and batch, there would be many similarities. The operating system also views CICS as it would any batch job with the exception that CICS is a very long-running job and usually has a very high priority (Figure 2-1).

Before we continue, let's assume that we arrive at our company and decide to work with CICS. We go to the terminal and find that CICS is not active. At this time, we call the computer operations department and request them to bring up CICS. The operations department will submit the CICS bring-up deck (job control). Figure 2-2 is an example of OS job control.

Figure 2-1.

```
          C  P  U
 -----------------------------------------------------------------
 :        :               :        :        :          :
 : BATCH  :  PRODUCTION   : BATCH  :  TEST  :  BATCH   :
 :        :               :        :        :          :
 : JOB    :     CICS      : JOB    :  CICS  :   JOB    :
 :_____:_____:_____:_____:_____:
```

Figure 2-2.

```
//CICSPROD JOB CLASS=W,REGION=4096K
//VERIFY    EXEC PGM=IDCAMS
//SYSPRINT DD SYSOUT=A
//DFHINTRA DD DSN=CICS.PROD.DFHINTRA,DISP=OLD
//DFHTEMP  DD DSN=CICS.PROD.DFHTSDS,DISP=OLD
//CUSTMAS  DD DSN=CUSTOMER.MASTER,DISP=SHR
//PARTMAS  DD DSN=PART.NUMBER.MASTER,DISP=SHR
//SYSIN    DD *
VERIFY FILE(DFHINTRA)
VERIFY FILE(DFHTSDS)
VERIFY FILE(CUSTMAS)
VERIFY FILE(PARTMAS)
//CICS      EXEC PGM=DFHSIP,
//          PARM=('SIT=01','FCT=01','DCT=01','PCT=01',
//               'PPT=01','TCT=01','MONITOR=(ACC,PER,EXC)'
//               'CMP=NO','OSCOR=102400','PLTPI=01')
//STEPLIB  DD DSN=CICS.LOADLIB,DISP=SHR
//SYSUDUMP DD SYSOUT=A
//DFHRPL   DD DSN=CICS.LOADLIB,DISP=SHR
//****    DUMP DATA SETS                  ********
//DFHDMPA  DD DSN=CICS.DUMPA,DISP=SHR
//DFHDMPB  DD DSN=CICS.DUMPB,DISP=SHR
//DFHSNAP  DD SYSOUT=A,OUTLIM=0
//****    AUTOMATIC STATISTICS DATA SET   ********
//DFHSTM   DD DSN=CICS.STATM,DISP=SHR
//DFHSTN   DD DSN=CICS.STATN,DISP=SHR
//****    INTRAPARTITION DATA SET         ********
//DFHINTRA DD DSN=CICS.DFHINTRA,DISP=(OLD,KEEP)
//****    AUXILIARY TEMPORARY STORAGE     ********
//DFHTEMP  DD DSN=CICS.DFHTSDS,DISP=OLD
//****    RESTART DATA SET                ********
//DFHRSD   DD DSN=CICS.DFHRSD,DISP=OLD
//****    EXTRAPARTITION DATA SETS        ********
//STATS    DD SYSOUT=*,DCB=(DSORG=PS,RECFM=V,BLKSIZE=136)
//INTRDR1  DD SYSOUT=(A,INTRDR),
//           DCB=(RECFM=FB,LRECL=80,BLKSIZE=80)
//****    JOURNAL DATA SETS               ********
//DFHJ01A  DD DSN=CICS.DFHJ01A,DISP=OLD
//****    APPLICATION DATASETS            ********
//CUSTMAS  DD DSN=CUSTOMER.MASTER,DISP=SHR
//PARTMAS  DD DSN=PART.NUMBER.MASTER,DISP=SHR
//****    THE FOLLOWING LIST THE DUMP DATASETS    *
//DUMP01   EXEC PGM=DFHDUP,PARM=SINGLE,COND=EVEN
//STEPLIB  DD DSN=CICS.LOADLIB,DISP=SHR
//DFHDMPDS DD DSN=CICS.DUMPA,DISP=SHR
//DFHPRINT DD SYSOUT=A
//DUMP02   EXEC PGM=DFHDUP,PARM=SINGLE,COND=EVEN
//STEPLIB  DD DSN=CICS.LOADLIB,DISP=SHR
//DFHDMPDS DD DSN=CICS.DUMPB,DISP=SHR
//DFHPRINT DD SYSOUT=A
```

Figure 2-3.

```
// JOB CICS
// OPTION LOG,NOFASTTR
// UPSI 001
// ASSGN SYS019,X'385'
// ASSGN SYS030,X'071'
// ASSGN SYS040,DISK,VOL=CICS01,SHR
// DLBL DFHJ01A,'CICS SYSTEM JOURNAL',0,SD
// EXTENT SYS012,MSTR02,1,0,14220,30
// DLBL DFHTEMP,'CICS.TEMP.STORAGE',,VSAM
// DLBL DFHNTRA,'CICS.INTRA.TRANS.DATA',,VSAM
// DLBL DFHDMPA,'CICS.DUMPA',0,SD
// EXTENT SYS040,CICS01,1,0,612,12
// DLBL DFHDMPB,'CICS.DUMPB',0,SD
// EXTENT SYS040,CICS01,1,0,624,12
// DLBL DFHSTM,'CICS.AUTO.STATS',0,SD
// EXTENT SYS040,CICS01,1,0,636,12
// DLBL DFHSTN,'CICS.STATN',0,SD
// EXTENT SYS040,CICS01,1,0,648,12
// DLBL CUSTMAS,'CUSTOMER.MASTER.CLUSTER',,VSAM
// DLBL PARTMAS,'PART.MASTER.CLUSTER',,VSAM
LIBDEF CL,SEARCH=(PRODPCL,PLANPCL),TEMP
// EXEC DFHSIP,SIZE=3200K
/*
/&
```

Figure 2-3 is an example of DOS job control.

Once the job has been submitted, CICS will go through a phase called initialization. All this means is that the necessary files will be opened, terminal communication established, programs loaded and any other initial work that must take place prior to CICS actually becoming available for user activity (our use). Figure 2-4 represents a typical CICS region after the initialization process has been completed.

Components of a CICS Region

Let's examine the terms in Figure 2-4. First we have the nucleus. It is comprised of all the management modules of CICS along with their respective tables. (The tables will be explained as they are encountered. Remember, we are trying to get the big picture!) Another part of the nucleus is the Common System Area (CSA) which contains the addresses of all CICS control blocks and storage areas. An area which is appended to the CSA is the Common Work Area (CWA) which is an installation (company) defined. The CWA could hold critical information such as interest rates, next customer number to assign, next invoice number to assign; all programs within CICS can then access the information.

The next area we have is the resident area. Programs which are frequently used can be kept in this area. This is a good idea since it will help to improve response time, which we mentioned was critical in an on-line environment. Following the resident area is the Dynamic Storage Area (DSA) where all CICS work is processed. So, let's take another look at the region with additional information. We will view the region as being comprised of only two parts: the nucleus and the dynamic storage area (DSA). See Figure 2-5.

Figure 2-4.

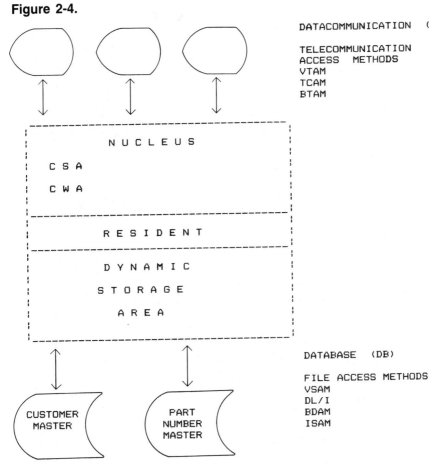

DATACOMMUNICATION   (DC)

TELECOMMUNICATION
ACCESS   METHODS
VTAM
TCAM
BTAM

DATABASE   (DB)

FILE ACCESS METHODS
VSAM
DL/I
BDAM
ISAM

Figure 2-5.

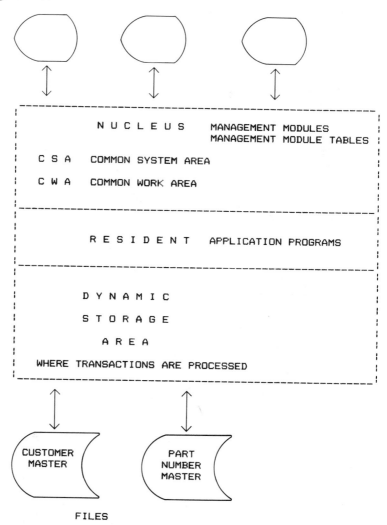

FILES

The preceding illustrations should give you, the application programmer, a good overall understanding of how a CICS region is set up. There are other internal areas, but they are not needed by the application programmer and are better left to the system programmer.

Next, we will go into a little more detail about how work gets processed in CICS. Let's assume in our example that before the operator accepts the customer order, the operator would like to know if the customer is already on the customer master file. The operator would enter the following on the cathode ray tube (CRT):

Figure 2-6.

```
INQX,SMITH_
```

and the enter key would now be pressed.

The first four characters (INQX) make up the transaction code. A transaction as known to CICS is made up of one or more application programs and the necessary resources needed to accomplish a unit of work. The unit of work in our example is the operator checking to determine if the customer is already on the file, which is a VSAM file. The operator is notifying CICS that there is work to do by pressing the enter key. One of the first things CICS must do is get the information which was on the CRT and bring it into the DSA of the region. The management module responsible for this is the terminal control program (TCP). To get the information, one of the following telecommunication access methods will be used: VTAM, TCAM, or BTAM. We will use VTAM (Figure 2-7) for our examples.

Figure 2-7.

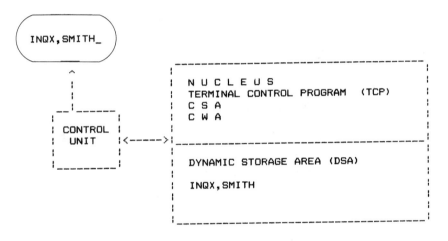

Now that the information (INQX,SMITH) is in the DSA, it can be processed. We stated that the customer master file must be read to determine if the name SMITH exists. This request is made by the application program. The management module needed to accomplish this is the file control program (FCP) which resides in the nucleus. The FCP will issue a VSAM request to get SMITH (Figure 2-8).

Let's assume that Smith is not on the file. The FCP will notify the application program of this and the application program will send a message back to the terminal informing the operator of the situation and our transaction will be terminated (see Figure 2-9).

Figure 2-8.

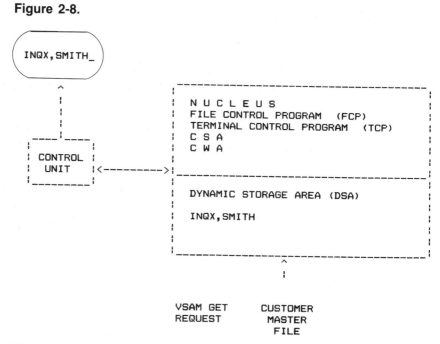

VSAM GET   CUSTOMER
REQUEST   MASTER
             FILE

Figure 2-9.

RECORD NOT FOUND_

Let's review what we have learned thus far by answering the following questions.

EXERCISE

1. Describe the general layout of a CICS region and explain the function of each area.
2. Explain a transaction and what it comprises.
3. a) Explain the function of the terminal control program.
   b) State the teleprocessing access methods that are supported.
4. a) Explain the function of the file control program.
   b) State the file access methods that are supported.
5. What is on-line processing?

3 Transaction Processing

We will build on our knowledge from the previous chapters and see in more technical detail how a transaction is processed by using the example from Chapter 2.

When the operator presses the enter key, the terminal control program (TCP) eventually gets control and detects that there is some input data (message) to process at terminal E567 (see Figure 3-1).

Figure 3-1.

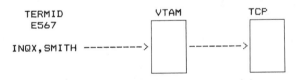

The TCP has to verify that this terminal is valid. TCP is able to do this by searching its terminal control table (TCT). The TCT contains all the terminals that are known to this particular version of CICS, with each terminal being uniquely named by a four-character terminal ID. Each terminal will have its own control block. A control block is simply a piece of storage containing information. The control block for each terminal is called a terminal control table terminal entry (TCTTE). Some of the information about the terminal would be: terminal ID, model number, screen size, and status. So, if we had a small network of ten terminals, there would be ten TCTTEs in the TCT (Figure 3-2). The TCT table resides in the nucleus along with the TCP.

Figure 3-2.

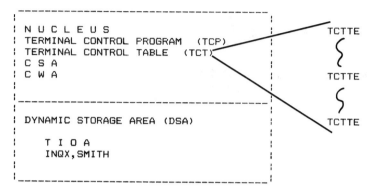

When the terminal has been verified, storage must be acquired so that the data (message) which came in can be saved. Since this area is associated with a terminal, the area is called a terminal input/output area (TIOA). The TIOA resides in the DSA (see Figure 3-2).

The storage control program (SCP) acquired the storage for the TIOA. The SCP, another management module, resides in the nucleus and uses the page allocation map (PAM), which is created at CICS system initialization, to manage the DSA. SCP's function is to manage the DSA.

The TCTTE resides in the nucleus and the TIOA resides in the DSA, so to associate these two control blocks, the address of the TIOA is placed in the TCTTE (see Figure 3-3). The two control blocks are now chained together.

Figure 3-3.

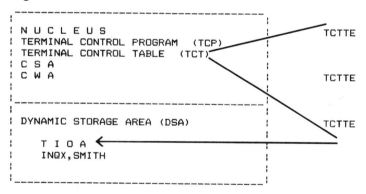

Next, the four-character transaction code (INQX) must be verified. The management module responsible for this is the task control program (KCP). It will search its associated table, the program control table (PCT), for the transaction code. This table contains all the transaction codes known to CICS. Before we stated that a transaction consists of one or more programs and the necessary resources needed to accomplish a unit of work. So the first program to be called by the transaction must also be in the PCT. Figure 3-4 illustrates a typical PCT entry.

Figure 3-4.

```
Program Control Table

TRANSID    PROGRAM        TWA
INQX       INQXPGM         0
```

After the transaction is found, a task control area (TCA) is acquired. The TCA may have an optional transaction work area (TWA) appended (see Figure 3-5). The size of the TWA is stated in the PCT for each transaction. The TWA can be used to pass information between programs within a transaction.

Figure 3-5.

```
--------
| TCA  |
|------|
| TWA  |
|------|
```

The TCA control block can reside anywhere in the DSA. We stated before that the TCTTE and the TIOA were chained together because they resided in different locations. The same is true for the TCA. The address of the TCTTE will be placed in the TCA and vice versa. Thus, all three control blocks are chained together (see Figure 3-6).

Figure 3-6.

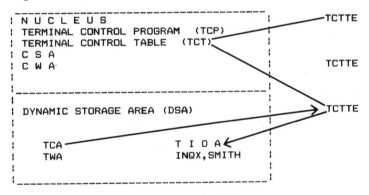

Let's examine our ten terminal network. If there were 10 operators and each operator keyed in the same transaction INQX and a name, CICS would get very confused because the same transaction is coming from 10 different terminals. To avoid this confusion, CICS assigns each incoming transaction a unique number. This number is called the task sequence number. Wait a minute! We have changed our terminology from transaction to task! A task is simply one iteration of a transaction. CICS must work with tasks and the user works with transactions.

Going back to our example, the TCA is created, and a unique task sequence number is assigned and placed in the TCA. An executive interface block (EIB) is also created and becomes part of the TCA. The EIB contains selected information from the various control blocks. This allows the Command Level program to obtain system information, if needed, without accessing system control blocks. Next, TCP will get control back and finish processing all the other terminals in our network. Eventually another management module, the program control program (PCP), will get control and will begin to process our task.

For our task to begin, CICS must locate the object module for program INQXPGM. The function of the program control program (PCP) is to locate application programs by using its associated table, the processing program table (PPT). Hence, the PPT will be searched for program INQXPGM. The PPT will also indicate whether the object module is in memory or out on the object load library disk. If out on the load library disk, the program must be brought into memory. The language the application program is written in, i.e., COBOL, PL/I, Assembler, or RPG II, is defined in the PPT as well (see Figure 3-7).

Figure 3-7.

```
Processing Program Table (PPT)

PROGRAM    LANGUAGE     CORE      DISK

INQXPGM    COBOL        0000      XXXX
```

Next, the PCP will determine if this is a Command Level program (our program is) and will make a unique copy of the original Working-Storage Section (thus becoming another control block in the DSA) and chain it off the TCA. Since our task has its own unique copy of Working-Storage, the program can modify any part of it without destroying the program's reentrancy.

You may be asking yourself why this is being mentioned. Let's examine our ten-terminal network again. We stated that 10 operators could enter the same transaction and CICS will not get confused because each transaction would become a task and assigned its own task sequence number. In addition, each task would have its own copy of Working-Storage. So far everything is fine, but the tasks would be using the same program. Remember, each task DID NOT get its own copy of the program; hence, all 10 tasks would be using the same program.

In CICS, whenever a program issues a CICS command, the program loses control and the task has the potential to lose control. Thus, if our task loses control, another task will get a chance to run. In CICS this is known as multitasking, which is simply the process of handling more than one task at a time. But it presents a problem. If our task loses control and another task gains control, the second task might be using the same program. To reduce the potential problems, the application program must be written as a reentrant program. A reentrant program is one that does not modify itself. We can modify Working-Storage since each task gets its own copy. The Linkage Section is also reentrant since it references areas which are external to our application program. Thus, in Command Level CICS, we do not have to concern ourselves with application program reenterability, providing Working-Storage and/or the Linkage Section is used.

At this point, our application program is given control. The program will do the following:

Receive the input data (message) from the terminal
Process the input message
Send the output data (message) to the terminal
Return control to CICS, thereby terminating the task

In general, all CICS programs do very similar processing to our program. Editing of the input is usually very similar to batch programming (Figure 3-8).

Figure 3-8.

CICS	BATCH
RECEIVE INPUT FROM TERMINAL	READ A RECORD
PROCESS THE MESSAGE	PROCESS THE RECORD
SEND MESSAGE TO TERMINAL	PRINT A MESSAGE
TERMINATE PROGRAM	GO BACK TO READ A RECORD

The relevant differences between on-line and batch are:

1. Response time is CRITICAL in on-line.
2. CICS interfaces with humans.

EXERCISE

Let's review what we have already learned.

1. Indicate the differences between a transaction and a task.
2. a) Describe a reentrant program.
   b) Why must CICS programs be reentrant?
3. a) Explain the function of the task control program.
   b) What is the purpose of the program control table?
4. a) Explain the function of the program control program.
   b) What is the purpose of the processing program table?
5. Define multitasking.
6. What is the EIB?

4 CICS Essentials

CICS COMMAND PARAMETERS

Before proceeding any further, let's review what we have learned from the previous three chapters. To begin with, CICS and batch jobs are similar because the operating system views them as single entities that run in their own regions. In a batch application (e.g., credit report, audit trail), only one program is using the resources associated with that job at any given time. The resources could be files, storage areas, programs, etc. Also the application (programs) directly communicates with the operating system.

CICS is very different. Within the region, many applications (e.g., order entry, customer maintenance, credit, shipping, etc.) could be run concurrently. Remember that this is possible because of the multitasking capability of CICS. Since many tasks will be active at the same time in the region, they must all SHARE the same resources (e.g., files, storage areas, programs, etc.). If the sharing is not done efficiently, bottlenecks will appear. The result will be tasks waiting for other tasks. This will cause the response time to slow down, creating an irate user! As we learn about the facilities of CICS, the sharing concept will also be mentioned.

It was stated before that a batch program communicates directly with the operating system. For a batch program to read a record, it must first open the file, read the record, wait for the I/O to complete, finish the edit, close the file, and terminate. Again, this is very logical, since the application program is not concerned with sharing. But in CICS this would create chaos!

If task 1 began to process, opened a file and read a record, it would have to wait for the I/O to complete. While task 1 is waiting, task 2 starts up (multitasking) and perhaps it uses the same program as task 1. When task 2 tries to open the file, problems immediately occur because the file is already opened and the results would be unpredictable. To alleviate this condition, certain rules must be adhered to in CICS.

The first rule is that an application program should not communicate directly with the operating system as in batch programming. When a program wants to make a request of the operating system, it must make the request to CICS, which in turn will communicate with the operating system. The way to do this is by having the application program issue a CICS command (Figure 4–1).

Figure 4-1.

```
APPL <----------> CICS <----------> OPERATING <----------> VSAM
PGM                                 SYSTEM                 FILE
```

The next rule is that application programs, in general, should not open or close files. This is done by CICS at the appropriate times.

The last rule pertains to COBOL only. In a batch COBOL program, a STOP RUN/GOBACK verb is needed. If the application program does not provide one, the COBOL compiler usually inserts one after the last paragraph in the program. When the verb is executed, the batch region is terminated. We must be careful in a CICS program. Why? Remember that the operating system views CICS as a long-running batch job. If a STOP RUN verb is executed, the CICS region will terminate. The entire network will shut down! Hopefully we want to avoid this situation.

We need a method to keep the COBOL compiler happy and CICS happy. The way to do this is by placing the STOP RUN/GOBACK verb somewhere in our program where it will never be executed. The place to do this is after a RETURN or XCTL command (Chapter 6).

Every CICS program must have a RETURN or XCTL command in it. Only one of these two commands is needed. If we forget to use a STOP RUN/GOBACK verb, the COBOL compiler will insert one after the last statement in the program and could cause disastrous results.

In addition to these rules other guidelines need to be followed to ensure good response. The application program should transmit as few characters as possible to the terminal. The number of file input/output requests should be kept to a minimum since I/O is very slow. In addition, the application program should try to use fall-through logic minimizing PERFORMs and GO TOs. This is essential because of virtual storage paging. To obtain a complete list of guidelines consult the IBM Application Programmer Reference Manual (APRM) for the release of CICS you are using.

You may be asking yourself, "Where can these CICS commands be inserted in a program?" Answer: anywhere in a program where an executable statement can be placed.

Let's see how to properly code a CICS command.

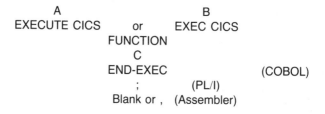

```
        A                      B
   EXECUTE CICS      OR    EXEC CICS
                C
            END-EXEC
```

All commands must begin with option A or B and end with option C. The form of option C differs by programming language.

```
        A                      B
   EXECUTE CICS      or    EXEC CICS
            FUNCTION
                C
            END-EXEC              (COBOL)
                 ;        (PL/I)
            Blank or ,  (Assembler)
```

The FUNCTION is mandatory. It represents the request the program is making such as READ, WRITE, or DELETE a record. The various functions will be explained in the following chapters. There are a few commands that have only a FUNCTION, but

```
   EXEC CICS FUNCTION
            OPTION
            END-EXEC
```

generally the commands have one or more options. DATASET, INTO, and FROM are only some of the many possibilities. Again, the options will be explained with the commands as they are encountered. The order of the options is not important.

```
   EXEC CICS FUNCTION
            OPTION (ARGUMENT)
            OPTION
            END-EXEC
```

Associated with each OPTION there may or may not be an ARGUMENT.

After the commands have been placed in an application program, the source program code is processed by the command language translator. It translates the commands into the programming statements for the language being used (i.e., COBOL) so the program can be compiled and link-edited. As an example, the command language translator would translate:

```
   EXEC CICS RECEIVE MAP(X') END-EXEC
```

to

```
   MOVE '             ' to DFHEIV0
   MOVE 'X' TO DFHEIV1
   CALL 'DFHEIV1' USING DFHEIV0 DFHEIV1 AI
```

The DFHEIVs are names automatically included in Working-Storage as part of the translate and compile process and are reserved. Here is a copy of the DFHEIV member from a COBOL program.

```
COPY DFHEIVAR.
01    DFHEIV.
      02 DFHEIV0      PICTURE X(26).
      02 DFHEIV1      PICTURE X(8).
      02 DFHEIV2      PICTURE X(8).
      02 DFHEIV3      PICTURE X(8).
      02 DFHEIV4      PICTURE X(6).
      02 DFHEIV5      PICTURE X(4).
      02 DFHEIV6      PICTURE X(4).
      02 DFHEIV7      PICTURE X(2).
      02 DFHEIV8      PICTURE X(2).
      02 DFHEIV9      PICTURE X(1).
      02 DFHEIV10     PICTURE S9(7) USAGE COMP-3.
      02 DFHEIV11     PICTURE S9(4) USAGE COMP.
      02 DFHEIV12     PICTURE S9(4) USAGE COMP.
      02 DFHEIV13     PICTURE S9(4) USAGE COMP.
      02 DFHEIV14     PICTURE S9(4) USAGE COMP.
      02 DFHEIV15     PICTURE S9(4) USAGE COMP.
      02 DFHEIV16     PICTURE S9(9) USAGE COMP.
      02 DFHEIV17     PICTURE X(4).
      02 DFHEIV18     PICTURE X(4).
      02 DFHEIV19     PICTURE X(4).
      02 DFHEIV97     PICTURE S9(7) USAGE COMP-3   VALUE ZERO.
      02 DFHEIV98     PICTURE S9(4) USAGE COMP     VALUE ZERO.
      02 DFHEIV99     PICTURE X(1)                 VALUE SPACE.
```

The translate and compile process will also insert the executive interface block (EIB) as the first area in the Linkage Section of the program and at execution time CICS provides automatic addressability to the EIB. The following is a copy of the EIB. The EIB control block contains information extracted from various CICS control blocks which allows us to obtain the information without accessing the actual control blocks. We have included a list of the field names along with their offset and the length.

The fields in the EIB will contain zeros if no meaningful value is present and the fields should not be modified.

EIBAID	Contains the one character hex representation of the key pressed by the operator.
EIBCALEN	Contains the size of the communication area passed from the previous program by use of the COMMAREA and LENGTH options. When no communication area is present, the field will contain zeros.
EIBCPOSN	Contains the cursor position associated with the last terminal input operation.
EIBDATE	Contains the date the task was initiated.
EIBDS	Contains the name of the DATASET last referenced in a file control request.
EIBFN	Contains a value representing the last command executed by the task (updated when the function has been completed).
EIBRCODE	Contains the response code returned after the command has been completed.

HEX OFFSET	EXEC FIELD NAME	LENGTH BYTES
0	EIBTIME	4
4	EIBDATE	4
8	EIBTRNID	4
C	EIBTASKN	4
10	EIBTRMID	4
14	EIBRSVD1	2
16	EIBCPOSN	2
18	EIBCALEN	2
1A	EIBAID	1
1B	EIBFN	2
1D	EIBRCODE	6
23	EIBDS	8
2B	EIBREQID	8
33	EIBRSRCE	8
3B	EIBSYNC	1
3C	EIBFREE	1
3D	EIBRECV	1
3E	EIBSEND	1
3F	EIBATT	1
40	EIBEOC	1
41	EIBFMH	1

EIBRSRCE   Contains the name of the resource last used in an I/O request.
EIBTASKN   Contains the task's sequence number.
EIBTIME   Contains the time the task was started.
EIBTRMID   Contains the term ID associated with the task.
EIBTRNID   Contains the transaction ID of the task.

The above is a partial list of the fields in the EIB. They are also the most often referenced fields by a program. For a complete listing consult the IBM APRM.

ARGUMENT VALUES

The possible argument values that can be specified in commands are:

    NAME
    POINTER-REF
    DATA-AREA
    LABEL
    DATA-VALUE

Let's use the following COBOL example to illustrate the argument values. Remember the options will be explained later.

As illustrated in our task example, we wanted to see if a customer was already on the CUSTMAS file. When the request to read the file was passed to CICS, it had to include the NAME of the file. We will see this is coded as DATASET(NAME). Another way to indicate a NAME would be:

```
WORKING-STORAGE SECTION.
01   WSWORKAREA.
     02 CUSTNAME              PIC X(8)      VALUE 'CUSTMAS'.
PROCEDURE DIVISION.
     EXEC CICS READ
          DATASET(CUSTNAME)    or      DATASET('CUSTMAS')
```

Therefore the NAME argument can either be a literal or a label where a value has been placed. The next type of argument, DATA-AREA would be used to indicate where in Working-Storage we would like the record placed-INTO(DATA-AREA). We would have to replace DATA-AREA with the label of a group or elementary item.

```
WORKING-STORAGE SECTION.
01   WSWORKAREA.
     02 CUSTNAME              PIC X(8)      VALUE 'CUSTMAS'.
01   CUSTREC.
     02  CUSTLASTNAME         PIC X(20).
PROCEDURE DIVISION.
     EXEC CICS READ
          DATASET(CUSTNAME)    or      DATASET('CUSTMAS')
          INTO(CUSTREC)        or      INTO(CUSTLASTNAME)
```

In addition, we must tell CICS the size of the area-LENGTH(DATA-AREA). In this instance the DATA-AREA must be an elementary item and either a half or fullword containing the length value. Lengths are generally specified as binary halfwords.

```
WORKING-STORAGE SECTION.
01   WSWORKAREA.
     02 CUSTNAME              PIC X(8)      VALUE 'CUSTMAS'.
     02 RECLEN                PIC S9(4)     COMP VALUE +20.
01   CUSTREC.
     02 CUSTLASTNAME          PIC X(20).
PROCEDURE DIVISION.
     EXEC CICS READ
          DATASET(CUSTNAME)    or      DATASET('CUSTMAS')
          INTO(CUSTREC)        or      INTO(CUSTLASTNAME)
          LENGTH(RECLEN)
```

Not only do we need to identify the file, but we also are requesting a specific customer's record. Therefore, we must supply the record ID (key)-RIDFLD(CUSTKEY). But perhaps the key of the file is actually last name, first name. We are only supplying the first part of the key. When doing this we must also tell CICS the length of the key we are supplying-KEYLENGTH(DATA-VALUE). A DATA-VALUE argument can be a constant KEYLENGTH('5') or a label of a half or fullword field containing the value.

```
WORKING-STORAGE SECTION.
01   WSWORKAREA.
        02 DNAME                      PIC X(8)        VALUE 'CUSTMAS'.
        02 RECLEN                     PIC S9(4) COMP  VALUE +20.
        02 KEYLEN                     PIC S9(4) COMP  VALUE +5.
        02 CUSTKEY                    PIC X(30)       VALUE 'SMITH'.
01   CUSTREC.
        02 CUSTLASTNAME                   PIC X(20).
PROCEDURE DIVISION.
     EXEC CICS READ
          DATASET(DNAME)        or       DATASET('CUSTMAST')
          INTO(CUSTREC)         or       INTO(CUSTLASTNAME)
          LENGTH(RECLEN)
          RIDFLD(CUSTKEY)
          KEYLENGTH(KEYLEN)     or       KEYLENGTH('5')
     END EXEC
```

There will be times when it is necessary to reference an area which is external (not part of) to our program. The CWA would be an example. Before we can access any information in the CWA, we need to get a pointer to it. This function uses a SET(POINTER-REF) option. The POINTER-REF argument is the name of a Linkage Section field (base locator) where we want CICS to place the pointer to (address of) the CWA.

```
LINKAGE SECTION.
01   FILLER.
        02 FILLER                 PIC S9(8) COMP.
        02 CWAPTR                 PIC S9(8) COMP.
PROCEDURE DIVISION.
     EXEC CICS ADDRESS CWA
          SET(CWAPTR)
     END EXEC
```

The last argument, LABEL, is how a Procedure Division paragraph or section name is specified. Perhaps a customer named Smith does not exist on our file. We would want CICS to handle this condition by branching to paragraph NEW-CUST.

```
PROCEDURE DIVISION.
     EXEC CICS HANDLE CONDITION
          NOTFOUND(NEW-CUST)
     END EXEC.


          ¦
          ¦
NEW-CUST.
```

Although we have been using commands to illustrate arguments, don't be confused. These commands will be fully explained later. What we're trying to understand now is arguments, so let's review.

NAME	Literal DATASET('CUSTMAS') or label DATASET(DCUST)
DATA-AREA	A group or elementary label INTO(CUSTREC) or INTO(CUSTNAME)
	An elementary label of a half or fullword LENGTH(RECLEN)
DATA-VALUE	A constant or an elementary label of a half or fullword KEYLENGTH('5') or KEYLENGTH(KEYLEN)

POINTER-REF Label of a Linkage Section base locator SET(CWAPTR)

LABEL   A Procedure Division paragraph or section name
          NOTFOUND(NEW-CUST).

Now let's start using and understanding commands.

ERROR HANDLING

Whenever commands are executed, there is always the possibility of something going wrong (i.e., record not found, duplicate record, etc.). The application program can check for possible errors by executing the following command:

```
EXEC CICS HANDLE CONDITION condition (LABEL)
                        condition (LABEL)
                        ERROR (LABEL)
                        END-EXEC
```

The command must be executed prior to the error situation arising. It sets up a number of GO TO branches depending on the condition listed. A condition is the error (i.e. not found, duplicate record, etc.). For each command in CICS there are a number of error conditions and these conditions are called Exception Conditions. As commands are explained in the following chapters, the Exception Conditions for them will be listed along with the default action.

Every HANDLE CONDITION can have a maximum of 12 conditions. If more are needed, another HANDLE CONDITION command can be executed. The HANDLE CONDITION command is valid only for the issuing program and remains active until the end of the program or until another HANDLE CONDITION command overrides it. The conditions can be coded in any order in the command. The ERROR condition provides a generalized routine to go to if no other Exception Condition has been provided. When control goes to the generalized routine, it is possible for the application program to check for specific errors. To do this, the EIB fields EIBFN and EIBRCODE would be used. The following tables on pages 24 and 25 give the hex representation and meaning of each.

If ERROR is included it will only take effect if no other conditions are processed in the command.

Normally if no HANDLE CONDITION command is executed, the application program will only get control back if the command request (i.e., READ, WRITE, etc.) is successful. An unsuccessful request will generally result in abnormal task termination.

As previously stated, the HANDLE CONDITION command causes unconditional branching. If the application program wants to get control back immediately after the CICS request (i.e., no branching) the following command would be used:

```
EXEC CICS IGNORE CONDITION condition
                        condition
                        END-EXEC
```

Figure 4-2. EXECUTIVE INTERFACE BLOCK FUNCTION CODES

CODES	COMMAND (FUNCTION)
02 02	ADDRESS
02 04	HANDLE CONDITION
02 06	HANDLE AID
02 08	ASSIGN
02 0A	IGNORE CONDITION
04 02	RECEIVE
04 04	SEND
04 06	CONVERSE
04 08	ISSUE EODS
04 0A	ISSUE COPY
04 0C	WAIT TERMINAL
04 0E	ISSUE LOAD
04 10	WAIT SIGNAL
04 12	ISSUE RESET
04 14	ISSUE DISCONNECT
04 16	ISSUE ENDOUTPUT
04 18	ISSUE ERASEAUP
04 1A	ISSUE ENDFILE
04 1C	ISSUE PRINT
04 1E	ISSUE SIGNAL
04 20	ALLOCATE
04 22	FREE
04 24	POINT
04 26	BUILD ATTACH
04 28	EXTRACT ATTACH
04 2A	EXTRACT TCT
06 02	READ
06 04	WRITE
06 06	REWRITE
06 08	DELETE
06 0A	UNLOCK
06 0C	STARTBR
06 0E	READNEXT
06 10	READPREV
06 12	ENDBR
06 14	RESETBR
08 02	WRITEQ TD
08 04	READQ TD
08 06	DELETEQ TD
0A 02	WRITEQ TS
0A 04	READQ TS
0A 06	DELETEQ TS
0C 02	GETMAIN
0C 04	FREEMAIN

CODES	COMMAND (FUNCTION)
0E 02	LINK
0E 04	XCTL
0E 06	LOAD
0E 08	RETURN
0E 0A	RELEASE
0E 0C	ABEND
0E 0E	HANDLE ABEND
10 02	ASKTIME
10 04	DELAY
10 06	POST
10 08	START
10 0A	RETRIEVE
10 0C	CANCEL
12 02	WAIT EVENT
12 04	ENQ
12 06	DEQ
12 08	SUSPEND
14 02	JOURNAL
14 04	WAIT JOURNAL
16 02	SYNCPOINT
18 02	RECEIVE MAP
18 04	SEND MAP
18 06	SEND TEXT
18 08	SEND PAGE
18 0A	PURGE MESSAGE
18 0C	ROUTE
1A 02	TRACE ON/OFF
1A 04	ENTER
1C 02	DUMP
1E 02	ISSUE ADD
1E 04	ISSUE ERASE
1E 06	ISSUE REPLACE
1E 08	ISSUE ABORT
1E 0A	ISSUE QUERY
1E 0C	ISSUE END
1E 0E	ISSUE RECEIVE
1E 10	ISSUE NOTE
1E 12	ISSUE WAIT
1E 14	ISSUE SEND
20 02	BIF DEEDIT

Figure 4-3. EXECUTIVE INTERFACE RETURN CODES

1st POS EIBFN	REL BYTE#	EIBRCODE BIT CONFIG	CONDITION
02	0	E0	INVREQ
04	0	04	EOF
04	0	10	EODS
04	0	C1	EOF
04	0	C2	ENDINPT
04	0	E1	LENGERR
04	0	E3	WRBRK
04	0	E4	RDATT
04	0	E5	SIGNAL
04	0	E6	TERMIDERR
04	0	E7	NOPASSBKRD
04	0	E8	NOPASSBKWR
04	0	EA	IGREQCD
04	0	EB	CBIDERR
04	0	D0	SYSIDERR
04	0	D2	SESSIONERR
04	0	D3	SYSBUSY
04	0	D4	SESSBUSY
04	0	D5	NOTALLOC
04	1	20	EOC
04	1	40	INBFMH
04	3	F6	NOSTART
04	3	F7	NONVAL
06	0	01	DSIDERR
06	0	02	ILLOGIC**
06	0	04	SEGIDERR*
06	0	08	INVREQ
06	0	0C	NOTOPEN
06	0	0F	ENDFILE
06	0	80	IOERR**
06	0	81	NOTFND
06	0	82	DUPREC
06	0	83	NOSPACE
06	0	84	DUPKEY
06	0	D0	SYSIDERR*
06	0	D1	ISCINVREQ
06	0	E1	LENGERR
08	0	01	QZERO
08	0	02	QIDERR
08	0	04	IOERR
08	0	08	NOTOPEN
08	0	10	NOSPACE
08	0	C0	QBUSY
08	0	D0	SYSIDERR*
08	0	D1	ISCINVREQ
08	0	E1	LENGERR
0A	0	01	ITEMERR
0A	0	02	QIDERR
0A	0	04	IOERR
0A	0	08	NOSPACE

1st POS EIBFN	REL BYTE#	EIBRCODE BIT CONFIG	CONDITION
0A	0	20	INVREQ
0A	0	D0	SYSIDERR*
0A	0	D1	ISCINVREQ*
0A	0	E1	LENGERR
0C	0	E2	NOSTG
0E	0	01	PGMIDERR
0E	0	E0	INVREQ
10	0	01	ENDDATA
10	0	04	IOERR
10	0	11	TRANSIDERR
10	0	12	TERMIDERR
10	0	14	INVTSREQ
10	0	20	EXPIRED
10	0	81	NOTFND
10	0	D0	SYSIDERR*
10	0	D1	ISCINVREQ*
10	0	E1	LENGERR
10	0	E9	ENVDEFERR
10	0	FF	INVREQ
12	0	32	ENQBUSY*
14	0	01	JIDERR
14	0	02	INVREQ
14	0	05	NOTOPEN
14	0	06	LENGERR
14	0	07	IOERR
14	0	09	NOJBUFSP
18	0	01	INVREQ
18	0	02	RETPAGE
18	0	04	MAPFAIL
18	0	08	INVMPSZ***
18	0	20	INVERRTERM
18	0	40	RTESOME
18	0	80	RTEFAIL
18	0	E3	WRBRK
18	0	E4	RDATT
18	1	10	INVLDC
18	1	40	IGREQCD
18	1	80	TSIOERR
18	2	01	OVERFLOW
1E	0	04	DSSTAT
1E	0	08	FUNCERR
1E	0	0C	SELNERR
1E	0	10	UNEXPIN
1E	0	E1	LENGERR
1E	1	11	EODS
1E	1	2B	IGREQCD
1E	2	04	EODS
1E	2	08	EOC
1E	2	10	IGREDID
1E	2	20	EOC

It is the responsibility of the application program to check for errors when using this command. More information about these two commands can be found in Chapter 13.

ADDRESSABILITY

The following is a conceptual presentation of addressability. Anyone already familiar with it may want to proceed to the end of the chapter.

Let's assume that a company has a number of application programs which need to do calculations based on state and federal taxes and that each program has a list of the taxes defined as constants. Taxes always seem to be changing, usually going upward. Whenever this occurs (unfortunately too frequently!), all the programs utilizing the taxes would have to be changed and recompiled. The process could be time-consuming and costly. A more logical and efficient way to handle this situation would be to put all of the taxes into a table and assemble the table as a program. The application programs could call the tax table whenever the table is needed. When any changes are needed, only the tax table would have to be reassembled. The application programs would not have to change.

The tax table would be accessible whenever the application programs find it necessary to reference it. Thus, Working-Storage could not be used since its use is for referencing data internal to the application program. The Linkage Section is used when referencing areas external to a program.

Figure 4-4.

```
core addr                     core addr

000200                        005000
    APPL                              TAX
    PGM                               TABLE
                                      PGM
001000                        006000
```

Figure 4-4 is a pictorial presentation of the application and tax table programs residing at different locations in memory. To reference the tax table, the application program needs to know its location (address) in memory. A way to do this in a batch program would be through the use of a CALL statement to a separate program. In CICS this could be accomplished by use of the LOAD command (Chapter 6). Once the location (address) has been obtained, it must be stored somewhere. The BLL cells in linkage would be used for this. Now that the location (address) has been found, names (labels) are needed to reference the information in the tax table. A dsect would be used to accomplish this. A dsect is simply an easy way of assigning labels in a program without reserving any storage.

Let's see what a BLL cell and a dsect would look like in a COBOL program.

```
LINKAGE SECTION.
01 PTRSLST.
    02 FILLER              PIC S9(8) COMP.           BLL
    02 TAXPTR              PIC S9(8) COMP.           CELLS
01 TAXTABLE.
    02 TAXI                PIC X(100).               DSECT
```

Each BLL cell must be defined as a fullword (four bytes) because it is going to contain an address and it can have any name. Each dsect (01 level) must have a corresponding BLL cell and the BLL cells must be in the same order as the 01 levels that follow, a COBOL requirement.

```
LINKAGE SECTION.
01 PTRSLST.
    02 FILLER              PIC S9(8) COMP.
    02 TAXPTR              PIC S9(8) COMP.
    02 RECPTR2             PIC S9(8) COMP.
    02 RECPTR3             PIC S9(8) COMP.
01 TAXTABLE.
    02 FEDTAX              PIC X(10).
    02 STATETAX            PIC X(10).
    02 CITYTAX             PIC X(10).
01 RECDESC2.
01 RECDESC3.
```

If the order of the 01 levels changes, the BLL cells must change accordingly.

Figure 4-5.

```
LINKAGE SECTION.
01 PTRSLST.
    02 FILLER              PIC S9(8) COMP.
    02 RECPTR3             PIC S9(8) COMP.
    02 TAXPTR              PIC S9(8) COMP.
    02 RECPTR2             PIC S9(8) COMP.
01 RECDESC3.
01 TAXTABLE.
    02 FEDTAX              PIC X(10).
    02 STATETAX            PIC X(10).
    02 CITYTAX             PIC X(10).
01 RECDESC2.
```

The COBOL compiler will make the proper associations of the BLL cells and the 01 levels.

You will notice that the dsects contain labels which have picture clauses. In Figure 4-5, TAXTABLE has a number of labels with picture clauses that total 30. This indicates that the dsect (TAXTABLE) can reference an area of 30 bytes. The area can only be referenced after a valid location (address) has been stored in its associated BLL cell (TAXPTR). It was stated before that a CALL statement can provide a program with a location (address).

Let's see how the computer could do this. Figure 4-4 is repeated with the addition of a Linkage Section to the application program.

```
core                 core addr

000200               005000
   APPL                       TAX
   PGM                        TABLE
                              PGM
001000               006000

LINKAGE SECTION.
01 PTRSLST.
   02 FILLER                 PIC S9(8) COMP.
   02 RECPTR3                PIC S9(8) COMP.
   02 TAXPTR                 PIC S9(8) COMP.
   02 RECPTR2                PIC S9(8) COMP.
01 RECDESC3.
01 TAXTABLE.
   02 FEDTAX                 PIC X(10).
   02 STATETAX               PIC X(10).
   02 CITYTAX                PIC X(10).
01 RECDESC2.
```

The application program will issue a CALL statement indicating that it wants the location (address) of the tax table returned in the label TAXPTR (BLL cell). After the CALL statement has been executed successfully, the application program can now reference the tax table. When the program references one of the labels (i.e., MOVE FEDTAX TO ------------) the following takes place. The computer will take the displacement (offset) of the label FEDTAX (which is zero because it is the first field in the dsect) and add it to the value (address) in memory (storage) and move 10 bytes (that is the picture clause size of FEDTAX). This is the way the computer finds data or locations.

Another way to state this: An address is resolved by adding the displacement of the label to the contents of its associated BLL cell or register.

EXERCISE

Let's review what we have already learned.

1. Why are resources shared in CICS?
2. State the function of a CICS command.
3. What is a dsect?
4. What is the difference between a HANDLE CONDITION and an IGNORE command?
5. Why is addressability important in CICS?

Each of the following chapters will deal with a specific function of CICS. The functions are terminal control, basic mapping, program control, file control, storage control, temporary storage, transient data, and interval control. The chapter will explain how each command works and illustrate various coding methods. Then we will proceed to put the commands in a typical application program.

The following is an explanation of what the entire program will do:

1. Accept input data (message).
2. Only the enter and clear keys are valid.
3. The PF1-24 and PA1-3 keys are invalid and if selected, a message will be sent back to the operator indicating an invalid key.
4. When an unformatted message has been received, send a formatted message back to the operator so that the necessary information about the customer to be added can be gathered.
5. Edit the input message.
   A. If OK, continue to #6.
   B. If not OK, highlight the fields that are incorrect so the operator can correct them and send back an error message.
6. Add the new customer to the file.
7. Send a message back to the operator indicating the operation has been successful.

This program illustrates the most typical function (adding a customer to a customer master file/data base) used by many organizations. By writing the program, we will learn to:

1. Use the most commonly used facilities of CICS.
2. Write an efficient, well-organized program for the computer and for ease of maintenance.
3. Get optimum response time by eliminating unnecessary character transmission.

In effect we will be logically putting the program together as we learn more about the capabilities of CICS. Proper coding techniques for CICS on-line programs will also be illustrated in our typical application program. Thus at the conclusion of reading this book, you will have a good working program shell to help you in writing future programs.

Remember that there are many ways to write programs and many variations on the way to code commands. It is beyond the scope of this book to show all possible combinations. Let's begin!

5 Terminal Control

RECEIVING DATA

As previously stated, the function of the management module terminal control is to handle communications between the terminals and CICS by utilizing a telecommunication access method (VTAM, TCAM, BTAM). Thus, when an application program wants to send or receive information from a terminal, it must request the TCP to do this via a CICS command. The terminal control program can work with two types of CRT formats. The first type is referred to as an unformatted screen. This type of screen allows the operator to enter data anywhere on the screen and the application program will receive exactly what was keyed in. Figure 5-1 illustrates an unformatted screen.

Figure 5-1.

```
INQX,SMITH_
```

The other type is referred to as a formatted screen. This type of screen will have predefined fields where data can be entered. There usually are title fields on the screen. The data fields received by the application program will be preceded by a three-byte control field (SBA/ADDR/ADDR). This control field is used by basic mapping support (Chapter 7). Figure 5-2 illustrates a formatted screen. Title fields are **NAME, ADDR, PRODUCT.**

Figure 5-2.

```
NAME: SMITH
ADDR: MAINE
PRODUCT: FLOWERS
```

The input data will appear as follows:

SBA:ADDR:ADDR:SMITH:SBA:ADDR:ADDR:MAINE:
SBA:ADDR:ADDR:FLOWERS

In our prior example, Figure 5-1, the operator had keyed the following:

```
INQX,SMITH_
```

and pressed the enter key. By pressing the enter key (or PF1-24, PA1-3, or clear, here referred to as function keys), the operator is letting CICS know there is work to be processed at the terminal. An attention identifier (AID), which is a one-character hex representation of the key that was pressed, will be returned in our task's executive interface block (EIB) in the label EIBAID. Since our program can reference that label, we can determine what key was actually pressed. You may be asking yourself: "Who cares what key was pressed!" Our program cares and this is why.

Whenever the enter key or PF1-24 keys are pressed, the terminal buffer will be read and the correct fields will be transmitted (sent) to our program. But if the operator had keyed in information and pressed any of the other function keys (clear or PA1-3) no data would be sent back except the one-character hex representation of the function key pressed. The terminal buffer is not read so our program would not receive any information. If we were expecting information and did not check the function key pressed, we could have erroneous data processed and this should be avoided.

There are two ways to determine which key the operator has pressed. The first way is to use the CICS command:

```
EXEC CICS HANDLE AID ENTER(LABEL)
                     PF1      (LABEL)
                     ⋮         ⋮
                     PF24     (LABEL)
                     PA1      (LABEL)
                     ⋮         ⋮
                     PA3      (LABEL)
                     CLEAR    (LABEL)
                     ANYKEY   (LABEL)    (PA1-3,PF1-24,CLEAR)
                     END-EXEC
```

This command establishes which label to go to depending on the attention identifier (AID) received. Any combination of 12 options can be selected and coded in any order. In the event that more than 12 options are required, an additional HANDLE AID command would be required. Again, this command creates a GO TO label environment. The only option that is not self-explanatory is the ANYKEY option. Remember the ERROR option with the HANDLE CONDITION command? The ANYKEY option works the same way. It simply means to GO TO a label if no other option has been chosen. Thus, HANDLE AID must be issued to create the environment and then a RECEIVE command must be executed to make the HANDLE AID options take effect. The two commands are needed just to determine what key was pressed. Think of the overhead!

Figure 5-3.

```
APPL PGM                    EIP                    M.MODULE
HANDLE AID
RECEIVE
```

Each command must go to the execute interface program (EIP) and then to the appropriate management module and then back to the EIP and back to the application program. This creates overhead and slows down response time. Keep in mind it is our responsibility to give good response time.

Another problem can arise. We learned previously that all commands have exception conditions. A problem can now arise because both the HANDLE CONDITION and the HANDLE AID commands must be executed prior to the RECEIVE command. Naturally, one of the commands (HANDLE CONDITION/HANDLE AID) must have priority. The order of their execution does not determine their priority. The HANDLE AID currently has priority over the HANDLE CONDITION.

Figure 5-4.

```
PROCEDURE DIVISION.
EXEC CICS HANDLE CONDITION ERROR(FATALERR) END-EXEC.
EXEC CICS HANDLE AID ENTER(EDITDATA)
                    CLEAR(END-SESSION)
                    ANYKEY(INVALID-KEY)
                    END-EXEC.
EXEC CICS RECEIVE
          END-EXEC.
EDITDATA.
END-SESSION.
INVALID-KEY.
FATALERR.
```

In this example (Figure 5-4) if a problem occurred during the transmission of data to CICS, when the program executes the RECEIVE command, the logic would branch to the paragraph label EDITDATA. Our program would be expecting good data and we received nothing. In this example, we really wanted the logic to go to paragraph label FATALERR but instead we go to EDITDATA because of the priority of the HANDLE

AID over the HANDLE CONDITION command. So we have two problems using the HANDLE AID command:

1. Much slower processing.
2. Invalid processing could occur.

There is a very easy way to avoid both of these situations. First, the copy member DFHAID (supplied to all CICS users by IBM) would have to be copied into Working-Storage.

Figure 5-5.

```
WORKING-STORAGE SECTION.
COPY DFHAID  ===>  01 DFHAID.
                      02 DFHNULL   PIC X VALUE IS ' '.
                      02 DFHENTER  PIC X VALUE IS QUOTE.
                      02 DFHCLEAR  PIC X VALUE IS '_'.
                      02 DFHPEN    PIC X VALUE IS '='.
                      02 DFHOPID   PIC X VALUE IS 'W'.
                      02 DFHMSRE   PIC X VALUE IS 'X'.
                      02 DFHSTRF   PIC X VALUE IS ' '.
                      02 DFHTRIG   PIC X VALUE IS '"'.
                      02 DFHPA1    PIC X VALUE IS '%'.
                      02 DFHPA2    PIC X VALUE IS '>'.
                      02 DFHPA3    PIC X VALUE IS ','.
                      02 DFHPF1    PIC X VALUE IS '1'.
                      02 DFHPF2    PIC X VALUE IS '2'.
                      02 DFHPF3    PIC X VALUE IS '3'.
                      02 DFHPF4    PIC X VALUE IS '4'.
                      02 DFHPF5    PIC X VALUE IS '5'.
                      02 DFHPF6    PIC X VALUE IS '6'.
                      02 DFHPF7    PIC X VALUE IS '7'.
                      02 DFHPF8    PIC X VALUE IS '8'.
                      02 DFHPF9    PIC X VALUE IS '9'.
                      02 DFHPF10   PIC X VALUE IS ':'.
                      02 DFHPF11   PIC X VALUE IS '#'.
                      02 DFHPF12   PIC X VALUE IS '@'.
                      02 DFHPF13   PIC X VALUE IS 'A'.
                      02 DFHPF14   PIC X VALUE IS 'B'.
                      02 DFHPF15   PIC X VALUE IS 'C'.
                      02 DFHPF16   PIC X VALUE IS 'D'.
                      02 DFHPF17   PIC X VALUE IS 'E'.
                      02 DFHPF18   PIC X VALUE IS 'F'.
                      02 DFHPF19   PIC X VALUE IS 'G'.
                      02 DFHPF20   PIC X VALUE IS 'H'.
                      02 DFHPF21   PIC X VALUE IS 'I'.
                      02 DFHPF22   PIC X VALUE IS ' '.
                      02 DFHPF23   PIC X VALUE IS '.'.
                      02 DFHPF24   PIC X VALUE IS '<'.
```

As can be seen in Figure 5-5 each function key has its own name (i.e., DFHENTER, DFHCLEAR, etc.) and picture and value clause. The EIBAID field is always filled in by CICS prior to giving our task control because the terminal control program issued the first receive. Thus there is no need to do a RECEIVE command to have this field filled. We also know that the attention identifier (AID) will be in the field EIBAID. All we have to do is compare EIBAID to one of the labels in the DFHAID copy member.

Let's recode the program in Figure 5-6.

Figure 5-6.

```
WORKING-STORAGE SECTION.
COPY DFHAID.
PROCEDURE DIVISION.
    EXEC CICS HANDLE CONDITION ERROR(FATALERR) END-EXEC.
    IF EIBAID = DFHENTER
       GO TO EDITDATA.
    IF EIBAID = DFHCLEAR
       GO TO END-SESSION.
    GO TO INVALID-KEY.
EDITDATA.
  EXEC CICS RECEIVE  .........END-EXEC
END-SESSION.
INVALID-KEY.
FATALERR.
```

Not only is the program more efficient, it is easier to read and understand and thus much easier to maintain. Also, we do not have to concern ourselves with the possibility of invalid processing as before since when an Exception Condition occurs during a RECEIVE command our program will execute the correct logic (i.e., GO TO FATALERR). This method will be used in all program examples because of its advantages over the prior HANDLE AID method. Let's continue with the program's input operation.

CICS went through all the necessary steps to establish a task and eventually our application program will get control. At this point the data entered by the operator is in our task's terminal input/output area (TIOA). The application program must execute the command:

EXEC CICS RECEIVE INTO(DATA-AREA) OR SET(POINTER-REF)
LENGTH(DATA-VALUE)
END-EXEC

to obtain the data. The data will be placed into Working-Storage or the Linkage Section of the application program.

Let's use Working-Storage first. An area where the input data is to be placed must be reserved along with a label containing the size of the reserved area.

Figure 5-7.

```
WORKING-STORAGE SECTION.
01 WSWORKAREA.
    02 IOLEN            PIC S9(4) COMP VALUE +25.
01 IOAREA.
    02 TRANIDNT         PIC X(4).
    02 FILLER           PIC X.
    02 CUSTNAME         PIC X(20).
```

An IOAREA was coded along with labels so we can reference the input data later. The command to execute would be coded as follows:

EXEC CICS RECEIVE INTO(IOAREA) LENGTH(IOLEN) END-EXEC

The data INQX,SMITH, which is currently in our task's TIOA, will be moved into our IOAREA group item label. Since the data is now in our

Working-Storage Section, the task's TIOA will be freed since it is no longer needed. The LENGTH option is mandatory on this RECEIVE command because the program is providing the storage area and we need to indicate how large the area is. After the data is moved from the TIOA into the Working-Storage Section (IOAREA), the LENGTH value will be changed to reflect the number of characters which originally came into the TIOA. This is why the argument associated with the LENGTH option must be a label defined as PIC S9(4) COMP and with a value. Think of it this way: We tell CICS how large an area we have reserved in Working-Storage and then after the data has been moved into that area, CICS tells us how many characters there were in the TIOA before the move.

Whenever the area provided with the INTO option is not large enough, CICS will only move in enough characters to fill the area and will truncate the remaining characters. When truncation occurs, CICS will also generate an Exception Condition, LENGERR. The default action when LENGERR occurs is to abnormally terminate the task. In our example, we have provided an area large enough to contain 25 characters. If that is all we need for our program, we do not care if more data is keyed in. But we do not want our task to abnormally terminate (abend). How can this be prevented? Prevent it with a HANDLE CONDITION or IGNORE CONDITION.

Figure 5-8.

```
WORKING-STORAGE SECTION.
01   WSWORKAREA.
     02 IOLEN        PIC S9(4) COMP VALUE +25.
01  IOAREA.
     02 TRANIDNT     PIC X(4).
     02 FILLER       PIC X.
     02 CUSTNAME     PICX(20).
COPY DFHAID
PROCEDURE DIVISION.
    EXEC CICS HANDLE CONDITION LENGERR(CONTEDIT)
              ERROR(FATALERR) END-EXEC.
    IF EIBAID = DEHENTER
       GO TO EDITDATA.
    IF EIBAID = DFHCLEAR
       GO TO END-SESSION.
    GO TO INVALID-KEY.
EDITDATA.
    EXEC CICS RECEIVE INTO(IOAREA) LENGTH(IOLEN) END-EXEC.
CONTEDIT.
END-SESSION.
INVALID-DATA.
FATALERR.
```

In this example, if 50 characters were keyed in by the operator, the first 25 would be moved into the IOAREA, the label IOLEN would be changed to 50, a LENGERR would occur and program logic would go to paragraph label CONTEDIT.

When the application program wants to process the data in the Linkage Section instead of the Working-Storage Section, our program would have to change.

Figure 5-9.

```
WORKING-STORAGE SECTION.
01   WSWORKAREA.
     02 IOLEN      PIC S9(4) COMP.
COPY DFHAID.
LINKAGE SECTION.
01   PTRSLST.
     02 FILLER     PIC S9(8) COMP.
     02 IOPTR      PIC S9(8) COMP.
01   IOAREA.
     02 TRANIDNT   PIC X(4).
     02 FILLER     PIC X.
     02 CUSTNAME   PIC X(20).
PROCEDURE DIVISION.
   EXEC CICS HANDLE CONDITION ERROR(FATALERR)
          END-EXEC.
   IF EIBAID = DFHENTER
      GO TO EDITDATA.
   IF EIBAID = DFHCLEAR
      GO TO END-SESSION.
  GO TO INVALID-KEY.
EDITDATA.
   EXEC CICS RECEIVE SET(IOPTR) LENGTH(IOLEN) END-EXEC.
END-SESSION.
INVALID-KEY.
FATALERR.
```

The first difference you notice between this program (Figure 5-9) and our previous program (Figure 5-8) is that the label IOLEN has no value clause. Whenever the SET option is chosen for a command, the application program is going to reference an area which is external to the program. This means that an area of sufficient size will be obtained by CICS on behalf of the application program and there is no chance of the LENGERR Exception Condition occurring. After the command has been successfully executed, the label specified with the LENGTH option will contain a value indicating the size of the area obtained. It is for informational purposes only. The program, for example, could use it to ensure that the obtained area is equal to or less than the dsect referencing it. This would help to ensure that no addressability problems occur. Conversely, if the obtained area is larger, the dsect would allow the program to correctly reference up to the size of the dsect. The INTO and SET options are mutually exclusive but one is needed to reference the input data.

SENDING DATA

Our program has now received the data and will process it. When the processing is complete, a message will be sent back to the terminal indicating the results. To send a message to a terminal, we will use the following command:

```
EXEC CICS SEND FROM(DATA-AREA)
              LENGTH(DATA-VALUE)
              ERASE                              optional
              CTLCHAR(DATA-AREA)                 optional
              END-EXEC
```

The FROM option is required and will contain the name of the label in our application program which contains the message. The label can be in Working-Storage or the Linkage Section (as long as we have proper addressability to it).

The LENGTH option is required and indicates how many characters of the message should be sent. The argument for the LENGTH option could be replaced with a decimal value not enclosed in quotes:

```
LENGTH (10)
```

or the argument could be a label defined as PIC S9(4) COMP with a value clause:

```
WORKING-STORAGE SECTION.
01   WSWORKAREA.
     02 MSGLEN          PIC S9(4) COMP VALUE +10.
```

The argument value should indicate the number of characters contained in the message. Leading and trailing spaces should not be sent since a space cannot be seen and extra character transmission slows down response time. Following are some examples of how a SEND command could be coded:

Figure 5-10

```
WORKING-STORAGE SECTION.
01   WSWORKAREA.
     02 MSGLEN          PIC S9(4) COMP VALUE +19.
01   OUTMSG.
     02 FILLER          PIC X(19)
                              VALUE 'INVALID KEY PRESSED'.
PROCEDURE DIVISION.
   EXEC CIC SEND FROM(OUTMSG) LENGTH(MSGLEN) END-EXEC.
```

or

```
WORKING-STORAGE SECTION.
01   OUTMSG.
     02 FILLER          PIC X(19).
PROCEDURE DIVISION.
   MOVE 'SESSION COMPLETED' TO OUTMSG.
   EXEC CICS SEND FROM (OUTMSG) LENGTH(17) END-EXEC.
```

Notice in this example we sent 17 characters even though OUTMSG is 19 bytes long. Remember never transmit unnecessary characters (i.e., spaces).

When the SEND command is executed, the terminal control program is notified to schedule a write to the terminal. When the data arrives at the terminal, by default, it will be written to wherever the cursor is currently residing. If response is slow, there is the possibility that while waiting for a response, the operator changed cursor positions. When this happens, the message will appear somewhere other than where it was originally intended. A way to avoid this would be by executing the following command (the labels from Figure 5-10 are used):

```
EXEC CICS SEND FROM(OUTMSG) LENGTH(17)
              ERASE
              END-EXEC
```

The screen will be erased, the cursor will be positioned at location 1,1 (the upper left corner of the screen, which is also referred to as the HOME position), and the data will then be written to the screen. This way is fine if we no longer need the data on the screen. But if the data is required, we could send a message to the screen with the proper control characters to position the cursor wherever desired. This is referred to as writing in native mode. This method is not discussed because it is not a very common technique. The other way is to use a formatted screen through the use of basic mapping support (Chapter 7).

The CTLCHAR option allows us to specify a write control character (WCC). The default WCC will restore the keyboard and turn off all the modified data tags (Chapter 7). Usually this is all that is necessary, so it need not be specified since that is the default. However, if we wish to get the operator's attention, the alarm can be sounded if the terminal has that feature. To free the keyboard, sound the alarm, and turn off all the modified data tags, we would do the following:

Figure 5-11.

```
WORKING-STORAGE SECTION.
  01   WSWORKAREA.
       02 MSGLEN          PIC S9(4) COMP VALUE +17.
       02 WSCTLCHAR       PIC X            VALUE '6'.
  01   OUTMSG.
       02 FILLER          PIC X(17)   VALUE 'SESSION COMPLETED'.
PROCEDURE DIVISION.
       EXEC CICS SEND FROM(OUTMSG) LENGTH(MSGLEN)
                 ERASE
                 CTLCHAR(WSCTLCHAR)
                 END-EXEC.
```

The argument associated with the option CTLCHAR must be a one-byte data area containing a value. The example in Figure 5-11 will erase the screen, send a message, and sound the alarm.

Some of the less frequently used terminal control commands for 3270-type terminals will be briefly mentioned.

```
EXEC CICS ISSUE PRINT END-EXEC
```

This command will print whatever data is currently displayed on the terminal to the printer which is attached to the same control unit as the terminal. The command is not valid for TCAM.

```
EXEC CICS ISSUE COPY
        TERMID(name)
        WAIT                          optional
        CTLCHAR(data-area)            optional
        END-EXEC
```

This command copies data from the buffer of a remote 3270 terminal into the buffer of the terminal attached to this task. Both terminals must be attached to the same control unit and the command is not valid for TCAM.

```
EXEC CICS ISSUE ERASEAUP END-EXEC
```

This command will erase all unprotected fields (fields where data can be entered) and set them to low-values, turn off all modified data tags, place the cursor in the first unprotected field, and unlock the keyboard. Remember it will NOT turn off any fields which were previously highlighted. In Chapter 7 we will see another way to accomplish all of the above including setting the field intensity from highlighted to normal.

EXCEPTION CONDITIONS

LENGERR   Default action is to abnormally terminate the task. This Exception Condition occurs when the input area is not large enough for the input message.

TERMIDERR   Default action is to abnormally terminate the task. This Exception Condition occurs when the term ID in the COPY command cannot be found in the terminal control table.

To obtain a complete listing of Exceptions Conditions, consult the IBM application programmer's Reference Manual.

EXERCISE

Let's review what we have already learned.

1. Describe the difference between an unformatted and formatted data stream.
2. Why is it preferable not to use the HANDLE AID command?
3. What is the difference between the INTO and SET options on the RECEIVE command?
4. Why is it recommended not to transmit extra characters (i.e., spaces)?

The following is an enhancement of what our typical application program is going to do:

1. Accept input data (message).
2. Only the enter and clear keys are valid.
3. The PF1-24 and PA1-3 keys are invalid and if selected, an unformatted message will be sent back to the operator indicating an invalid key.
4. When an unformatted message has been received, send a formatted message back to the operator so that the necessary information about the customer to be added can be gathered.
5. Edit the input message.
   A. If OK, continue to #6.
   B. If not OK, highlight the fields that are incorrect so the operator can correct them and send back an error message.
6. Add the new customer to the file.
7. Send a message back to the operator indicating the operation has been successful.

```
SOURCE PROGRAM LISTING

        IDENTIFICATION DIVISION.
        PROGRAM-ID.  COMMEXP.
        ENVIRONMENT DIVISION.
        DATA DIVISION.
        WORKING-STORAGE SECTION.
        01  WSWORKAREA.
            02 MSGLEN                 PIC S9(4) COMP VALUE +25.
        COPY DFHAID.
        01  IOAREA.
            02 TRANIDNT               PIC X(4).
            02 FILLER                 PIC X.
            02 CUSTNAME               PIC X(20).
     PROCEDURE DIVISION.
  **     IT IS A GOOD PRACTICE TO ESTABLISH A HANDLE CONDITION UPON   **
  **                       ENTRY TO A PROGRAM                         **
         EXEC CICS HANDLE CONDITION ERROR(FATALERR)
1                                   LENGERR(CONTPROCESS)
                                    END-EXEC.
  **     THE FOLLOWING WILL DETERMINE WHICH KEY THE OPERATOR SELECTED **
         IF EIBAID = DFHENTER
             NEXT SENTENCE
2        ELSE
             IF EIBAID = DFHCLEAR
                 MOVE 'SESSION COMPLETED' TO IOAREA
                 EXEC CICS SEND FROM(IOAREA) LENGTH(17) END-EXEC
             ELSE
                 MOVE 'INVALID KEY PRESSED' TO IOAREA
3                EXEC CICS SEND FROM(IOAREA) LENGTH (19) END-EXEC.
  **     THE FOLLOWING WILL OBTAIN THE INPUT MESSAGE                  **
         EXEC CICS RECEIVE INTO(IOAREA) LENGTH(MSGLEN) END-EXEC.
         CONTPROCESS.
4        FATALERR.
  **     THE FOLLOWING WILL PROCESS ANY EXCEPTION CONDITIONS          **
         MOVE 'PROCESSING PROBLEM' TO IOAREA.
         EXEC CICS SEND FROM(IOAREA) LENGTH(18) END-EXEC.
```

The above program was coded to accept the input message only if the operator had selected the enter or clear keys. Any other key selection will result in the following message being sent after the screen has been erased: "invalid key selection". When the clear key has been selected it will indicate that the operator desires to end the session so the following message will be sent: "session completed". There is no need to erase the screen when sending this message because when the operator presses the clear key the screen will automatically be erased. When the enter key has been chosen, the program will accept the input message and that is all for now.

COMMENTS:

1. If more than 25 characters are present when the RECEIVE command is executed, the program will continue to process since we are only concerned with the first 25 characters.

2. The AID value is being checked and the appropriate action is being taken. The SEND command is coded more than once but this helps to cut down on VS paging and allows fall-through logic. It is also easier to maintain.

3. The IOAREA is being used for both input and output since we no longer need the input when sending the output message. It would be fine if the output messages were defined as constants in Working-Storage but we must remember that each task gets its own copy of Working-Storage and if many tasks were using this program it would unnecessarily increase the demand for storage.

4. At FATALERR the program will send just a general message at this time indicating a process problem. After we have learned more about CICS this will be changed. The ERASE option has not been used; therefore the message will appear wherever the cursor is residing.

Notice that no Linkage Section has been coded in the source listing. After the program has been passed through the translator and compiler a Linkage Section will be automatically inserted. The Working-Storage and Linkage Sections will appear as the following:

Figure 5-12.

```
IDENTIFICATION DIVISION.
PROGRAM-ID. COMMEXP.
ENVIRONMENT DIVISION.
DATA DIVISION.
WORKING-STORAGE SECTION.
01  WSWORKAREA.
    02 MSGLEN                   PIC S9(4)   COMP   VALUE +25.
01  IOAREA.
    02 TRANIDNT                 PIC X(4).
    02 FILLER                   PIC X(1).
    02 CUSTNAME                 PIC X(20).
```

Figure 5-12 (continued).

```
01  DFHAID.
    02 DFHNULL   PIC X VALUE IS ' '.
    02 DFHENTER  PIC X VALUE IS QUOTE.
    02 DFHCLEAR  PIC X VALUE IS '_'.
    02 DFHPEN    PIC X VALUE IS '='.
    02 DFHOPID   PIC X VALUE IS 'W'.
    02 DFHMSRE   PIC X VALUE IS 'X'.
    02 DFHSTRF   PIC X VALUE IS ' '.
    02 DFHTRIG   PIC X VALUE IS '"'.
    02 DFHPA1    PIC X VALUE IS '%'.
    02 DFHPA2    PIC X VALUE IS '>'.
    02 DFHPA3    PIC X VALUE IS ','.
    02 DFHPF1    PIC X VALUE IS '1'.
    02 DFHPF2    PIC X VALUE IS '2'.
    02 DFHPF3    PIC X VALUE IS '3'.
    02 DFHPF4    PIC X VALUE IS '4'.
    02 DFHPF5    PIC X VALUE IS '5'.
    02 DFHPF6    PIC X VALUE IS '6'.
    02 DFHPF7    PIC X VALUE IS '7'.
    02 DFHPF8    PIC X VALUE IS '8'.
    02 DFHPF9    PIC X VALUE IS '9'.
    02 DFHPF10   PIC X VALUE IS ':'.
    02 DFHPF11   PIC X VALUE IS '#'.
    02 DFHPF12   PIC X VALUE IS '@'.
    02 DFHPF13   PIC X VALUE IS 'A'.
    02 DFHPF14   PIC X VALUE IS 'B'.
    02 DFHPF15   PIC X VALUE IS 'C'.
    02 DFHPF16   PIC X VALUE IS 'D'.
    02 DFHPF17   PIC X VALUE IS 'E'.
    02 DFHPF18   PIC X VALUE IS 'F'.
    02 DFHPF19   PIC X VALUE IS 'G'.
    02 DFHPF20   PIC X VALUE IS 'H'.
    02 DFHPF21   PIC X VALUE IS 'I'.
    02 DFHPF22   PIC X VALUE IS ' '.
    02 DFHPF23   PIC X VALUE IS '.'.
    02 DFHPF24   PIC X VALUE IS '<'.
01  DFHEIV.
    02 DFHEIV0   PICTURE X(26).
    02 DFHEIV1   PICTURE X(8).
    02 DFHEIV2   PICTURE X(8).
    02 DFHEIV3   PICTURE X(8).
    02 DFHEIV4   PICTURE X(6).
    02 DFHEIV5   PICTURE X(4).
    02 DFHEIV6   PICTURE X(4).
    02 DFHEIV7   PICTURE X(2).
    02 DFHEIV8   PICTURE X(2).
    02 DFHEIV9   PICTURE X(1).
    02 DFHEIV10  PICTURE S9(7) USAGE COMP-3.
    02 DFHEIV11  PICTURE S9(4) USAGE COMP.
    02 DFHEIV12  PICTURE S9(4) USAGE COMP.
    02 DFHEIV13  PICTURE S9(4) USAGE COMP.
    02 DFHEIV14  PICTURE S9(4) USAGE COMP.
    02 DFHEIV15  PICTURE S9(4) USAGE COMP.
    02 DFHEIV16  PICTURE S9(9) USAGE COMP.
```

Figure 5-12 (continued).

```
        02 DFHEIV17   PICTURE X(4).
        02 DFHEIV18   PICTURE X(4).
        02 DFHEIV19   PICTURE X(4).
        02 DFHEIV97   PICTURE S9(7) USAGE COMP-3   VALUE ZERO.
        02 DFHEIV98   PICTURE S9(4) USAGE COMP     VALUE ZERO.
        02 DFHEIV99   PICTURE X(1)                 VALUE SPACE.


    LINKAGE SECTION.
    COPY DFHEIBLK REPLACING EIBLK BY DFHEIBLK.
*       EIBLK EXEC INTERFACE BLOCK
    01  DFHEIBLK.
*           EIBTIME       TIME IN OHHMMSS FORMAT
        02 EIBTIME     PICTURE S9(7) USAGE COMP-3.
*           EIBDATE       DATE IN OOYYDDD FORMAT
        02 EIBDATE     PICTURE S9(7) USAGE COMP-3.
*           EIBTRNID      TRANSACTION IDENTIFIER
        02 EIBTRNID    PICTURE X(4).
*           EIBTASKN      TASK NUMBER
        02 EIBTASKN    PICTURE S9(7) USAGE COMP-3.
*           EIBTRMID      TERMINAL IDENTIFIER
        02 EIBTRMID    PICTURE X(4).
*           DFHEIGDI      RESERVED
        02 DFHEIGDI    PICTURE S9(4) USAGE COMP.
*           EIBCPOSN      CURSOR POSITION
        02 EIBCPOSN    PICTURE S9(4) USAGE COMP.
*           EIBCALEN      COMMAREA LENGTH
        02 EIBCALEN    PICTURE S9(4) USAGE COMP.
*           EIBAID        ATTENTION IDENTIFIER
        02 EIBAID      PICTURE X(1).
*           EIBFN         FUNCTION CODE
        02 EIBFN       PICTURE X(2).
*           EIBRCODE      RESPONSE CODE
        02 EIBRCODE    PICTURE X(6).
*           EIBDS         DATASET NAME
        02 EIBDS       PICTURE X(8).
*           EIBREQID      REQUEST IDENTIFIER
        02 EIBREQID    PICTURE X(8).
*           EIBRSRCE      RESOURCE NAME
        02 EIBRSRCE    PICTURE X(8).
*           EIBSYNC       SYNCPOINT REQUIRED
        02 EIBSYNC     PICTURE X.
*           EIBFREE       TERMINAL FREE REQUIRED
        02 EIBFREE     PICTURE X.
*           EIBRECV       DATA RECEIVE REQUIRED
        02 EIBRECV     PICTURE X.
*           EIBSEND       RESERVED
        02 EIBSEND     PICTURE X.
*           EIBATT        ATTACH DATA EXISTS
        02 EIBATT      PICTURE X.
*           EIBEOC        GOTTEN DATA IS COMPLETE
        02 EIBEOC      PICTURE X.
*           EIBFMH        GOTTEN DATA CONTAINS FMH
        02 EIBFMH      PICTURE X.
    01 DFHCOMMAREA PICTURE X(1).
    01 DFHBLLSLOT1 PICTURE X(1).
    01 DFHBLLSLOT2 PICTURE X(1).
```

Let's see how the program would change if we decided to use the
Linkage Section instead of Working-Storage.

```
SOURCE PROGRAM LISTING

        IDENTIFICATION DIVISION.
        PROGRAM-ID. COMMEXP.
        ENVIRONMENT DIVISION.
        DATA DIVISION.
        WORKING-STORAGE SECTION.
        01   WSWORKAREA.
             02 MSGLEN                    PIC S9(4) COMP VALUE +25.
        01   OUTMSG.
             02 FILLER                    PIC X(20).
        COPY DFHAID.
        LINKAGE SECTION.
        01   PTRSLST.
             02 FILLER                    PIC S9(8) COMP.
             02 IOPTR                     PIC S9(8) COMP.
        01   IOAREA.
             02 TRANIDNT                  PIC X(4).
             02 FILLER                    PIC X.
             02 CUSTNAME                  PIC X(20).
        PROCEDURE DIVISION.
     ** IT IS A GOOD PRACTICE TO ESTABLISH A HANDLE CONDITION UPON **
     **                  ENTRY TO A PROGRAM                         **
1        EXEC CICS HANDLE CONDITION ERROR(FATALERR)
                                       END-EXEC.
     ** THE FOLLOWING WILL DETERMINE WHICH KEY THE OPERATOR SELECTED **
        IF EIBAID = DFHENTER
            NEXT SENTENCE
2        ELSE
            IF EIBAID = DFHCLEAR
                MOVE 'SESSION COMPLETED' TO OUTMSG
                EXEC CICS SEND FROM(OUTMSG) LENGTH(17) END-EXEC
            ELSE
                MOVE 'INVALID KEY PRESSED' TO OUTMSG
3                EXEC CICS SEND FROM(OUTMSG) LENGTH(19)
                                        ERASE END-EXEC.
4        EXEC CICS RECEIVE SET(IOPTR) LENGTH(MSGLEN) END-EXEC.
        FATALERR.
     ** THE FOLLOWING WILL PROCESS ANY EXCEPTION CONDITIONS        **
        MOVE 'PROCESSING PROBLEM' TO OUTMSG.
        EXEC CICS SEND FROM(OUTMSG) LENGTH(18) END-EXEC.
```

COMMENTS

1. The LENGERR condition has been removed because CICS will acquire an
   area large enough to hold the input message.

2. The AID value is being checked and the appropriate action is being taken.
   The SEND command is coded more than once but this helps to cut down on
   VS paging and allows fall-through logic. It is also easier to maintain.

3. The OUTMSG is defined in Working-Storage because the area in the Linkage Section can only be used if the RECEIVE command is successful. At that
   time the program will have proper addressability to the IOAREA.

4. The SET option is used instead of the INTO option. Remember when using
   SET we are asking CICS to acquire the area and return the address of that

area to us in the data-area label provided. The LENGTH option will tell us how large the obtained area is.

In this example, a Linkage Section has been provided in the source listing. After the translate and compile, the Working-Storage and Linkage Sections will appear as follows:

```
IDENTIFICATION DIVISION.
PROGRAM-ID. COMMEXP.
ENVIRONMENT DIVISION.
DATA DIVISION.
WORKING-STORAGE SECTION.
01  WSWORKAREA.
    02 MSGLEN                PIC S9(4)   COMP   VALUE +25.
01  OUTMSG.
    02 FILLER             PIC X(20).
01  DFHAID.
    02 DFHNULL   PIC X VALUE IS ' '.
    02 DFHENTER  PIC X VALUE IS QUOTE.
    02 DFHCLEAR  PIC X VALUE IS '_'.
    02 DFHPEN    PIC X VALUE IS '='.
    02 DFHOPID   PIC X VALUE IS 'W'.
    02 DFHMSRE   PIC X VALUE IS 'X'.
    02 DFHSTRF   PIC X VALUE IS ' '.
    02 DFHTRIG   PIC X VALUE IS '"'.
    02 DFHPA1    PIC X VALUE IS '%'.
    02 DFHPA2    PIC X VALUE IS '>'.
    02 DFHPA3    PIC X VALUE IS ','.
    02 DFHPF1    PIC X VALUE IS '1'.
    02 DFHPF2    PIC X VALUE IS '2'.
    02 DFHPF3    PIC X VALUE IS '3'.
    02 DFHPF4    PIC X VALUE IS '4'.
    02 DFHPF5    PIC X VALUE IS '5'.
    02 DFHPF6    PIC X VALUE IS '6'.
    02 DFHPF7    PIC X VALUE IS '7'.
    02 DFHPF8    PIC X VALUE IS '8'.
    02 DFHPF9    PIC X VALUE IS '9'.
    02 DFHPF10   PIC X VALUE IS ':'.
    02 DFHPF11   PIC X VALUE IS '#'.
    02 DFHPF12   PIC X VALUE IS '@'.
    02 DFHPF13   PIC X VALUE IS 'A'.
    02 DFHPF14   PIC X VALUE IS 'B'.
    02 DFHPF15   PIC X VALUE IS 'C'.
    02 DFHPF16   PIC X VALUE IS 'D'.
    02 DFHPF17   PIC X VALUE IS 'E'.
    02 DFHPF18   PIC X VALUE IS 'F'.
    02 DFHPF19   PIC X VALUE IS 'G'.
    02 DFHPF20   PIC X VALUE IS 'H'.
    02 DFHPF21   PIC X VALUE IS 'I'.
    02 DFHPF22   PIC X VALUE IS ' '.
    02 DFHPF23   PIC X VALUE IS '.'.
    02 DFHPF24   PIC X VALUE IS '<'.
01  DFHEIV.
    02 DFHEIV0     PICTURE X(26).
    02 DFHEIV1     PICTURE X(8).
    02 DFHEIV2     PICTURE X(8).
    02 DFHEIV3     PICTURE X(8).
    02 DFHEIV4     PICTURE X(6).
    02 DFHEIV5     PICTURE X(4).
    02 DFHEIV6     PICTURE X(4).
```

```
          02 DFHEIV7      PICTURE X(2).
          02 DFHEIV8      PICTURE X(2).
          02 DFHEIV9      PICTURE X(1).
          02 DFHEIV10     PICTURE S9(7) USAGE COMP-3.
          02 DFHEIV11     PICTURE S9(4) USAGE COMP.
          02 DFHEIV12     PICTURE S9(4) USAGE COMP.
          02 DFHEIV13     PICTURE S9(4) USAGE COMP.
          02 DFHEIV14     PICTURE S9(4) USAGE COMP.
          02 DFHEIV15     PICTURE S9(4) USAGE COMP.
          02 DFHEIV16     PICTURE S9(9) USAGE COMP.
          02 DFHEIV17     PICTURE X(4).
          02 DFHEIV18     PICTURE X(4).
          02 DFHEIV19     PICTURE X(4).
          02 DFHEIV97     PICTURE S9(7) USAGE COMP-3  VALUE ZERO.
          02 DFHEIV98     PICTURE S9(4) USAGE COMP    VALUE ZERO.
          02 DFHEIV99     PICTURE X(1)                VALUE SPACE.

   LINKAGE SECTION.
   COPY DFHEIBLK REPLACING EIBLK BY DFHEIBLK.
*       EIBLK EXEC INTERFACE BLOCK
   01   DFHEIBLK.
*          EIBTIME      TIME IN 0HHMMSS FORMAT
          02 EIBTIME     PICTURE S9(7) USAGE COMP-3.
*          EIBDATE      DATE IN 00YYDDD FORMAT
          02 EIBDATE     PICTURE S9(7) USAGE COMP-3.
*          EIBTRNID     TRANSACTION IDENTIFIER
          02 EIBTRNID    PICTURE X(4).
*          EIBTASKN     TASK NUMBER
          02 EIBTASKN    PICTURE S9(7) USAGE COMP-3.
*          EIBTRMID     TERMINAL IDENTIFIER
          02 EIBTRMID    PICTURE X(4).
*          DFHEIGDI     RESERVED
          02 DFHEIGDI    PICTURE S9(4) USAGE COMP.
*          EIBCPOSN     CURSOR POSITION
          02 EIBCPOSN    PICTURE S9(4) USAGE COMP.
*          EIBCALEN     COMMAREA LENGTH
          02 EIBCALEN    PICTURE S9(4) USAGE COMP.
*          EIBAID       ATTENTION IDENTIFIER
          02 EIBAID      PICTURE X(1).
*          EIBFN        FUNCTION CODE
          02 EIBFN       PICTURE X(2).
*          EIBRCODE     RESPONSE CODE
          02 EIBRCODE    PICTURE X(6).
*          EIBDS        DATASET NAME
          02 EIBDS       PICTURE X(8).
*          EIBREQID     REQUEST IDENTIFIER
          02 EIBREQID    PICTURE X(8).
*          EIBRSRCE     RESOURCE NAME
          02 EIBRSRCE    PICTURE X(8).
*          EIBSYNC      SYNCPOINT REQUIRED
          02 EIBSYNC     PICTURE X.
*          EIBFREE      TERMINAL FREE REQUIRED
          02 EIBFREE     PICTURE X.
*          EIBRECV      DATA RECEIVE REQUIRED
          02 EIBRECV     PICTURE X.
*          EIBSEND      RESERVED
          02 EIBSEND     PICTURE X.
*          EIBATT       ATTACH DATA EXISTS
          02 EIBATT      PICTURE X.
*          EIBEOC       GOTTEN DATA IS COMPLETE
          02 EIBEOC      PICTURE X.
*          EIBFMH       GOTTEN DATA CONTAINS FMH
          02 EIBFMH      PICTURE X.
```

```
01   DFHCOMMAREA PICTURE X(1).
01   PTRSLST.
     02 FILLER              PIC S9(8) COMP.
     02 IOPTR               PIC S9(8) COMP.
01   IOAREA.
     02 TRANIDNT            PIC X(4).
     02 FILLER              PIC X.
     02 CUSTNAME            PIC X(20).
```

All this program does is receive a message and send one out. We have not included a GOBACK/STOP RUN verb which we previously stated was needed in a COBOL program. It was also stated that the verb should go after a RETURN or XCTL command which every CICS program needs. Let's proceed to the next chapter and learn about these two commands as well as some others.

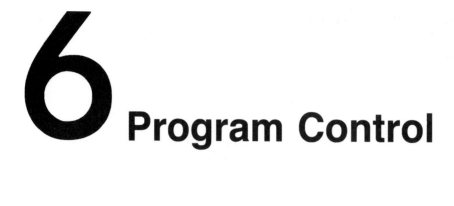

6 Program Control

LINKING AND TRANSFER CONTROL

The program control program (PCP) manages the flow of control between programs within the CICS system. All programs must have their names defined in the processing program table (PPT).

Recalling the definition of a task, we know a task can consist of one or more programs. Application programs execute at various logical levels within a task. There can be any number of logical levels within a task but only one program can be active at any given logical level. The more logical levels that are created, the slower response will be, so it is always desirable to keep logical levels to a minimum. The first program to receive control within a task is at the highest logical level. Let's see how these logical levels are created.

There may be instances when a program is written to handle a specific function (i.e. screen editing) and when finished, wants to give control to another program but does not want to get control back. An XCTL command would be used. This command does not create another lower logical level. Instead control stays at the same logical level but the program which issues the XCTL command will be removed since it is only possible to have one program active at a given logical level (Figure 6-1).

In our company there are subroutines which are needed by many application programs (e.g., date conversion, check digit, print routine,

Figure 6-1.

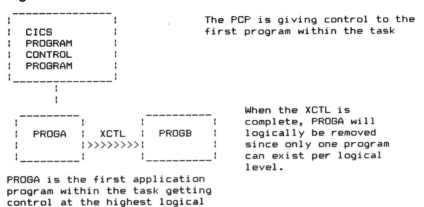

The PCP is giving control to the first program within the task

When the XCTL is complete, PROGA will logically be removed since only one program can exist per logical level.

PROGA is the first application program within the task getting control at the highest logical level.

etc.). One way to handle this would be to have all application programs call the particular subroutine whenever it is needed. The way to do this in CICS is to execute a LINK command. This will pass control down to the subroutine program thereby creating a lower logical level. When the subroutine is finished processing it will return to the linking program, thereby passing control back up to the higher logical level (Figure 6-2).

Figure 6-2.

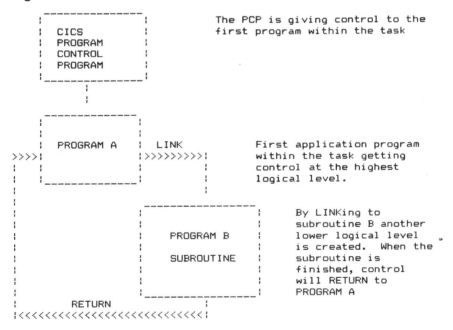

The PCP is giving control to the first program within the task

First application program within the task getting control at the highest logical level.

By LINKing to subroutine B another lower logical level is created. When the subroutine is finished, control will RETURN to PROGRAM A

Let's see how these two functions, XCTL and LINK, can be accomplished.

To transfer control to another program within the same task while staying at the same logical level, the following command would be used:

```
EXEC CICS XCTL PROGRAM(name)
            COMMAREA(data-area)    optional
            LENGTH(data-value)     optional
            END-EXEC
```

Using Figure 6-1, the command would be coded as follows:

```
#1 EXEC CICS XCTL PROGRAM('PROGB') END-EXEC
```

or

```
    WORKING-STORAGE SECTION.
    01 PGMNAME.
#2      02 FILLER                PIC X(8) VALUE 'PROGB'.
    PROCEDURE DIVISION.
        EXEC CICS XCTL PROGRAM(PGMNAME) END-EXEC
```

Example 1 shows how to code the command with the argument for the PROGRAM option as a literal enclosed in quotes. Example 2 shows how to code the command with the argument for the program option specified as a data-area. In this instance, the data-area must be specified as 8 characters even though the value clause contains 5. CICS wants 8 characters for a program name and if the data-area specified contains less than 8, the proper number will be added which in most cases will cause an error. When the program is specified as a literal it can be up to 8 characters. The program name must be in the processing program table (PPT).

Previously we learned that the HANDLE CONDITION commands were valid only for the issuing program. Thus when the program we are transferring control to (i.e., PROGB) receives control, it must establish its own HANDLE CONDITION commands even though we are still on the same logical level.

When it is necessary to transfer control to another program at a lower logical level and receive control back, i.e., calling a subroutine, the following command would be used:

```
EXEC CICS LINK PROGRAM(name)
            COMMAREA(data-area)    optional
            LENGTH(data-value)     optional
            END-EXEC
```

The program that executes this command will get control back when the linked-to program is finished at the next sequential executable instruction.

Using Figure 6-2, the command could be coded as follows:

```
#3 EXEC CICS LINK PROGRAM('PROGB') END-EXEC
```

or

```
         WORKING-STORAGE SECTION.
         01 PGMNAME.
   #4        02 FILLER                       PIC X(8)   VALUE 'PROGB'.
         PROCEDURE DIVISION.
               EXEC CICS LINK PROGRAM(PGMNAME) END-EXEC
```

Example 3 shows how to code the command with the argument for the PROGRAM option as a literal enclosed in quotes. Example 4 shows how to code the command with the argument for the program option specified as a data-area. In this instance, the data-area must be specified as 8 characters even though the value clause contains 5. CICS wants 8 characters for a program name and if the data-area specified contains less than 8, the proper number will be added which in most cases will cause an error. When the program is specified as a literal it can be up to 8 characters. The program name must be in the processing program table (PPT).

Again the program we are linking to must establish its own HANDLE CONDITION commands. When the program issuing the LINK command receives control back, its HANDLE CONDITION commands will automatically go back into effect and there is no need to reestablish them.

PASSING DATA TO ANOTHER PROGRAM

If we wish to pass data to another program the COMMAREA and LENGTH options can be used.

```
PROGRAM-ID. PROGA.
WORKING-STORAGE SECTION.
01 WSPASSDATA.
    02  PASSINFO         PIC X (25).        This program is
PROCEDURE DIVISION.                         SENDING data.
      EXEC CICS XCTL PROGRAM('PROGB')
                     COMMAREA(WSPASSDATA)
                     LENGTH(25)
                     END-EXEC


PROGRAM-ID.  PROGB.
LINKAGE SECTION.
01 DFHCOMMAREA.                             This program is
    02 PASSINFO          PIC X (25).        RECEIVING data
PROCEDURE DIVISION.
      IF EIBCALEN = 25
         MOVE PASSINFO TO .......
```

The sending program (i.e., PROGA) can send data from any area to which it has addressability. The receiving program (PROGB) MUST receive the data in the DFHCOMMAREA which is in the Linkage Section. Addressability to DFHCOMMAREA is automatically provided by CICS when an area exists. The way to determine if there is an area associated with DFHCOMMAREA is by checking the label EIBCALEN in the EIB for a value greater than zero or checking for the exact length of data that the program expects (which is the preferred way since it leads to fewer errors).

When EIBCALEN is equal to zero it means no communication area exists. The receiving program does not have to provide for a dsect which is equal in size to the area being passed to it. The size can be smaller but it MUST NEVER be larger since the longer length will be assumed and addressability problems will arise and the results will be unpredictable.

When it is necessary to pass data to another program and get control back, as in the case of calling a subroutine, the following method would be used:

```
PROGRAM-ID. PROGA.
WORKING-STORAGE SECTION.
01 WSPASSDATA.
   02  PASSINFO              PIC X(25).        This program is
PROCEDURE DIVISION.                            SENDING data.
    EXEC CICS LINK PROGRAM('PROGB')
                   COMMAREA(WSPASSDATA)
                   LENGTH(25)
                   END-EXEC

PROGRAM-ID.  PROGB.
LINKAGE SECTION.
01 DFHCOMMAREA.                                This program is
   02 PASSINFO               PIC X (25).       RECEIVING data
PROCEDURE DIVISION.
    IF EIBCALEN = 25
       MOVE PASSINFO TO .......
```

When PROGA issues the LINK command using the COMMAREA option, PROGB will get control and receive the passed area in its own DFHCOMMAREA. If PROGB makes any changes to the data in the DFHCOMMAREA, the changes will be available to PROGA when PROGB is finished processing and returns control to PROGA.

LOADING PROGRAMS

Previously we learned that to avoid recompiling many programs, it would be advantageous to have only one copy of a table for many programs to use if the particular table frequently changed (e.g., the tax table example from Chapter 4). The way an application program would gain access to the table at execution time would be through the use of the following command:

```
EXEC CICS LOAD PROGRAM(name)
               SET(pointer-ref)        optional
               LENGTH(data-area)       optional
               ENTRY(pointer-ref)      optional
               HOLD                    optional
               END-EXEC
```

In addition to gaining access to a table, the command can be used to load programs and maps. The argument name associated with the option PROGRAM indicates the name of the program, table, or map to be loaded. The name can be up to 8 characters and must be defined in the processing program table (PPT) and if not found in the PPT, the PGMIDERR Exception Condition will occur.

The option SET indicates where we want the program control program to return the address of the loaded program.

The option LENGTH, though not required, will indicate the size of the acquired program, table, or map.

The option ENTRY indicates an entry point into the loaded program, table, or map.

The option HOLD indicates to CICS to maintain the program in the dynamic storage area (DSA) until a RELEASE command is issued.

Let's see how this command could be coded to gain access to our tax table from the previous discussion.

```
WORKING-STORAGE SECTION.
01   WSWORKAREA.
     02   TAXTBLEN          PIC S9 (4) COMP.
LINKAGE SECTION.
01   PTRSLST.
     02 FILLER              PIC S9(8) COMP.
     02 TAXPTR              PIC S9(8) COMP.
01   TAXTABLE.
     02 FEDTAX              PIC X(10).
     02 STATETAX            PIC X(10).
     02 CITYTAX             PIC X(10).
PROCEDURE DIVISION.
     EXEC CICS LOAD PROGRAM('TAXPGM')
               SET(TAXPTR)    LENGTH(TAXTBLEN)
               END-EXEC
```

When the task has terminated the program, table, or map loaded will be released. If the HOLD option had been specified, the loaded program, table, or map will remain in storage until the following command is executed:

```
EXEC CICS RELEASE PROGRAM(name) END-EXEC
```

Using the previous example with the addition of the HOLD option, the program would appear as follows:

```
WORKING-STORAGE SECTION.
01   WSWORKAREA.
     02 TAXTBLEN                PIC S9(4) COMP.
LINKAGE SECTION.
01   PTRSLST.
     02 FILLER                  PIC S9(8) COMP.
     02 TAXPTR                  PIC S9(8) COMP.
01   TAXTABLE.
     02 FEDTAX                  PIC X(10).
     02 STATETAX                PIC X(10).
     02 CITYTAX                 PIC X(10).
PROCEDURE DIVISION.
     EXEC CICS LOAD PROGRAM('TAXPGM')    HOLD
               SET(TAXPTR)    LENGTH(TAXTBLEN)
               END-EXEC.
               :
               :
     EXEC CICS RELEASE PROGRAM('TAXPGM') END-EXEC
     MOVE ZEROS TO TAXPTR.
```

After the RELEASE command has been executed, the program, table, or map has been freed and our program no longer has valid addressability to it. To ensure that we do not inadvertently try to alter the area after the RELEASE command, which could cause unpredictable results to other tasks, the program will zero out the pointer-ref containing the address of the loaded program. Thus, if the application does reference the area after the RELEASE command, CICS will know that the program is trying to reference an area outside of the CICS region and abnormally terminate only this task. The use of the HOLD option and the RELEASE command should be used only after consulting a system programmer.

PROGRAM RETURN

We know that one way to end processing in a program is to use an XCTL command. The second way is by the use of the following command:

```
EXEC CICS RETURN
          TRANSID(name)              optional
          COMMAREA(data-area)        optional
          LENGTH(data-value)         optional
          END-EXEC
```

When the RETURN command is executed, control will be given to CICS which will determine if there are any other higher logical levels in this task. If so, the program at the next higher logical level will be given control. When a program at the highest logical level in the task executes this command, control is given to CICS which will terminate the task.

Using the same example from Figure 6-2, when PROGB, which is the linked-to program and thus at a lower logical level, is finished processing, it wants to give control back to PROGA. It will do this by executing the RETURN command.

```
PROGRAM-ID. PROGA.
WORKING-STORAGE SECTION.
01   WSPASSDATA.
     02  PASSINFO       PIC X(25).     This program is
PROCEDURE DIVISION.                     SENDING data
     EXEC CICS LINK PROGRAM('PROGB')
                    COMMAREA(WSPASSDATA)
                    LENGTH(25)
                    END-EXEC.
     EXEC CICS RETURN END-EXEC.

PROGRAM-ID.PROGB.
LINKAGE SECTION.
01   DFHCOMMAREA.                       This program is
     02  PASSINFO       PIC X(25).      RECEIVING data
PROCEDURE DIVISION.
     IF EIBCALEN = 25
        MOVE PASSINFO TO ......
                  :
                  :
     EXEC CICS RETURN END-EXEC.
```

Control passes back to PROGA at the next sequential executable instruction and when it is finished a RETURN command must also be executed.

```
PROGRAM-ID. PROGA.
WORKING-STORAGE SECTON.
01   WSPASSDATA.
     02  PASSINFO        PIC X(25).      This program is
PROCEDURE DIVISION.                      SENDING data
     EXEC CICS XCTL PROGRAM('PROGB')
                    COMMAREA(WSPASSDATA)
                    LENGTH(25)
                    END-EXEC


PROGRAM-ID. PROGB.
LINKAGE SECTION.
01   DFHCOMMAREA.                        This program is
     02   PASSINFO       PIC X(25).      RECEIVING data
PROCEDURE DIVISION.
     IF EIBCALEN = 25
        MOVE PASSINFO TO ..........
     EXEC CICS RETURN END-EXEC.
```

Control passes to PROGB which is at the same logical level. When it issues a RETURN, the task will terminate since we are at the highest logical level in the task.

The TRANSID option, which is valid only for terminal-oriented tasks, allows the program to specify the next transaction to be started at this terminal regardless of what is entered by the operator. Why would you want to do this?

PSEUDO-CONVERSATIONAL VERSUS CONVERSATIONAL PROGRAMMING

In our typical application program which we started coding in the previous chapter, if the data was incorrect, we were going to send a message to the operator indicating that perhaps the name entered could not be found on the file. When the message is sent we would like to have the operator only reenter what is really necessary (i.e., the customer name) and not the transaction. There are two ways to accomplish this. One way would be to send a message to the operator and have the task wait on a reply from the operator. This is very efficient for the operator because only the incorrect data would have to be reentered and the operator thinks he or she is in a conversation with the computer. From CICS' standpoint this is NOT a good idea. Suppose the operator has to go to another area to obtain the correct information; this could take some time. Perhaps the operator decides it is time to go to lunch or take a break. By the time the operator replies, much time has passed. This is bad because in CICS all tasks share the same resources and thus if the operator doesn't reply fast enough other tasks could be deprived of some valuable resources. The way to get around this problem and still have the operator think he or she is in a conversation with the computer, is by terminating the task and specifying at that time the next transaction to be started when the operator presses one of the function keys. This is called pseudo-conversational programming and is the most efficient way to code in a very high percentage of applications. In reality, to the operator, pseudo-conversational appears to be one session, even though that one session is comprised of several executions of a transaction. The first method described is called conversational programming which means to have the task wait on a reply from the operator. This method will NOT be discussed or illustrated in this book.

We stated that the operator in pseudo-conversational programming would only have to reenter the fields which were incorrect. If this is so, we need a place to store the correct fields. A way to store data beyond task termination is through the use of the COMMAREA and LENGTH options on the RETURN command. These options are valid only for the program at the highest logical level in the task. If a lower level program in the task tries to execute a RETURN command using these two options, an INVREQ Exception Condition will occur.

When the COMMAREA option is used, the argument data-area can reference any area in Working-Storage or any area in the Linkage Section to which it has addressability. The LENGTH option indicates the size of the area we are saving beyond task termination. The COMMAREA area option can be used with the XCTL, LINK, or RETURN command to pass data to another program or another task. The receiving program will receive the data in the DFHCOMMAREA of the Linkage Section. EIBCALEN will contain the value specified in the LENGTH option of the RETURN, XCTL, or LINK commands. EIBCALEN will contain zeros if no data has been passed.

How long will an area being passed between tasks exist at the terminal? An area will exist until an application program at the highest logical level in a task at the terminal issues a RETURN command without the COMMAREA option specified or with the COMMAREA option but pointing to a new area.

The following is an example of a one-program transaction which will go into pseudo-conversational programming by executing a RETURN command with the TRANSID option. It will also pass data to the next task which in this case happens to be itself. Thus we can say that this is an example of a returning program invoking itself.

COMMENTS

1. The EIBCALEN, which is part of the EIB, is checked to see if a communication area exists. If not, information will be moved to an area in Working-Storage to save beyond task termination. Data CANNOT be moved to the DFHCOMMAREA because the EIBCALEN equals zero indicating the area does NOT exist. If data were moved there, the results would be unpredictable because of invalid addressability.

2. The information to be saved is moved.

SOURCE LISTING:

```
IDENTIFICATION DIVISION.
PROGRAM-ID. PROGA.
ENVIRONMENT DIVISION.
DATA DIVISION.
WORKING-STORAGE SECTION.
01  WORK-AREA.
    02 WSCOUNT            PIC 9(3).
    02 WSINFO             PIC X(20).
    LINKAGE SECTION.
    01  DFHCOMMAREA
        02 OLD COUNT      PIC 9(3).
        02 OLD-INFO       PIC X(20).
    PROCEDURE DIVISION
1       IF EIBCALEN = ZERO
            MOVE 444 TO WSCOUNT
2           MOVE 'SMITH' TO WSINFO
3           EXEC CICS RETURN TRANSID('ACCO')
                COMMAREA(WORK-AREA)  LENGTH(23)   END-EXEC
        ELSE
4           PERFORM USE COMMAREA-DATA
5           EXEC CICS RETURN TRANSID('ACCO')
6               COMMAREA(DFHCOMMAREA) LENGTH(EIBCALEN) END-EXEC
7           GOBACK.
```

3. The task is terminating and saving the data for the next incoming task which will be ACCO. This transaction is associated with program PROGA in the PCT.

4. The EIBCALEN is not equal to zero which means we have a communication area that can be referenced in the Linkage Section.

5. This is the same as #3.

6. We are now saving data which is residing in the DFHCOMMAREA. Notice that the argument EIBCALEN is used with the LENGTH option. Since EIBCALEN contains the same value (23) it can be used instead of the decimal value. This is a good technique because if the size of the communication area changes, only one field would have to change. The program is much easier to maintain.

7. The COBOL verb GOBACK has been inserted in the program in a place where it will never be executed. This keeps the COBOL compiler and the CICS system happy.

TRANSACTION INITIATION

Perhaps you are wondering how CICS determines what transaction to initiate. Let's assume that CICS has just been initialized for today's processing and the terminal screen contains the following message:

```
GOOD MORNING
WELCOME TO THE HAPPY SEED COMPANY
PRESS THE CLEAR KEY, ENTER A TRANSACTION
AND PRESS THE ENTER KEY
```

You press the clear key and the screen is immediately erased and the one-character hex representation of the clear key is sent to CICS. The terminal control program eventually gets to servicing the terminal and will perform the following logic:

1. Is this a print request (a PA key can be defined to initiate a printing of data on the screen)? If so, initiate printing.

2. Is this a basic mapping support paging request? If so, initiate the CSPG transaction.

3. Is an attach function management header (FMH) in the data stream? If so, and test 4 and 5 fail, initiate the CSMI transaction. This transaction is used when desiring to process a request in another CICS system.

4. Is this terminal established with a permanent transaction (stated when the terminal is defined in the TCT)? If so, initiate the transaction specified.

5. Did a prior task at this terminal issue a RETURN specifing the TRANSID option? If so, initiate the transaction.

6. Is this a 3270-type terminal? If so, is this a task request (stated in the program control table)? If so, initiate the transaction.

7. If this is not a task request or this terminal is not a 3270, does the input data stream begin with a transaction? If so, initiate the transaction.

8. If no transaction is present, has the clear key been pressed? If so, free the keyboard (i.e., use the SEND command with a LENGTH of zero). If the clear key has not been pressed, send the following message:

DFH2001 INVALID TRANSACTION IDENTIFICATION—PLEASE RESUBMIT

In this case, the logic path #8 is taken. You now enter the following information:

INQX,SMITH—

and press the enter key.

The terminal control program receives control and performs the same logic. This time, logic path #7 is taken, the task is initiated, and the program associated with the transaction sends out a screen containing information about the customer and terminates by issuing the following command:

EXEC CICS RETURN TRANSID('INQX') END-EXEC.

The following screen appears:

```
NAME: JOHN SMITH        ADDRESS: P.O.B.  1432

CITY: NEW YORK          STATE: NEW YORK   ZIP: 99007
```

You find the information shown satisfies your requirements and decide to clear the screen via the clear key.

The terminal control program receives control, performs the usual logic, and path #5 is taken. But wait a minute! The clear key was pressed and previously logic path #8 was taken. Has something gone wrong? NO! Path #5 is taken because a prior task at this terminal issued a RETURN command with the NEXT TRANSID option specified. This allows the program to send out a message instead of just having the screen remain blank. The following message appears on the screen:

```
SESSION COMPLETED
```

and the task terminates with a RETURN command and no TRANSID option.

You press the clear key and the terminal control program takes logic path #8 and frees the keyboard without going through the overhead of initiating a task!

You have a clear screen and decide to press the enter key. The terminal control program gets control and path #8 is taken. The following message appears on the screen:

DFH2001 INVALID TRANSACTION IDENTIFICATION—PLEASE RESUBMIT

You decide to press PF8 which is not a task request. The terminal control program gets control and path #6 is taken and falls to #8 and the same DFH2001 message is written to the screen starting wherever the cursor is residing. Since there is not enough room on the current screen line, the message will wrap around and continue on the following line. A task request was previously mentioned. What is it? It's possible in CICS to establish a function key (i.e., PF4) to initiate a transaction. This would save the operator from knowing and entering a transaction. This provides a more user-friendly interface between the operator and the computer. Let's establish a task-request key using the PF4 function key to initiate program CUSTPGM. The entry in the program control table would be:

```
DFHPCT TYPE = ENTRY,
       TASKREQ = PF4,
       PROGRAM = CUSTPGM
```

Notice there is no transaction specified. PF4 actually becomes the transaction!

To perform an inquiry for customer SMITH, the following would be entered:

```
SMITH_
```

and the PF4 key pressed (this assumes the prior task at this terminal issued a RETURN command with NO TRANSID option). No transaction needs to be entered.

The terminal control program receives control and the logic path #6 is taken. Program CUSTPGM receives control and displays the appropriate information and terminates. It was possible to obtain the information without knowing a transaction which is much more user friendly!

Both methods (i.e., transaction versus PF4) will be compared.

INQX,SMITH_

        ENTER

SMITH_

        PF4

The operator must know the transaction code. In addition, extra characters are transmitted.

The operator needs to enter the name and press PF4. This is more user-friendly and creates less character transmission. This method could lead to more productivity because less keystrokes are required and this should result in more work being processed by the operator.

The end result is the same for both methods. The task-request method is limited by the number of available function keys on the keyboard (i.e., if each keyboard has 12 function keys, only 12 requests can be established).

Logic path #1 is similiar to a task-request function because a PA key must be established to initiate the print request.

Logic path #2 will be examined in Chapter 13.

The last logic path to examine is #4. It is possible to establish a specific transaction with a terminal by the following entry in the TCT:

```
DFHTCT TYPE = TERMINAL,
       TRANSID = ACCO
```

This means that any function key pressed except logic path #1 and 2, will invoke the transaction specified in the TCT. The operator can't override it by keying in a transaction nor can a task override it by issuing a RETURN and specifing a TRANSID. A task request can't override it. This method might be useful in an environment where a terminal runs a single transaction all day long. Since it is virtually impossible to override, care should be exercised before selecting this method.

That's how the terminal control program determines the task to initiate.

ABEND PROCESSING

Instances may arise during task processing (i.e., VSAM illogic) when it is necessary to immediately terminate our task. The following command would be used:

```
EXEC CICS ABEND
        ABCODE(name)          optional
        END-EXEC
```

When the command is issued without the ABCODE option:

```
EXEC CICS ABEND END-EXEC
```

our task will terminate without a transaction dump.

When we need to terminate the task and acquire a transaction dump, the command would be coded as follows:

```
EXEC CICS ABEND ABCODE('MYDP') END-EXEC
```

The ABCODE option will generate a transaction dump with the four-character argument specified printed at the top of the dump. The four-character code will also appear on the terminal screen. The code should not start with the letter A (Chapter 13).

Previously we learned that the HANDLE CONDITION command created an environment which was to take effect if an exception condition occurred during the execution of a command. When something went wrong, the HANDLE CONDITION allowed us to branch to a routine in our program to perform some special processing i.e.,

```
   EXEC CICS HANDLE CONDITION ERROR(FATALERR) END-EXEC
FATALERR.
   EXEC CICS ABEND ABCODE('CMMX') END-EXEC
```

In this example whenever anything other than a normal return from a command occurs, our program will go to paragraph label FATALERR and execute an ABEND command to invoke a dump and terminate the task.

That's fine for exception conditions within commands but suppose our program is unfortunate enough to receive a data check (e.g., performing an arithmetic operation on two fields one of which contains alpha characters). This will generate a dump (ASRA) and cause our task to terminate. If the dump occurs and we would like to send a message to the operator before task termination, it would appear impossible. Fortunately the following command will allow us to branch to a routine or program and perform any necessary cleanup work before terminating.

```
   EXEC CICS HANDLE ABEND
        LABEL(label) or PROGRAM(name)
        CANCEL
        RESET
        END-EXEC
```

This command creates an exit which is active for each logical level in a task. HANDLE CONDITION commands are established for each program regardless of logical levels and when the program terminates so do its associated HANDLE CONDITION commands. This is not true for HANDLE ABEND commands which stay in effect for each task until canceled. Task termination always cancels an exit.

At least one of the following options is required.

The LABEL option specifies the paragraph label in the program to go to.

The PROGRAM option specifies the program which will be given control (XCTL).

The CANCEL option will cancel any previously established exit at this logical level.

The RESET option will reset the previously deactivited exit.

CICS cancels the exit after it is taken to prevent a recursive situation (i.e., if not canceled and the task abends in the exit routine, a looping condition would arise).

Since exits are valid for each logical level, it is wise to cancel an exit which was established with the LABEL option prior to issuing an XCTL command. Why is this important? Take the following situation:

```
        PROGRAM A                               PROGRAM B

   EXEC CICS HANDLE ABEND                            ¦

        LABEL(FATALERR)                              ¦

        END-EXEC.                                  ASRA

             ¦

             ¦

   EXEC CICS XCTL PROGRAM('B')

        END-EXEC

FATALERR.
```

Program A establishes an exit to a label (FATALERR). If nothing goes wrong, control is transferred to program B at the same logical level. The exit remains in effect but program A is gone since only one program can be active per logical level. Program B obtains control and an ASRA occurs. CICS looks for the active exit label which is now gone. The result is abending of the task with no exit processing taking place. This could lead to problems so remember to cancel an exit with a label before transferring control. The following command would be issued before the XCTL command in our previous example:

EXEC CICS HANDLE ABEND CANCEL END-EXEC

The exits should always be tested prior to going into production. How can they be tested if we are lucky enough to go through testing without an abend (rare indeed!)? The ABEND command can be used. Let's see how this can be accomplished.

```
SOURCE CODE

PROCEDURE DIVISION.

1    EXEC CICS HANDLE CONDITION ERROR(FATALERR) END-EXEC.

2    EXEC CICS HANDLE ABEND PROGRAM('ERRORPGM') END-EXEC.

     normal processing logic

3    EXEC CICS ABEND END-EXEC.

4 FATALERR.

        ┊

        ┊
```

COMMENTS

1. A HANDLE CONDITION is established to trap any exception conditions generated by CICS commands.

2. An exit is established in the event an ASRA (for example) occurs. The exit will transfer control to program ERRORPGM.

3. The ABEND command without the ABCODE option will force an abend and in this way the exit logic can be tested. This command should be removed after successful testing.

4. The necessary logic has been included for HANDLE CONDITION processing.

EXCEPTION CONDITIONS

PGMIDERR   Default action is to abnormally terminate the task. This Exception Condition occurs when the program name cannot be found in the processing program table (PPT) or the program has been disabled.

INVREQ   Default action is to abnormally terminate the task. This Exception Condition occurs when the RETURN command with the COMMAREA option is used in a program that is not at the highest logical level for the task or the RETURN command with the TRANSID option is used in a program for a task not attached to a terminal.

EXERCISE

Let's review what we have already learned.

1. Indicate the difference between a LINK and XCTL command.

2. Describe the COMMAREA option on LINK, XCTL, and RETURN commands.

3. Why is pseudo-conversational programming better than conversational programming?
4. State the purpose of the TRANSID option on the RETURN command.
5. What is the HANDLE ABEND command used for?

The following is a repeat of what our typical application program is going to do:

1. Accept input data (message).
2. Only the enter and clear keys are valid.
3. The PF1-24 and PA1-3 keys are invalid and if selected, an unformatted message will be sent back to the operator indicating an invalid key.
4. When an unformatted message has been received, send a formatted message back to the operator so that the necessary information about the customer to be added can be gathered.
5. Edit the input message. A. If OK, continue to #6. B. If not OK, highlight the fields that are incorrect so the operator can correct them and send back an error message.
6. Add the new customer to the file.
7. Send a message back to the operator indicating the operation has been successful.

We will code our program to accept the input message only if the operator has selected the enter or clear keys. Any other key selection will result in the following message being sent after the screen has been erased: "invalid key selection". When the clear key has been selected it will indicate that the operator desires to end the session so the following message will be sent: "session completed". There is no need to erase the screen when sending this message because when the operator presses the clear key the screen will automatically be erased. When the enter key has been chosen, the program will accept the input message and that is all for now.

```
SOURCE PROGRAM LISTING

        IDENTIFICATION DIVISION.
        PROGRAM-ID.  COMMEXP.
        ENVIRONMENT DIVISION.
        DATA DIVISION.
        WORKING-STORAGE SECTION.
        01 WSWORKAREA.
           02 MSGLEN                    PIC S9(4) COMP VALUE +25.
        COPY DFHAID.
        01  IOAREA.
           02 TRANIDNT                  PIC X(4).
           02 FILLER                    PIC X.
           02 CUSTNAME                  PIC X(20).
        PROCEDURE DIVISION.
**    IT IS A GOOD PRACTICE TO ESTABLISH A HANDLE CONDITION UPON     **
**                    ENTRY TO A PROGRAM                             **
        EXEC CICS HANDLE CONDITION ERROR(FATALERR)
                            LENGERR(CONTPROCESS)
                            END-EXEC.
```

```
 **     THE FOLLOWING WILL DETERMINE WHICH KEY THE OPERATOR SELECTED   **
        IF EIBAID = DFHENTER
            NEXT SENTENCE
        ELSE
            IF EIBAID = DFHCLEAR
                MOVE 'SESSION COMPLETED' TO IOAREA
                EXEC CICS SEND FROM(IOAREA) LENGTH(17) END-EXEC
1               EXEC CICS RETURN END-EXEC
        ELSE
                MOVE 'INVALID KEY PRESSED' TO IOAREA
                EXEC CICS SEND FROM(IOAREA) LENGTH (19) END-EXEC
2               EXEC CICS RETURN END-EXEC.
 **     THE FOLLOWING WILL OBTAIN THE INPUT MESSAGE                      **
        EXEC CICS RECEIVE INTO(IOAREA) LENGTH(MSGLEN) END-EXEC.
     CONTPROCESS.
     FATALERR.
 **     THE FOLLOWING WILL PROCESS ANY EXCEPTION CONDITIONS              **
3        EXEC CICS ABEND ABCODE('CMEX') END-EXEC.
4        GOBACK.
```

COMMENTS

1,2. The RETURN command is being issued after the message is sent to the terminal. The task will terminate at this time since we are at the highest logical level in the task.

3. The ABEND command has been inserted. This will generate a transaction dump and abnormal task termination in the event of any unexpected problems.

4. The necessary GOBACK/STOP RUN verb has been inserted in a place where it will never be executed.

7 Basic Mapping Support

DEFINING FORMATTED SCREENS

We previously learned that the terminal control program handled the sending and receiving of data between the application program and CICS, in addition to working with both formatted and unformatted screens. It was also shown that a formatted screen would produce a formatted data stream in which a three-byte control field preceded the data.

|SBA|ADDR|ADDR|DATA|SBA|ADDR|ADDR|DATA . . . .

When working with an unformatted screen which produces an unformatted data stream, the application program did not need to concern itself with the three-byte control field because it did not exist. Unfortunately not many applications use unformatted screens so we need an easy method of working with the three-byte control field.

Basic mapping support (BMS) is the answer! It will handle any formatted data stream and interpret the stream for us. But it can only work with formatted data streams. If it tries to work with an unformatted data stream, an error will occur and the default will be for our task to terminate.

BMS actually is an interface between the terminal control and application programs. It will interpret input data streams and format output data streams so that the application program does not have to concern itself with the type of physical terminal it is dealing with. In this way, the application program becomes device independent. BMS is also used to define the way a terminal screen will appear (i.e., titles, input/output fields, and messages). The act of defining the screen is referred to as a map generation. Thus a screen can be defined to contain one or more maps. BMS will support many different terminal types which are listed in the APRM. In this chapter we will be addressing 3270-type terminals because of their high popularity.

Before our application program can work with the maps, they must be generated. The following is an example of a typical screen which will be used to explain the parameters needed to define maps.

Figure 7-1.

```
            1                   2                   3                   4                   5                   6 ......
   12345678901234567890123456789012345678901234567890123456789012345678901234567
01
02                                #INVENTORY CONTROL
03
04   #CUST NO:#      #CUST NAME#                             #
05
06   #PART NO:#      #
07
08   #QTY:#      #
09
10   #ADD OR SUBTRACT:# #
11
12
13
14
15
16
17
18
19
20
21
22   #CLEAR TO END SESSION
23   #see note 1
24

     Note 1   This is the error message line which is 76 bytes long

     Note 2   The # represents the attribute byte
```

The screen (Figure 7-1) will be defined using BMS. Though this method is not always used (screen-generator programs are becoming very popular and rightly so because of the tremendous amount of time saved), it is good to understand because it will help us to understand the way screens function.

There are only three assembler macros needed to define maps and they are:

DFHMSD   Defines a map set which can contain one or more maps and gives the overall characteristics of the maps to follow. A map set is similar to the cover of a book in the sense that a book cover gives us an idea of what is to follow.

DFHMDI   Defines the map within a map set. A map set can contain one or more maps just as a book can be composed of one or more chapters. Some installations (companies) store all the maps for a given application into one map set. This may appear to be a good idea since all maps would be easy to find. But from an execution standpoint it may not be good, since all maps of a map set must be copied into a program at one time whether they are referenced or not. This should be discussed with the system programmer.

DFHMDF   Defines each individual field within the map. A map can contain a number of fields just as a chapter of a book can contain a number of pages.

Each macro will be listed the possible options along with a brief description of each option. For specific details refer to the APRM. After listing the options, we will use Figure 7-1 to illustrate how each macro is used. All assembler macros begin in column 1, the DFH starts in column 10, and the options begin in column 16. The order of the options is not positional, so the options can be coded in any order. If more than one line is needed, the continuation character goes in column 72 and coding continues in column 16 of the next line.

```
mapset   DFHSD   TYPE=DSECT!MAP!FINAL
                 ,TERM=3270,1050...ALL
                 ,LANG=ASM!COBOL!PLI
                 ,BASE=NAME
                 ,MODE=IN!OUT!INOUT
                 ,CTRL=(PRINT,L40,FREEKB,ALARM,FRSET)
                                 L64
                                 L80
                                 HONEOM
                 ,DATA=FIELD!BLOCK
                 ,TIOAPFX=YES!NO
                 ,STORAGE=AUTO
                 ,COLOR=DEFAULT!BLUE!RED!GREEN!TURQUOISE!YELLOW!
                         PINK!NEUTRAL
                 ,EXTATT=NO!MAPONLY!YES
                 ,HILIGHT=OFF!BLINK!REVERSE!UNDERLINE
                 ,HTAB=tab ....
                 ,LDC=MNEMONIC
                 ,OBFMT=YES!NO
                 ,PS=BASE!PSID
                 ,SUFFIX=N
                 ,VTAB=tab .....
                 ,VALIDN=((mustfill) (,mustenter))
```

mapset   The 1-7 character name of the mapset. This name must be in the processing program table because maps are considered to be programs in CICS. A one-character suffix is added to the name based on the terminal type or SUFFIX operand during the mapset assemble.

TYPE   DSECT will create the symbolic map description which appears in the application program. MAP specifies the physical map which is used at task execution and does not appear in the application program. FINAL is coded to indicate the end of the mapset.

TERM   Defines the terminal type associated with the mapset.

LANG	Specifies the language the dsect should be generated in.
BASE	Allows one storage area to be shared by more than one mapset.
MODE	Indicates whether the mapset is to be used for input operations, output operations, or both.
CTRL	Specifies the write control character.
DATA	Indicates whether the data will be referenced as individual fields or as a block.
TIOAPFX	Specifies if a 12-byte prefix should be added. For command level programs, it must be YES.
STORAGE	Specifies whether the maps within the mapset should share storage or have separate storage (AUTO).
COLOR	Specifies default color for color-supported devices.
EXTATT	Specifies whether the extended attributes are supported (COLOR, PS, VALIDN, HILIGHT).
HILIGHT	Specifies the default highlighting.
HTAB	Specifies tab positions for horizontal forms control.
LDC	Specifies the mnemonic to determine the logical device code.
OBFMT	Specifies whether outbound formatting is needed.
PS	Indicates whether program symbols are to be used.
SUFFIX	Indicates the character to append to the mapset name.
VTAB	Specifies tab positions for vertical forms control.
VALIDN	Specifies whether the field must be filled completely or whether only some data must be entered.

The first macro to define our screen will be:

```
ICMSET DFHMSD
TYPE = &DSECT,TERM = 3270,TIOAPFX = YES,LANG = COBOL,      X
MODE = INOUT,                                              X
CTRL = FREEKB,                                             X
EXTATT = YES
```

1. The TYPE operand indicates a symbolic parameter which will be replaced with the proper option by means of the JCL during the assembly.
2. A 3270-type terminal will be used.
3. This is a command program so TIOAPFX = YES is mandatory.
4. The application program using this mapset is COBOL; thus a COBOL dsect is needed.
5. The mapset will be used for both input and output.
6. The CTRL operand indicates the keyboard should be freed (unlocked).
7. The EXTATT operand indicates we wish to use the extended attributes.

The next part that needs to be described is the individual map within the mapset.

```
map       DFHMDI SIZE=(line,colunm)
                ,LINE=number,NEXT,SAME
                ,COLUMN=number,NEXT,SAME
                ,JUSTIFY=(LEFT,FIRST)|(RIGHT,LAST)
                ,HEADER=YES
                ,TRAILER=YES
                ,CTRL=(PRINT,L40,FREEKB,ALARM,FRSET)
                            L64
                            L80
                            HONEOM
                ,DATA=FIELD|BLOCK
                ,TIOAPFX=YES|NO
                ,STORAGE=AUTO
                ,COLOR=DEFAULT|BLUE|RED|GREEN|TURQUOISE|YELLOW|
                        PINK|NEUTRAL
                ,HILIGHT=OFF|BLINK|REVERSE|UNDERLINE
                ,OBFMT=YES|NO
                ,PS=BASE|PSID
                ,SUFFIX=N
                ,VALIDN=((mustfill) (,mustenter))
```

map   The 1-7 character name of the map and this name is not defined in any tables. The map name can be identical to the mapset name ONLY when there is one map in the mapset.

SIZE   Specifies the dimensions of the map.

LINE   Specifies the starting line number for the map.

COLUMN   Specifies the starting column of the map and establishes the margin for the map.

JUSTIFY   Indicates LEFT or RIGHT margin for the column. FIRST specifies a new page. LAST specifies the bottom of the page.

HEADER   allows map to be used when the OVERFLOW condition occurs. The map will appear at the top.

TRAILER   allows map to be used when the OVERFLOW condition occurs. The map will appear at the bottom.

The following are used only when it is necessary to override any operand previously used in the DFHMSD macro. The meaning of each is the same as previously defined.

    CTRL, DATA, TIOAPFX, COLOR, OBFMT, HILIGHT,
    PS, VALIDN

The second macro to define our screen will be:

```
ICMSET    DFHMSD TYPE=&DSECT,TERM=3270,TIOAPFX=YES,      x
                LANG=COBOL,                              x
                MODE=INOUT,                              x
                CTRL=FREEKB,                             x
                EXTATT=YES
ICMAP     DFHMDI SIZE=(24,80),LINE=1,COLUMN=1
```

1. The screen is 24 lines by 80 columns.
2. The map is to be written to the screen starting on line 1 in column 1.

All formatted screens must contain at least one attribute byte. The attribute is used to define the characteristics of the field associated with the attribute byte. An attribute has the following characteristics.

1. It controls the characteristics of all the following buffer locations on the screen until another attribute byte is encountered.

2. It occupies a position on the screen but it cannot be displayed or printed and it is protected from operator keying except the clear key.

3. It is entered by being written by an application program. Most often it is·defined through the use of basic mapping when the screen is defined.

4. It can act as a tab stop.

The attribute byte is composed of 8 bits and its format is:

```
 --------------------------------------------
 ! X ! X ! U/P ! A/N ! D/SPD ! RES ! MDT !
 --------------------------------------------
  0   1    2      3     4 5     6     7
```

BIT

BIT		
0,1		its value is determined by the values of bits 2-7.
2		0 = unprotected field Usually used for input fields.
	1 = protected field	Usually used for fields which are not to be entered, i.e., titles.
3	0 = alpha	Any character can be entered and the default justification is left.
	1 = numeric	Puts the keyboard into the numeric lock if the keyboard has the feature and the default justification is right.
2,3	1,1 = autoskip	The field will be protected and the cursor will not stop (skip) at this field and is usually used for title fields.
4,5	0,0 = normal intensity 0,1 = normal intensity	Indicates the brightness of the field.
	1,0 = high intensity	Usually used to indicate an error.
	1,1 = dark	Usually used for passwords and security information-nondisplay.
6	must be 0	
7	0 = not modified	The contents of this field will NOT be transmitted to CICS.
	1 = modified	The contents of the field will be transmitted to CICS.

Bit 7 is referred to as the modified data tag (MDT). It is used for input operations only. The MDT can be turned on or off three different ways.

1. It can be set when it is defined, usually done with the DFHMDF macro.
2. It can be set during the execution of a program within a task. This is often referred to as changing it dynamically.
3. The operator can set the MDT. Whenever a character is entered into a field the MDT is turned ON. Whenever the EOF key is pressed, the MDT is turned ON. Whenever the ERASE INPUT key is pressed, all the unprotected fields are set to low-values and the MDTs are turned OFF.

The next part that needs to be defined is all the individual fields within the map.

```
FIELDNAME  DFHMDF POS=number,(line,column)
                 ,ATTRB=(ASKIP,NUM,BRT,DET,IC,FSET)
                        PROT      DRK
                        UNPROT    NORM
                 ,LENGTH=number
                 ,JUSTIFY=(LEFT,BLANK) ¦ (RIGHT,ZERO)
                 ,INITIAL='     ' ¦ XINIT='    '
                 ,GRPNAME=user group name
                 ,OCCURS=number
                 ,PICIN='value'
                 ,PICOUT='value'
                 ,COLOR=DEFAULT¦BLUE¦RED¦GREEN¦TURQUOISE¦YELLOW¦
                        PINK¦NEUTRAL
                 ,HILIGHT=OFF¦BLINK¦REVERSE¦UNDERLINE
                 ,OBFMT=YES¦NO
                 ,PS=BASE¦PSID
                 ,VALIDN=((mustfill) (,mustenter))
```

FIELDNAME	A 1-7 character name. The FIELDNAME operand should only be used when desiring to reference the field in the application program.
POS	Indicates the position of the attribute byte. The position can be stated as a number relative to zero or the line and column position. The use of the line and column is common.
ATTRB	Specifies the attribute characteristics.
LENGTH	Indicates the size of the field NOT counting the attribute byte.
JUSTIFY	The default for numeric fields is justify right and zero fill; for nonnumeric fields it is left justify and space fill.
GRPNAME	Specifies one name to contiguous fields.
OCCURS	Specifies a field is to be repeated "number" of times.
PICIN	Specifies the picture to be associated with the input field.
PICOUT	Specifies the picture to be associated with the output fields.

The following are used only when it is necessary to override any operand previously used in the DFHMSD macro.

COLOR	Specifies default color for color-supported devices.
OBFMT	Specifies whether outboard formatting is needed.

PS   Indicates whether program symbols are to be used.

VALIDN   Specifies whether the field must be filled completely or whether only some data must be entered.

HILIGHT   The default OFF specifies no highlighting. BLINK specifies the field is to blink. REVERSE indicates the field will be displayed in reverse video, i.e., black characters against a white background. UNDERLINE indicates the field is to be underlined. When a field is UNDERLINEd, only the data will be transmitted and not the underline characters. This is an excellent way to indicate the length of a field to the operator.

The terminal must be defined in the terminal control table as supporting these features. If not so defined, the features will be ignored.

Let's use Figure 7-1 and the DFHMDF macro and finish defining our map.

We will examine each statement in our source map program and determine what the operands of the DFHMDF macro are doing.

1. A field name has not been assigned because we do not want to reference this field in the program. The POS operand indicates the start of the field including the attribute byte. The LENGTH operand specifies how large the field is NOT counting the attribute byte. In this case, the field is only 17 bytes long. The INITIAL operand specifies the initial value to be displayed in this field when the map is written to the screen. Since the ATTRB operand was omitted, it assumes we want the default values which are normal intensity, auto skip field, and modified data tag off. Remember we stated that the attribute will control all the following buffer locations until another attribute byte is encountered. In Figure 7-1, this means that all buffer locations between line 2, column 29 and line 4, column 04 will be normal intensity, auto skip, and MDT off.

2. This statement is the same as #1 except for the initial value being displayed.

3. A field name, CUSTNO, has been assigned because we are going to reference it in the application program. Remember the name can only be up to 7 characters long. This name will appear in the dsect which the map assembly will generate. An ATTRB operand has been specified because the default values are not needed. This operand is indicating that the field is NUM (giving right justification and zero fill, the keyboard will be put into numeric lock if it has that feature) and when the screen is displayed, the cursor (IC) will appear in the beginning of this field. This saves the operator from tabbing over to the first unprotected field. Remember that there is only one cursor so it can only be displayed in one field at a time. If the IC option is used in more than one ATTRB operand the cursor will appear in the last field whose ATTRB operand has specified the IC option. Even though the UNPROT and NORM intensity options have not been coded, the field will take on those characteristics.

4. This statement is almost the same as #1 and 2. The default attribute is the same as #1 but the attribute is going to allow the operator to enter only four characters in the previous field. When the cursor encounters this attribute it

Figure 7-1.

```
           1         2         3         4         5         6 ......
  1234567890123456789012345678901234567890123456789012345678901234567
01
02                             #INVENTORY CONTROL
03
04  #CUST NO:#     #CUST NAME#                        #
05
06  #PART NO:#     #
07
08  #QTY:#    #
09
10  #ADD OR SUBTRACT:# #
11
12
13
14
15
16
17
18
19
20
21
22  #CLEAR TO END SESSION
23  #see note 1
24
```

```
    Note 1   This is the error message line which is 76 bytes long

    Note 2   The # represents the attribute byte

    ICMSET    DFHMSD TYPE=&DSECT,TERM=3270,TIOAPFX=YES,          x
                     LANG=COBOL,                                 x
                     MODE=INOUT,                                 x
                     CTRL=FREEKB,                                x
                     EXTATT=YES
    ICMAP     DFHMDI SIZE=(24,80),LINE=1,COLUMN=1
 1            DFHMDF POS=(02,29),LENGTH=17,INITIAL='INVENTORY CONTROL'
 2            DFHMDF POS=(04,04),LENGTH=08,INITIAL='CUST NO:'
 3  CUSTNO    DFHMDF POS=(04,13),LENGTH=04,ATTRB=(NUM,IC)
 4            DFHMDF POS=(04,18),LENGTH=09,INITIAL='CUST NAME'
 5  CUSTNM    DFHMDF POS=(04,28),LENGTH=20,ATTRB=UNPROT
 6            DFHMDF POS=(04,49),LENGTH=01
 7            DFHMDF POS=(06,04),LENGTH=08,INITAL='PART NO:'
 8  PARTNO    DFHMDF POS=(06,13),LENGTH=04,ATTRB=NUM
 9            DFHMDF POS=(06,18),LENGTH=01
10            DFHMDF POS=(08,04),LENGTH=04,INITIAL='QTY:'
11  QTY       DFHMDF POS=(08,09),LENGTH=03,ATTRB=NUM,PICIN='999'
12            DFHMDF POS=(08,13),LENGTH=01
13            DFHMDF POS=(10,04),LENGTH=16,INITIAL='ADD OR SUBTRACT:'
14  ACTCD     DFHMDF POS=(10,21),LENGTH=01,ATTRB=UNPROT
15            DFHMDF POS=(10,23),LENGTH=01
16            DFHMDF POS=(22,04),LENGTH=20,INITIAL='CLEAR TO END SESSION'
17  ERRMSG    DFHMDF POS=(23,04),LENGTH=76
18            DFHMSD TYPE=FINAL
```

will automatically skip to the next unprotected field. We can say that the attribute is acting as both a field delimiter and tab skip.

5. Again, this statement has a field name, CUSTNM, specified because we want

to reference it in the application program. Since the default attribute is not desired, the UNPROT option has been selected.

6. This statement again is similar to #4 because it is acting as a field delimiter and tab skip. The LENGTH indicates 1 byte and is necessary.

7. This statement is similar to #1, 2, and 4.

8. A field name, PARTNO, has been specified and since we want numeric data to be entered, the attribute of numeric has been selected. The field will be normal intensity and unprotected. Remember the data the program receives will be right justified and zero filled.

9. This statement is similar to #6.

10. This statement is similar to #1, 2, 4, and 7.

11. A field name, QTY, has been provided and is similar to #8. The operand PICIN has been added. All this operand will do is to generate a picture clause of 999 instead of the usual XXX. This is a good idea if the input is needed in an arithmetic operation AFTER it has been determined to be a valid numeric field by saving an extra move statement.

12. This statement is similar to #6 and 9.

13. This statement is similar to #1, 2, 4, 7, and 10.

14. This statement is similar to #11.

15. This statement is similar to #6, 9 and 12.

16. This statement is similar to #1, 2, 4, 7,10, and 13.

17. This statement is specifying an error message line. It is a good idea to allow one line for an error message at the top or bottom of the terminal screen. The reason line 24 was not chosen is because that line is usually reserved for system type messages, e.g., the CICS system will be down in 5 minutes, etc. This allows messages to be sent through the network without destroying the screen the operator is working on.

18. This macro is needed after the last map in the mapset has been defined.

This is the source code needed for defining a map and mapset. Much of the information is standard and it can tend to get rather boring coding all this information. That is the reason a good map-generating program is a common way to develop the map. After the mapset and maps have been coded the source code will be passed through a two-step assembly. The first step is to assemble the mapset and maps and link them to the CICS LOAD LIB. The name used in the step is the mapset name which is specified on the DFHMSD macro. This name must also be specified in the processing program table because mapsets are considered to be programs in CICS. This step is assembling the physical map (DFHMSD TYPE = MAP). The physical map is only used at execution time and will never appear in the application program. The second step will assemble the dsect needed by the application program. The dsect generated for our application program must be a COBOL dsect because our program is written in COBOL. The output from step two will be cataloged by the mapset name to the source statement library. The dsect is copied into the application program and becomes part of the program compile. The physical map and the dsect are

brought together (merged) at task execution time. Figure 7-2 illustrates this
procedure.

Figure 7-2.

```
                              SOURCE
                               CODE
                                :
                                :
STEP 1.    TYPE=MAP      - ASSEMBLE  and LINK EDIT BY MAP  SET  NAME

                          (PHYSICAL MAP) to the CICS LOAD LIBRARY.

STEP 2.    TYPE=DSECT    - ASSEMBLE  and  CATALOG  by MAP  SET  NAME

                          (DSECT) to the SOURCE STATEMENT LIBRARY.

TASK EXECUTION           - The PHYSICAL MAP and DSECT are MERGED
```

Let's see how the dsect would appear after the assembly.

```
01  ICMAPI.                              01   ICMAPO REDEFINES ICMAPI.
    02 FILLER      PIC X(12).                 02 FILLER     PIC X(12).
    02 CUSTNOL     PIC S9(4) COMP             02 FILLER     PIC X(3).
    02 CUSTNOF     PIC X.                      02 CUSTNOC    PIC X.
    02 FILLER REDEFINES CUSTNOF.              02 CUSTNOP    PIC X.
       03 CUSTNOA  PIC X.                     02 CUSTNOH    PIC X.
    02 FILLER      PIC X(4).                  02 CUSTNOV    PIC X.
    02 CUSTNOI     PIC X(4).                  02 CUSTNOO    PIC X(4).
    02 CUSTNML     PIC S9(4) COMP             02 FILLER     PIC X(3).
    02 CUSTNMF     PIC X.                     02 CUSTNMC    PIC X.
    02 FILLER REDEFINES CUSTNMF.              02 CUSTNMP    PIC X.
       03 CUSTNMA  PIC X.                     02 CUSTNMH    PIC X.
    02 FILLER      PIC X(4).                  02 CUSTNMV    PIC X.
    02 CUSTNMI     PIC X(20).                 02 CUSTNMO    PIC X(20).
    02 PARTNOL     PIC S9(4) COMP             02 FILLER     PIC X(3).
    02 PARTNOF     PIC X.                     02 PARTNOC    PIC X.
    02 FILLER REDEFINES PARTNOF.              02 PARTNOP    PIC X.
       03 PARTNOA  PIC X.                     02 PARTNOH    PIC X.
    02 FILLER      PIC X(4).                  02 PARTNOV    PIC X.
    02 PARTNOI     PIC X(4).                  02 PARTNOO    PIC X(4).
    02 QTYL        PIC S9(4) COMP             02 FILLER     PIC X(3).
    02 QTYF        PIC X.                     02 QTYC       PIC X.
    02 FILLER REDEFINES QTYF.                 02 QTYP       PIC X.
       03 QTYA     PIC X.                     02 QTYH       PIC X.
    02 FILLER      PIC X(4).                  02 QTYV       PIC X.
    02 QTYI        PIC 999.                   02 QTYO       PIC X(3).
    02 ACTCDL      PIC S9(4) COMP             02 FILLER     PIC X(3).
    02 ACTCDF      PIC X.                     02 ACTCDC     PIC X.
    02 FILLER REDEFINES ACTCDF.               02 ACTCDP     PIC X.
       03 ACTCDA   PIC X.                     02 ACTCDH     PIC X.
    02 FILLER      PIC X(4).                  02 ACTCDV     PIC X.
    02 ACTCDI      PIC X.                     02 ACTCDO     PIC X.
    02 ERRMSGL     PIC S9(4) COMP.            02 FILLER     PIC X(3).
    02 ERRMSGF     PIC X.                     02 ERRMSGC    PIC X.
    02 FILLER REDEFINES ERRMSGF.              02 ERRMSGP    PIC X.
       03 ERRMSGA  PIC X.                     02 ERRMSGH    PIC X.
    02 FILLER      PIC X(4).                  02 ERRMSGV    PIC X.
    02 ERRMSGI     PIC X(76).                 02 ERRMSGO    PIC X(76).
```

The first thing you will notice is that the output map redefines the
input map. Next both maps contain an initial FILLER of X(12) because
command level CICS requires the operand TIOAPFX = YES.

The L appended to the input field name indicates the length of the field. When used with an input operation, it represents the number of characters which were in the field prior to justification. In output operations, it is used for symbolic cursor positioning (discussed later in this chapter).

The I appended to the field name represents the input data.

The F appended to the field name represents the flag field. Whenever the cursor is placed at the beginning of a field and the EOF (erase until end of field) key is pressed, the modified data tag is turned on and a HEX 80 is placed in the field. It is for input operations only.

The A appended to the field name represents the attribute field. It is used ONLY for output operations. It appears in the input map section only because of the assembly procedure.

The O appended to the field name indicates the output data.

The C appended to the field name represents the extended color attribute.

The P appended to the field name represents the extended programmed symbols.

The H appended to the field name represents the extended highlight feature.

The V appended to the field name represents the extended validation feature (i.e., whether the field must be partially or completely filled).

The dsect must be copied into the application program. The dsect can be used in the Working-Storage Section or the Linkage Section of the program. One of two copy statements is needed depending on the version of COBOL you are working with. Both ways are shown in Figure 7-3.

Figure 7-3.

```
WORKING-STORAGE SECTION.            WORKING-STORAGE SECTION.
COPY MAP SET NAME                   01 MAPI/O COPY MAP SET NAME
```

Using the source code from before, let's fill in the necessary information.

```
SOURCE LISTING
WORKING-STORAGE SECTION.            WORKING-STORAGE SECTION.
COPY ICMSET                         01 ICMAPI COPY ICMSET
```

In both examples, the ENTIRE MAPSET will be copied into the application program. Next we will see how to set up a map in the Linkage Section of a program.

```
SOURCE LISTING

LINKAGE SECTION.                    LINKAGE SECTION.
01  PTRSLST.                        01 PTRSLST.
      02 FILLER     PIC S9(8) COMP.       02 FILLER     PIC S9(8) COMP.
      02 MAPPTR     PIC S9(8) COMP.       02 MAPPTR     PIC S9(8) COMP.
COPY ICMSET                         01 ICMAPI COPY ICMSET
```

Since we are going to work with an area external to the program, a BLL cell must be associated with our map.

SENDING FORMATTED DATA

Once the necessary mapsets have been copied into the application program, we can begin to work with them. Let's discover how to send a map to the terminal. This is a good idea because if the application program wants to receive one, a map must be sent first! The command to send a map to the terminal is:

```
EXEC CICS SEND MAP(name)
                MAPSET(name)                          optional
                MAPONLY or DATAONLY                   optional
                ERASE or ERASEUP                      optional
                CURSOR or CURSOR(data-value)          optional
                FROM (data-area)                      optional
                LENGTH(data-value)                    optional
```

The following are merely overrides of what was previously coded with the mapset and map definition.

```
                ALARM                                 optional
                FREEKB                                optional
                FRSET                                 optional
                PRINT                                 optional
                HONEOM or L40 or L64 or L80)          optional
                END-EXEC
```

To send a map to the screen we must provide the map name. In addition, the mapset name is required because only the mapset name is in the processing program table and both names can be up to 7 characters long. When the MAP and MAPSET names are identical, the MAPSET option need not be specified. When the MAPSET option is omitted, CICS assumes that the MAP and MAPSET names are the same.

```
EXEC CICS SEND MAP('ICMAP') MAPSET('ICMSET') END-EXEC
```

The FROM and LENGTH options are used only if the data to be sent to the terminal resides in an area other than the map dsect.

The MAPONLY and DATAONLY options are mutually exclusive. When the MAPONLY option is used, it means to only send the default data which is located in the physical map and DO NOT send any data from the application program dsect. The DATAONLY option means to send only the data which is in the application program dsect and DO NOT use any data from the physical map. When neither option is specified, it means to merge the data in the application program dsect with the default data in the physical map and send all the information to the terminal. It is important to know which option to use because it is essential to transmit only necessary characters to try to optimize response time. When is the correct time to use each? When the map is initially sent to the terminal, if the application program only wants the default data to be sent, then MAPONLY would be used. Perhaps the application wants to send only messages to the terminal (i.e., field titles and data already displayed) then the DATAONLY option should be used. When default data and application program data are to be sent (i.e., send a map containing information about a customer) then neither should be used.

The option ERASE or ERASEAUP are mutually exclusive. The ERASE option will erase the screen setting it to low-values before the map is written to the terminal. It is good to use this option when the map is initially displayed. The ERASEAUP option will only erase the unprotected fields on the screen and set those fields to low-values. This option is good to use after information has been accepted and is good. The input data may only need to be erased to indicate the operation was successful.

The CURSOR option is used when it is necessary to override what was previously coded with the IC option when the mapset/map was defined.

Let's examine a number of ways the SEND command could be coded to send information to the terminal. The mapset which we just coded will be used.

The following example will illustrate the way to send the initial map to the screen after the operator has entered a transaction code. To remove the transaction code entered by the operator, the screen needs to be erased and the cursor will appear in the first unprotected field as specified when the map was created. Only default data will be sent.

```
SOURCE LISTING

WORKING-STORAGE SECTION.
COPY ICMSET
PROCEDURE DIVISION.
    EXEC CICS SEND MAP('ICMAP') MAPSET('ICMSET')
              ERASE MAPONLY END-EXEC
```

The next example will illustrate sending a map to an operator who has requested information about a particular customer by keying in the transaction: INQX,SMITH. The application program will read the customer record and move the contents of the record to the map dsect and then the map will be sent to the operator after the screen has been erased. The MAPONLY or DATAONLY option will not be used because we will be merging data in our application program with the default data in the physical map.

```
SOURCE LISTING

WORKING-STORAGE SECTION.
COPY ICMSET
RECORD DESCRIPTION
PROCEDURE DIVISION.
    Acquire  the record and move the information from the
      record to the map dsect
  EXEC CICS  SEND  MAP('ICMAP')  MAPSET('ICMSET')  ERASE  END-EXEC
```

The next example will illustrate the method of sending data to the screen which already contains a map. This is usually done when in an editing session and the operator has made mistakes and only a few fields need correction. The screen does not need to be erased. The CURSOR option will be used. This means that the application will indicate where the cursor is to be located. We want to position the cursor at the first occurrence of an error as the program edits the input data. During the program edit, whenever an error occurs a minus 1 (-1) will be moved to the field name which was wrong and that has an L appended to it. This method is called symbolic cursor positioning. It is possible that there could be many errors encountered during the edit and for each one a minus 1 will be moved. Thus if 5 fields are wrong, the minus 1 will be moved five times. When the map is written out, the cursor will appear in only the FIRST field. Before we stated that during the map define, if the IC option was used more than once, the cursor appeared in the LAST field containing the IC option. During task execution, the reverse happens. The cursor appears in the first field and this is because of the way BMS handles symbolic cursor positioning.

```
SOURCE LISTING

WORKING-STORAGE SECTION.
COPY ICMSET
PROCEDURE DIVISION.
    edit input data
    EXEC CICS SEND MAP('ICMAP') MAPSET('ICMSET') CURSOR
            DATAONLY END-EXEC
```

As we were learning the ways to send data to the terminal, we did not have to concern ourselves with the actual physical location of where the data was going to be placed on the screen. This is how BMS helps us. The application program actually becomes independent of the device to which it is sending data. Thus BMS is a very effective interface between the application program and the terminal control program.

APPL	BMS	TERM CNTL
PGM	PGM	PGM

The APPL PGM sends a message containing data. The BMS PGM takes the message and inserts the necessary control characters and then the TERM CNTL PGM gets the message and sends it to the screen.

RECEIVING FORMATTED DATA

We have found out how easy it is to send data to the terminal using BMS so let's see how easy it is to receive data from the terminal again using BMS. In this instance the reverse of the send logic is going to take place. The terminal control program will get the message and make it available to the application program, but preceding each piece of data will be a three-byte control field containing information such as where the data was actually residing out at the terminal. When the application program gets the data, it does not want to concern itself as to where the data was physically positioned on the screen. It just wants to edit the data. To resolve this situation, we will need the services of BMS again. What BMS will do is interpret the three-byte control field preceding the data and using information from the physical map will determine where the data is to be placed in the application program dsect. It will also perform any required justification for us. After it gets done interpreting the input data stream, BMS will give our application program control and now we can reference the data by symbolic labels and not concern ourselves with anything else. As you can probably see, BMS is somewhat complicated but it is also very powerful and makes our programming job MUCH easier!

TERM CNTL	BMS	APPL
PGM	PGM	PGM

The TERM CNTL PGM acquires the message and stores it in memory. The BMS PGM takes the message and removes the necessary control characters and performs the necessary justification and then the APPL PGM gets the message and edits the data.

To acquire the input data, the application program will have to execute the following command:

```
EXEC CICS RECEIVE MAP(name)
                  MAPSET(name)                          optional
                  INTO(data-area) or SET(pointer-ref)   optional
                  FROM(data-area)                       optional
                  LENGTH(data-value)                    optional
                  END-EXEC
```

The MAP option specifies the 1-7 character map name within the mapset. The I or O which is appended to the map name during the map assembly is not to be used. The MAPSET option specifies the 1-7 character mapset name in the processing program table, to which the map belongs. When the MAP and MAPSET names are identical, the MAPSET option need not be specified. When MAPSET name is omitted, CICS assumes that the MAP and MAPSET names are the same.

The INTO and SET options are mutually exclusive. The INTO option is used when it is necessary to place the mapped data in an area OTHER than the map dsect. The SET option is used when desiring to reference the mapped input data via the Linkage Section.

When both the INTO and SET options are omitted, the data will be placed wherever the map dsect resides. If the map dsect is residing in the Linkage Section, be sure storage has been previously acquired (Chapter 9) to ensure proper addressability.

The FROM and LENGTH options are used if the data to be mapped is already available to the program.

Let's examine a number of ways the RECEIVE command could be coded to receive information from the terminal. The mapset which we just coded and used in the SEND examples will also be used here.

The following example will illustrate the way to receive data into the application program. It is assumed here that a prior task had sent out the map and the operator had entered information.

```
SOURCE LISTING

WORKING-STORAGE SECTION.
COPY ICMSET
PROCEDURE DIVISION.
    EXEC CICS RECEIVE MAP('ICMAP') MAPSET('ICMSET') END-EXEC
```

The input data which is residing in the TIOA prior to the RECEIVE command will be interpreted by BMS and moved into the dsect residing in Working-Storage. Since the TIOA is no longer needed, it will be freed.

The following example will illustrate a program receiving the data in the Linkage Section of the application program. Again it is assumed that a prior task had sent out the map and the operator had entered information.

```
SOURCE LISTING

LINKAGE SECTION.
01  PTRSLST.
    02 FILLER       PIC S9(8) COMP.
    02 MAPPRT       PIC S9(8) COMP.
COPY ICMSET.
PROCEDURE DIVISION.
    EXEC CICS RECEIVE MAP('ICMAP') MAPSET('ICMSET')
                      SET(MAPPTR)
                      END-EXEC.
```

Perhaps the data is already available to the application program and it is necessary to move it into the map dsect. The following example will illustrate how this can be accomplished. The FROM and LENGTH options are needed and the data label argument for the LENGTH option must be initialized. Zeros are moved to the IOPTR because the area associated with the label is freed. This will help to insure data integrity within the CICS region.

```
SOURCE LISTING

WORKING-STORAGE SECTION.
01  WSWORKAREA.
    02 IOLEN        PIC S9(4) COMP.
COPY ICMSET.
LINKAGE SECTION.
01  PTRSLST.
    02 FILLER       PIC S9(8) COMP.
    02 IOPTR        PIC S9(8) COMP.
01  IOAREA.
    02 FILLER       PIC X(100).
PROCEDURE DIVISION.
    EXEC CICS RECEIVE SET(IOPTR)
                      LENGTH(IOLEN)
                      END-EXEC.

process checking


EXEC CICS RECEIVE MAP('ICMAP') MAPSET('ICMSET')
                  FROM(IOAREA)
                  LENGTH(IOLEN)
                  END-EXEC.

MOVE ZEROS TO IOPTR.
```

Situations may arise when it is necessary to determine if the data coming in from the screen is unformatted (i.e., MENU, SMITH) or formatted (i.e., SBA|ADDR|ADDR|SMITH|SBA|ADDR|ADDR|4444 . . . . .). A typical example of this situation is when the operator can enter a transaction and/or data and the program responds with a screen where the operator can enter data and invoke the same program. The application program must be able to know the difference between the two types of screens. Why? If the program tries to issue a RECEIVE MAP command and the data stream is unformatted a MAPFAIL Exception Condition will result. The method used to distinguish the difference is to check for the presence of the set buffer address (SBA). Since a formatted data stream begins with an SBA (hex 11), that's what to check for! Let's see how this is accomplished using Working-Storage first.

```
      SOURCE LISTING

      WORKING-STORAGE SECTION.
      01   WSWORKAREA.
           02 WSLEN        PIC S9(4) COMP VALUE +100.
           02 INPUTAREA.
              04 INTRANS  PIC X(4).
 1            04 FILLER   PIC X.
              04 INNAME   PIC X(20).
              04 FILLER   PIC X(75).
           02 FILLER       REDEFINES INPUTAREA.
 2            04 INSBA    PIC X.
              04 FILLER   PIC X(99).
 3         02 WSDECVAL     PIC S9(4) COMP VALUE +17.
 4         02 FILLER       REDEFINES WSDECVAL.
              04 FILLER   PIC X.
              04 WSHEX11  PIC X.
      COPY ICMSET
      PROCEDURE DIVISION.
 5        EXEC CICS RECEIVE INTO(INPUTAREA)
                            LENGTH(WSLEN)
                            END-EXEC.
 6        IF INSBA = WSHEX11
 7            EXEC CICS RECEIVE
                     MAP('ICMAP')
                     MAPSET('ICMSET')
                     FROM(INPUTAREA)
                     LENGTH(WSLEN)
                     END-EXEC
              GO TO EDIT-MAP-DATA
           ELSE
 8            process unformatted message.
      EDIT-MAP-DATA.
```

COMMENTS

1. An input area has been established to receive both types of data streams. Since it is possible to receive formatted data, the area should be as large as the MAP dsect.

2. The input area has been redefined and a label has been set in the first position to check for the presence of a SBA.

3. A field has been set to contain the decimal value of hex 11 which is decimal 17. The field must be set to S9(4) COMP because two bytes are required.

4. The decimal field is redefined so that the second byte of the field will contain the hex 11.

5. The first RECEIVE command can handle both unformatted and formatted data streams.

6. Now the check will be done to determine if the input stream is formatted.

7. When the input stream is formatted, the RECEIVE MAP command will use the data which already resides in the program. This requires the use of the FROM and LENGTH options.

8. The data stream is formatted and the necessary logic will be executed.

A more efficient way of doing the same thing would be by using the Linkage Section of the program. This method is better because there is less data movement and the size of Working-Storage is kept to a minimum. Let's see how this is done.

```
        SOURCE LISTING

        WORKING-STORAGE SECTION.
        01  WSWORKAREA.
            02 WSLEN          PIC S9(4) COMP.
            02 WSDECVAL       PIC S9(4) COMP VALUE +17.
            02 FILLER         REDEFINES
               WSDECVAL.
               04 FILLER      PIC X.
               04 WSHEX11     PIC X.
2       COPY ICMSET.
        LINKAGE SECTION.
        01  PTRSLST.
            02 FILLER         PIC S9(8) COMP.
            02 INPTR          PIC S9(8) COMP.
        01  INAREA.
            02 INPUTAREA.
               04 INTRANS     PIC X(4).
1              04 FILLER      PIC X.
               04 INNAME      PIC X(20).
               04 FILLER      PIC X(75).
            02 FILLER         REDEFINES
               INPUTAREA.
               04 INSBA       PIC X.
               04 FILLER      PIC X(99).
        PROCEDURE DIVISION.
3           EXEC CICS RECEIVE SET(INPTR)
                              LENGTH(WSLEN)
                              END-EXEC.
            IF INSBA = WSHEX11
4           EXEC CICS RECEIVE
                        MAP('ICMAP')
                        MAPSET('ICMSET')
                        FROM(INAREA)
                        LENGTH(WSLEN)
                        END-EXEC
              GO TO EDIT-MAP-DATA
            ELSE
              process unformatted message.
        EDIT-MAP-DATA.
```

COMMENTS

The following will point out only the areas which have changed from the previous example.

1. The input area has been established to receive both types of data streams in the Linkage Section.
2. The mapset remains in Working-Storage.
3. The RECEIVE command will establish addressability to the TIOA. Since only an address is returned, it eliminates the movement of data from the TIOA into the Working-Storage Section as in the prior example until absolutely necessary.
4. The data will now be moved from the TIOA into the area reserved for the mapset.

EXCEPTION CONDITIONS

INVMPSZ   Indicates the map currently being sent will not fit on the terminal. The default action is to abnormally terminate the task.

MAPFAIL   Indicates that a RECEIVE MAP command was issued and the input data stream was unformatted or there is no data to receive, hence a length of zero. In both cases, it simply means that the input data stream does contain at least one set buffer address (SBA). The default action is to abnormally terminate the task.

To obtain a complete listing of Exception Conditions, consult the IBM Application Programmer's Reference Manual.

EXERCISE

Let's review what we have learned about basic mapping.

1. Define the function of basic mapping support.
2. Define a formatted data stream.
3. What is a map and how is it defined?
4. A-What is the difference between the MAPONLY and DATAONLY option of the SEND command?
   B- What happens if neither is specified?
5. What is the difference between the ERASEAUP option on the SEND MAP command and the terminal control command EXEC CICS ERASEAUP END-EXEC?
6. Describe what happens when the SEND MAP command is executed.
7. Describe what happens when the RECEIVE MAP command is executed.

8. In what table must mapset names be defined and why?

9. How can the modified data tag (MDT) be turned on and off?

10. What is symbolic cursor positioning?

11. Why is it a good practice to save data beyond task termination?

The following is an enhancement of what our typical application program is going to do:

1. Accept input data (message).

2. Only the enter and clear keys are valid.

3. The PF1-24 and PA1-3 keys are invalid and if selected, a message will be sent back to the operator indicating an invalid key.

4. When an unformatted message has been received, send a formatted message back to the operator so that the necessary information about the customer to be added can be gathered.

5. Edit the input message. All fields are required but only a customer name or number is needed. A. If OK, continue to /6. B. If not OK, highlight the fields that are incorrect so the operator can correct them and send back an error message.

6. Add the new customer to the file.

7. Send a message back to the operator indicating the operation has been successful.

We will code our program to accept the input message only if the operator has selected the enter or clear keys. Any other key selection will result in the following message being sent after the screen has been erased: "invalid key selection". When the clear key has been selected it will indicate that the operator desires to end the session so the following message will be sent: "session completed". There is no need to erase the screen when sending this message because when the operator presses the clear key the screen will automatically be erased. When the enter key has been chosen, the program will accept the input message which can only consist of the transaction code. At this time the label EIBCALEN will be equal to zero since no COMMAREA has been previously saved. This also indicates that it is the first time into this program and a map will be sent to the operator so data can be entered and a COMMAREA will be created at this time. Thus when we enter this program the second time the label EIBCALEN will be greater than zero indicating a map is to be received. When the data has been correctly edited, a record will be added to the customer master file. If any errors exist, a message will be sent back to the operator and the incorrect fields will be highlighted.

A very high percentage of CICS online programs are typical of ours.

The following gives a good overview of what the program will accomplish. It can be referred to as a road map because it helps us to navigate through a program. Since many on-line programs are the same, by using this road map, changes become easy even if you were not the original

CHECK FUNCTION KEYS

DETERMINE IF COMMAREA PRESENT (EIBCALEN)

1ST TIME	2ND TIME
EIBCALEN = ZERO	EIBCALEN > ZERO
RECEIVE DATA (UNFORMATTED)	RECEIVE MAP (FORMATTED)
PROCESS INPUT	MERGE NEW DATA WITH PREVIOUS
	DATA
SEND MAP	RESET ATTRIBUTES TO ORIGINAL
	MAPSET SETTINGS
RETURN TRANSID	MOVE LOW-VALUES TO OUTPUT
COMMAREA	FIELDS
LENGTH	EDIT DATA
	CHECK FOR ERRORS
	NO ERRORS
	UPDATE LOGIC
	SEND MAP INDICATING A
	SUCCESSFUL UPDATE
	RETURN
	ERRORS
	SEND MAP DATAONLY
	CURSOR
	RETURN TRANSID
	COMMAREA LENGTH

author of the program. Debugging also becomes easier since all programs have very similar logic.

COMMENTS

1. The Exception Condition MAPFAIL has been established to take effect when no data has been sent (i.e., all modified data tags off) or an unformatted data stream has been sent (i.e., no set buffer address (SBA)). This establishes an unconditional branch.

2. When the enter key has been pressed, a check will be made to determine if this is the first or second time into our the program. The label EIBCALEN is acting as an indicator. When it is equal to zero it means it is the first time into the program. Otherwise it is the second time.

3. When it is the first time into the program, the map will be sent to the terminal

```
      IDENTIFICATION DIVISION.
      PROGRAM-ID. COMMEXP.
      ENVIRONMENT DIVISION.
      DATA DIVISION.
      WORKING-STORAGE SECTION.
      COPY DFHAID.
      COPY ICMSET.
      COPY DFHBMSCA.
      01  WSWORKAREA.
          02 MSGLEN              PIC S9(4)   COMP VALUE +25.
          02 IOAREA              PIC X(20).
          02 WSDEC128            PIC S9(4)   COMP  VALUE +128.
          02 FILLER              REDEFINES
             WSDEC128.
             04 FILLER           PIC X.
             04 WSHEX80          PIC X.
          02 WSCOMM              PIC X(32)   VALUE  LOW-VALUES.
          02 WSERRIND            PIC 9       VALUE  ZERO.
          02 WSQMRK.
             04 FILLER           PIC X       VALUE '?'.
             04 FILLER           PIC X(19)   VALUE LOW-VALUES.
      LINKAGE SECTION.
      01  DFHCOMMAREA.
          02 CCUSTNO             PIC X(4).
          02 CCUSTNM             PIC X(20).
          02 CPARTNO             PIC X(4).
          02 CQTY                PIC X(3).
          02 CQTYN               REDEFINES
             CQTY                PIC 9(3).
          02 CACTCD              PIC X.
      PROCEDURE DIVISION.
 **      IT IS A GOOD PRACTICE TO ESTABLISH A HANDLE CONDITION UPON   **
 **                      ENTRY TO A PROGRAM                           **
         EXEC CICS HANDLE CONDITION ERROR(FATALERR)
1                                   MAPFAIL(NODATA)
                                    END-EXEC.
 **      THE FOLLOWING WILL DETERMINE WHICH KEY THE OPERATOR SELECTED **
         IF EIBAID = DFHENTER
2            IF EIBCALEN = 32
6                EXEC CICS RECEIVE MAP('ICMAP') MAPSET('ICMSET') END-EXEC
             ELSE
3                EXEC CICS SEND MAP('ICMAP') MAPSET('ICMSET')
                             MAPONLY
                             ERASE    END-EXEC
             EXEC CICS RETURN
4                        TRANSID(EIBTRNID)
                         COMMAREA(WSCOMM)   LENGTH(32)
                         END-EXEC
         ELSE
            IF EIBAID = DFHCLEAR
               MOVE  'SESSION COMPLETED' TO IOAREA
               EXEC CICS SEND FROM(IOAREA) LENGTH(17) END-EXEC
               EXEC CICS RETURN END-EXEC
            ELSE
               MOVE 'INVALID KEY PRESSED'  TO IOAREA
               EXEC CICS SEND FROM(IOAREA) LENGTH(19)
                             ERASE END-EXEC
               EXEC CICS RETURN END-EXEC.
 **      THE INPUT DATA WILL BE MERGED WITH THE PREVIOUSLY SAVED DATA **
7        IF CUSTNOL IS GREATER THAN ZERO
            MOVE CUSTNOI TO CCUSTNO
```

```
                ELSE
                    IF CUSTNOF = WSHEX80
                        MOVE LOW-VALUES TO CCUSTNO.
                IF CUSTNML IS GREATER THAN ZERO
                    MOVE CUSTNMI TO CCUSTNM
                ELSE
                    IF CUSTNMF = WSHEX80
                        MOVE LOW-VALUES TO CCUSTNM.
                IF PARTNOL IS GREATER THAN ZERO
                    MOVE PARTNOI TO CPARTNO
                ELSE
                    IF PARTNOF = WSHEX80
                        MOVE LOW-VALUES TO CPARTNO.
                IF QTYL IS GREATER THAN ZERO
                    MOVE QTYI TO CQTY
                ELSE
                    IF QTYF = WSHEX80
                        MOVE LOW-VALUES TO CQTY.
                IF ACTCDL IS GREATER THAN ZERO
                    MOVE ACTCDI TO CACTCD
                ELSE
                    IF ACTCDF = WSHEX80
                        MOVE LOW-VALUES TO CACTCD.
  **    THE INPUT FIELDS WILL BE SET TO LOW-VALUES TO REDUCE       **
  **                     CHARACTER TRANSMISSION                    **
8      MOVE LOW-VALUES TO CUSTNO CUSTNMO PARTNOO QTYO ACTCDO.
  **    THE ATTRIBUTES WILL BE RESTORED TO THEIR ORIGINAL SETTINGS **
9      MOVE DFHBMUNP TO CUSTNOA CUSTNMA PARTNOA QTYA.
   CONTPROCESS.
  **    EDIT THE DATA WHICH NOW RESIDES IN DFHCOMMAREA             **
10     IF CCUSTNO = LOW-VALUES AND CCUSTNM = LOW-VALUES
            MOVE WSQMRK TO CUSTNOO
            MOVE  -1    TO CUSTNOL
            MOVE   1    TO WSERRIND
            MOVE DFHBMBRY TO CUSTNOA.
       IF CPARTNO = LOW-VALUES
            MOVE WSQMRK TO PARTNOO
            MOVE  -1   TO PARTNOL
            MOVE   1   TO WSERRIND
            MOVE DFHBMBRY TO PARTNOA.
       IF CQTY = LOW-VALUES
            MOVE WSQMRK TO QTYO
            MOVE  -1    TO QTYL
            MOVE   1    TO WSERRIND
            MOVE DFHBMBRY TO QTYA.
       ELSE
            IF CQTY IS NOT NUMERIC
                MOVE -1 TO QTYL
                MOVE 1 TO WSERRIND
                MOVE DFHBMBRY TO QTYA.
       IF CACTCD = LOW-VALUES
            MOVE WSQMRK TO ACTCDO
            MOVE  -1    TO ACTCDL
            MOVE   1    TO WSERRIND
            MOVE DFHBMBRY TO ACTCDA.
  **    CHECK TO DETERMINE IF ANY ERRORS EXIST                     **
       IF WSERRIND = ZERO
            GO TO ADD-RECORD.
11     MOVE 'ERRORS HIGHLIGHTED    PLEASE CORRECT AND RESUBMIT' TO
            ERRMSGO.
   SEND-DATAONLY-MAP.
  **    SEND BACK TO THE TERMINAL ONLY THE ATTRIBUTES, QUESTIONS   **
  **    MARKS AND AN ERROR MESSAGE.  LOW-VALUES ARE NEVER          **
```

```
    **                          TRANSMITTED                          **
         EXEC CICS SEND MAP('ICMAP') MAPSET('ICMSET')
12                           DATAONLY
                             CURSOR          END-EXEC.
    **   THE PROGRAM WILL BE RE-INVOKING ITSELF AND SAVING THE        **
    **                          DFHCOMMAREA                           **
         EXEC CICS RETURN
13                 TRANSID(EIBTRNID)
                   COMMAREA(DFHCOMMAREA)
                   LENGTH(EIBCALEN)
                   END-EXEC.
    ADD-RECORD.
    **   ADD LOGIC                                          **
14       MOVE -1 TO CUSTNOL.
15       MOVE 'UPDATE SUCCESSFUL' TO ERRMSGO.
    **   THE MESSAGE WILL BE SENT, ATTRIBUTES SET TO THEIR ORIGINAL   **
    **   AND ALL THE UNPROTECTED FIELDS ON THE SCREEN WILL BE ERASED  **
16       EXEC CICS SEND MAP('ICMAP') MAPSET('ICMSET')
                   ERASEAUP
                   CURSOR
                   DATAONLY
                   END-EXEC.
    **   THE COMMAREA WILL BE REFRESHED                       **
17       MOVE LOW-VALUES TO DFHCOMMAREA.
18       EXEC CICS RETURN
                   TRANSID(EIBTRNID)
                   COMMAREA(DFHCOMMAREA)
                   LENGTH(EIBCALEN)
                   END-EXEC.
    NODATA.
19       MOVE LOW-VALUES TO ICMAPO.
    **   WHEN THE DFHCOMMAREA CONTAINS LOW-VALUES, IT INDICATES NO    **
    **                   HAS BEEN ENTERED                     **
         IF DFHCOMMAREA = LOW-VALUES
20         MOVE 'NO DATA ENTERED' TO ERRMSGO
           MOVE -1    TO CUSTNOL.
21       GO TO SEND-DATAONLY-MAP.
    FATALERR.
    **   THE FOLLOWING WILL PROCESS ANY EXCEPTION CONDITIONS          **
    **   A TRANSACTION DUMP WILL BE TAKEN AND THE TASK WILL TERMINATE **
    **                   IMMEDIATELY                          **
         EXEC CICS ABEND ABCODE('CMEX') END-EXEC.
5        GOBACK.
```

after the screen has been erased. The screen must be erased in this instance to remove the four-character transaction code and any other data on the screen. The MAPONLY option indicates that only the default data in the physical map should be sent.

4. The RETURN command is being issued along with the next transaction to invoke when the operator presses a function key. The program is coded with multiple RETURN commands. The program could have used GO TO a particular paragraph in the program which contained the RETURN command. Why is one preferred over the other? In a large program (this program will be, when we are finished), using controlled redundant code helps cut down VS paging and makes the program easier to maintain. The label EIBTRNID has been used as the argument because we want to use the same transaction which initiated this task. Also by using this method, less maintenance is required if the trans id is changed. The COMMAREA and LENGTH

options establish the COMMAREA. The COMMAREA contains low-values because it reflects what is currently displayed in the unprotected fields on the screen. The DFHCOMMAREA in Linkage cannot be used because EIB-CALEN equals zero and indicates no area currently exists.

5. The necessary GOBACK/STOP RUN verb has been inserted in a place where it will never be executed.

6. When the label EIBCALEN is greater than zero (in this example equal to 32) it indicates that a map has been previously sent by a prior task to the terminal. At this time we know a formatted screen exists and to obtain the data, a RECEIVE MAP command needs to be issued. If the operator did not key in any data, all the modified data tags would be off and a MAPFAIL Exception Condition would result. At this time let's assume data has been entered by the operator and the modified data tags are on. The data in our TIOA will be interpreted by BMS and will be placed in our dsect (Working-Storage) after proper justification has taken place. When the mapping operation has been completed, the TIOA will be released since we now have the data in Working-Storage. If the Linkage Section is used with the SET option on the RECEIVE command, the TIOA will NOT be released.

7. The incoming data will now be merged with the old data residing in DFHCOMMAREA. Let's examine how the data is being checked. The length field is being checked for the presence of data because a binary compare is faster than an alphanumeric compare. If the length is greater than zero the input data will be moved to the associated label in the DFHCOMMAREA. When the length is zero it means that no data was entered or that the operator erased the entire field with the EOF key. This can be determined by checking for the presence of a HEX 80 in the flag field (i.e., CUSTNOF, CUSTNMF). The constant WSHEX80 has been defined in Working-Storage. When this is the case, low-values will be moved to the associated label in the DFHCOM-MAREA.

8. Low-values, which are never transmitted, will be moved to the output fields. Since the output map redefines the input map the effect will be to overlay all input. But this is fine since we saved all data in the DFHCOMMAREA. Low-values could also be moved to the group label ICMAPO.

9. The attributes will be restored to their original settings. Also this will turn off any highlighting of previous errors. Thus we will not have the problem of good data being highlighted. The labels can be found in the copy member DFHBMSCA, which is supplied to CICS users by IBM. The following is a typical copy member from a program. The value clauses are not exact because many characters are not printable. Next to each field is its associated meaning. Many installations append their own fields to this list if the need arises.

```
COPY DFHBMSCA

01 DFHBMSCA.
   02 DFHBMPEM  PIC X    PRINTER END OF MESSAGE
              VALUE IS ' '.
   02 DFHBMPNL  PIC X    PRINTER NEW-LINE CHARACTER
              VALUE IS ' '.
```

```
02 DFHBMASK  PIC X    AUTOSKIP
         VALUE IS ZERO.
02 DFHBMUNP  PIC X    UNPROTECTED
         VALUE IS ' '.
02 DFHBMUNN  PIC X    UNPROTECTED NUMERIC
         VALUE IS '&'.
02 DFHBMPRO  PIC X    PROTECTED
         VALUE IS '-'.
02 DFHBMBRY  PIC X    BRIGHT INTENSITY
         VALUE IS 'H'.
02 DFHBMDAR  PIC X    NONDISPLAY
         VALUE IS '<'.
02 DFHBMFSE  PIC X    MDT ON
         VALUE IS 'A'.
02 DFHBMPRF  PIC X    PROTECTED, MDT ON
         VALUE IS '/'.
02 DFHBMASF  PIC X    AUTOSKIP, MDT ON
         VALUE IS '1'.
02 DFHBMASB  PIC X    AUTOSKIP, BRIGHT INTENSITY
         VALUE IS '8'.
02 DFHBMEOF  PIC X    FIELD ERASED
         VALUE IS ' '.
02 DFHDFCOL  PIC X    DEFAULT COLOR
         VALUE IS ' '.
02 DFHBMDET  PIC X    FIELD DETECTED
         VALUE IS ' '.
02 DFHDFT    PIC X    DEFAULT OVERRIDE FOR MAP ATTRIBUTES
         VALUE IS ' '.
02 DFHBLUE   PIC X    BLUE
         VALUE IS '1'.
02 DFHRED    PIC X    RED
         VALUE IS '2'.
02 DFHPINK   PIC X    PINK
         VALUE IS '3'.
02 DFHGREEN  PIC X    GREEN
         VALUE IS '4'.
02 DFHTURQ   PIC X    TURQUOISE
         VALUE IS '5'.
02 DFHYELLO  PIC X    YELLOW
         VALUE IS '6'.
02 DFHNEUTR  PIC X    NEUTRAL
         VALUE IS '7'.
02 DFHBASE   PIC X    PROGRAMMED SYMBOL SET
         VALUE IS ' '.
02 DFHDFHI   PIC X    DEFAULT, NO HIGHLIGHT
         VALUE IS ' '.
02 DFHBLINK  PIC X    BLINK
         VALUE IS '1'.
02 DFHREVRS  PIC X    REVERSE VIDEO
         VALUE IS '2'.
02 DFHUNDLN  PIC X    UNDERLINE
         VALUE IS '4'.
02 DFHMFIL   PIC X    MANDATORY FILL
         VALUE IS 'D'.
02 DFHMENT   PIC X    MUST ENTER
         VALUE IS 'B'.
02 DFHMFE    PIC X    MUST ENTER AND FILL
         VALUE IS 'F'.
```

10. The data residing in DFHCOMMAREA will be edited. Since all fields are required, a check is made to determine the presence of data. When none is found, a question mark (WSQMRK) will be moved to the output field. Notice

---

that the label WSQMRK starts with a question mark followed by low-values. This is because COBOL will pad with spaces if only the literal "?" is moved. This is not desired bacause spaces are transmitted. Thus the label WSQMRK should always be as large as the largest output field in the map. A minus 1 (-1) is moved to the length field to take advantage of symbolic cursor positioning. This should be done whenever an error is found. A 1 is moved to the error indicator (WSERRIND) and the field is highlighted and the modified data tag is turned off. This is the standard procedure to follow when editing data in CICS. As many fields as possible should be edited in a task and single-field editing should be avoided.

11. The error indicator (WSERRIND) is being checked. If errors exist a general message will be sent to the operator. Otherwise the program will branch to the ADD-RECORD logic. This logic will be changed in Chapter 8.

12. The MAP is sent to the operator and contains only the attributes and question marks and message. None of the input data will be sent back because it already resides in the DFHCOMMAREA. The DATAONLY option is used which means to only send the data in the dsect in our application program and do NOT send the default data in the physical map. The CURSOR option has also been chosen. This will insert the cursor in the FIRST output field whose length field contains high-values. The length field was set to high-values by moving a minus 1 (-1) to the length field during editing. This is the way to set an S9(4) COMP field to high-values in COBOL.

13. The RETURN command is issued with the TRANSID option indicating we wish to reinvoke the same transaction. The COMMAREA option indicates we wish to save the area associated with the label DFHCOMMAREA beyond task termination. Since its size is the same as the previous task we can use the value contained in the label EIBCALEN.

14. When the MAP has been sent, the cursor will appear at the CUSTNO field.

15. The update message is being moved to the message line.

16. When the MAP is sent, all unprotected fields will be erased and set to low-values, the attributes will be set to their original settings and the message will be sent. There is no need to resend the title fields since they are already on the screen.

17. Since all the fields on the screen have be set to low-values, the COMMAREA will also be set to low-values since it reflects what is currently displayed on the screen.

18. The RETURN command is being issued and has specified the same TRAN-SID but with a refreshed COMMAREA.

19. When a MAPFAIL Exception Condition occurs, it could mean no data was entered by the operator. So why are we moving low-values to the output map? This is done to ensure no unwanted characters get transmitted.

20. If the DFHCOMMAREA contains low-values, it means that no data resides in the input fields and the message "NO DATA ENTERED" can be sent. If the DFHCOMMAREA does not contain low-values, it means data does exist on the screen but all the modified data tags are off (i.e., during an error correction cycle) and sending of the message "NO DATA ENTERED" might con-

fuse the operator. In this situation, nothing will be sent to the terminal except the write control character which will free the keyboard and remove the inhibit indicator. This process varies depending upon the application design.

21. The previous SEND and RETURN logic will be used.

Remember that various coding techniques could be used but all techniques should try to minimize character transmission and VS paging, in addition to being easy to maintain.

8 File Control

The file control program (FCP) of CICS handles the accessing of the following direct access files: VSAM, BDAM, and ISAM. Files are accessed by application programs which specify the name of the file. These names are collectively kept in the file control table (FCT), which will also indicate the type of processing allowed for the file (i.e., read, write, add, etc.), the type of file (VSAM, BDAM, ISAM), buffers allocated, etc. VSAM FCT entries will contain the number of strings but the key size and location and record size, etc. are stored in the VSAM catalog. Since application programs don't normally open and/or close files, information pertaining to a file's open/ close status is also stored in the FCT. The following is a VSAM entry from an FCT:

```
DFHFCT TYPE=DATASET,DATASET=CUSTMAS,                          X
       ACCMETH=(VSAM,KSDS),                                   X
       BUFND=3,                                               X
       BUFNI=2,                                               X
       FILSTAT=(ENABLED,OPEN),                                X
       LOG=YES,                                               X
       JID=NO,                                                X
       RECFORM=(FIXED,BLOCKED),                               X
       SERVREQ=(GET,UPDATE,NEWREC,BROWSE,DELETE,PUT),         X
       STRNO=3
```

Don't be confused by the DATASET parameter. DATASET really indicates the DD name on the OS JCL and the DLBL name on the DOS

JCL (Figure 8-1 CUSTMAS & PARTMAS). The examples in this chapter will assume VSAM as the access method because of its popularity.

Figure 8-1.

```
OS  JCL

//CICSPROD JOB CLASS=W,REGION=4096K
//VERIFY   EXEC PGM=IDCAMS
//SYSPRINT DD SYSOUT=A
//DFHINTRA DD DSN=CICS.PROD.DFHINTRA,DISP=OLD
//DFHTEMP  DD DSN=CICS.PROD.DFHTSDS,DISP=OLD
//CUSTMAS  DD DSN=CUSTOMER.MASTER,DISP=SHR
//PARTMAS  DD DSN=PART.NUMBER.MASTER,DISP=SHR
//SYSIN    DD *
VERIFY FILE(DFHINTRA)
VERIFY FILE(DFHTSDS)
VERIFY FILE(CUSTMAS)
VERIFY FILE(PARTMAS)
//CICS     EXEC PGM=DFHSIP,
//         PARM=('SIT=01','FCT=01','DCT=01','PCT=01',
//               'PPT=01','TCT=01','MONITOR=(ACC,PER,EXC)'
//               'CMP=NO','OSCOR=102400','PLTPI=01')
//STEPLIB  DD DSN=CICS.LOADLIB,DISP=SHR
//SYSUDUMP DD SYSOUT=A
//DFHRPL   DD DSN=CICS.LOADLIB,DISP=SHR
//****   DUMP DATA SETS               ********
//DFHDMPA  DD DSN=CICS.DUMPA,DISP=SHR
//DFHDMPB  DD DSN=CICS.DUMPB,DISP=SHR
//DFHSNAP  DD SYSOUT=A,OUTLIM=0
//****     AUTOMATIC STATISTICS DATA SET    ********
//DFHSTM   DD DSN=CICS.STATM,DISP=SHR
//DFHSTN   DD DSN=CICS.STATN,DISP=SHR
//****     INTRAPARTITION DATA SET          ********
//DFHINTRA DD DSN=CICS.DFHINTRA,DISP=(OLD,KEEP)
//****     AUXILIARY TEMPORARY STORAGE      ********
//DFHTEMP  DD DSN=CICS.DFHTSDS,DISP=OLD
//****     RESTART DATA SET                 ********
//DFHRSD   DD DSN=CICS.DFHRSD,DISP=OLD
//****     EXTRAPARTITION DATA SETS         ********
//STATS    DD SYSOUT=*,DCB=(DSORG=PS,RECFM=V,BLKSIZE=136)
//INTRDR1  DD SYSOUT=(A,INTRDR),
//            DCB=(RECFM=FB,LRECL=80,BLKSIZE=80)
//****     JOURNAL DATA SETS               ********
//DFHJ01A  DD DSN=CICS.DFHJ01A,DISP=OLD
//****     APPLICATION DATASETS            ********

//CUSTMAS  DD DSN=CUSTOMER.MASTER,DISP=SHR
//PARTMAS  DD DSN=PART.NUMBER.MASTER,DISP=SHR

//****     THE FOLLOWING LIST THE DUMP DATASETS    *
//DUMP01   EXEC PGM=DFHDUP,PARM=SINGLE,COND=EVEN
//STEPLIB  DD DSN=CICS.LOADLIB,DISP=SHR
//DFHDMPDS DD DSN=CICS.DUMPA,DISP=SHR
//DFHPRINT DD SYSOUT=A
//DUMP02   EXEC PGM=DFHDUP,PARM=SINGLE,COND=EVEN
//STEPLIB  DD DSN=CICS.LOADLIB,DISP=SHR
//DFHDMPDS DD DSN=CICS.DUMPB,DISP=SHR
//DFHPRINT DD SYSOUT=A
```

```
// JOB CICS
// OPTION LOG,NOFASTTR
// UPSI 001
// ASSGN SYS019,X'385'
// ASSGN SYS030,X'071'
// ASSGN SYS040,DISK,VOL=CICS01,SHR
// DLBL DFHJ01A,'T1 CICS SYSTEM JOURNAL',0,SD
// EXTENT SYS012,MSTR02,1,0,14220,30
// DLBL DFHTEMP,'CICS.TEMP.STORAGE',,VSAM
// DLBL DFHINTRA,'CICS.INTRA.TRANS.DATA',,VSAM
// DLBL DFHDMPA,'CICS.DUMPA',0,SD
// EXTENT SYS040,CICS01,1,0,612,12
// DLBL DFHDMPB,'CICS.DUMPB',0,SD
// EXTENT SYS040,CICS01,1,0,624,12
// DLBL DFHSTM,'CICS.AUTO.STATS',0,SD
// EXTENT SYS040,CICS01,1,0,636,12
// DLBL DFHSTN,'CICS.STATN',0,SD
// EXTENT SYS040,CICS01,1,0,648,12

// DLBL CUSTMAS,'CUSTOMER.MASTER.CLUSTER',,VSAM
// DLBL PARTMAS,'PART.MASTER.CLUSTER',,VSAM

   LIBDEF CL,SEARCH=(PRODPCL,PLANPCL),TEMP
// EXEC DFHSIP,SIZE=3200K
/*
/&
```

READING RECORDS

To access a record, an application program would issue the following command:

```
EXEC CICS READ DATASET(name)
        INTO(data-area) or SET(pointer-ref)
        LENGTH(data-area)                        optional
        RIDFLD(data-area)
        EQUAL                                    optional
        END-EXEC
```

We stated before that an application program can process information in the Working-Storage or Linkage Section. Let's see how to do this when reading a record for inquiry and searching for a record with a full key equal to the one specified by the application program.

The argument CUSTMAS associated with the DATASET option indicates the DDNAME of the dataset we wish to access.

The INTO option specifies the area where we want the record placed.

The LENGTH option indicates the size of the area reserved. For fixed-length records this is optional but it is always a good idea to supply it since record sizes can change and if the program assumes eventually an error will occur.

```
WORKING-STORAGE SECTION.
01 WSWORKAREA.
    02 RECLEN          PIC S9(4) COMP VALUE +100.
    02 RECKEY          PIC X(8).
01 RECDESC.
    02 CUSTNO          PIC X(8).
    02 CUSTNAME        PIC X(20).
    02 CUSTADDR        PIC X(30).
    02 CUSTINFO        PIC X(42).
PROCEDURE DIVISION.
    EXEC CICS HANDLE CONDITION ERROR(FATALERR)
            NOTFOUND(NOREC)
            END-EXEC.
    MOVE INKEY TO RECKEY.
    EXEC CICS READ DATASET('CUSTMAS')
            INTO(RECDESC) LENGTH(RECLEN)
            RIDFLD(RECKEY) EQUAL
            END-EXEC
```

The RIDFLD option contains the key of the record we wish to read.
The argument RECKEY, as you can see, is external to the record description. This is a good idea since results are unpredictable whenever the
argument specifies a label within the actual record description.

The option EQUAL has been specified but is not needed because
EQUAL is the default.

A HANDLE CONDITION has been established in case the record
can't be found. That's all there is to reading a record!

If we wish to process the record in the Linkage Section, the program
would change to the following:

```
WORKING-STORAGE SECTION.
01 WSWORKAREA.
    02 RECLEN          PIC S9(4) COMP VALUE +100.
    02 RECKEY          PIC X(8).
LINKAGE SECTION.
01 PTRSLST.
    02 FILLER          PIC S9(8) COMP.
    02 RECPTR          PIC S9(8) COMP.
01 RECDESC.
    02 CUSTNO          PIC X(8).
    02 CUSTNAME        PIC X(20).
    02 CUSTADDR        PIC X(30).
    02 CUSTINFO        PIC X(42).
PROCEDURE DIVISION.
    EXEC CICS HANDLE CONDITION ERROR(FATALERR)
            NOTFOUND(NOREC)
            END-EXEC.
    MOVE INKEY TO RECKEY.
    EXEC CICS READ DATASET('CUSTMAS')
            SET(RECPTR)  LENGTH(RECLEN)
            RIDFLD(RECKEY) EQUAL
            END-EXEC.
```

When this command is executed, the file control program will acquire
a piece of storage and ask VSAM to get the record. The record will be
placed in the acquired area and the address of the acquired area will be
passed back to our application program in the RECPTR label. We learned
before that results were unpredictable if the argument associated with the

RIDFLD option contained a label within the record description. When working in the Linkage Section, the label containing the record key MUST be external to the record description. Why? Remember that the area associated with the record description is only acquired after the command has been executed. Thus if we try to move data to an area we do not own, our task could clobber another task's area and thereby cause the other task to abend or the worst yet, cause CICS to abend!

You may be asking yourself, "If this can cause a task to abend or the CICS system to crash, why use it?" Suppose we were working with a variable length record whose size could vary from 500 to 7000 bytes and 90% of the records were only 1000 bytes. If we wanted to process the records in the Working-Storage Section, the maximum size area must be obtained (i.e., 7000). This means that every time a task utilizes this program all the storage would be allocated even though it is needed 10% of the time. This is very wasteful. By using the Linkage Section the exact amount of storage would be acquired only at the proper time.

We learned how to access a record by specifying a full key equal. There are times when it will be necessary to access a record which is equal to or greater than the key specified. In this case, the option GTEQ would be used in place of EQUAL. Remember if both are omitted, the default is EQUAL.

Perhaps there will be a need to access a record when knowing only part of the key (e.g., name search or a range of customer numbers). In these instances we need to do a partial key or generic search. This is easily accomplished by using the GENERIC and KEYLENGTH options. Let's see how this is done by first illustrating Working-Storage.

```
WORKING-STORAGE SECTION.
01 WSWORKAREA.
    02 RECLEN        PIC S9(4) COMP VALUE +100.
    02 RECKEY        PIC X(8).
01 RECDESC.
    02 CUSTNO        PIC X(8).
    02 CUSTNAME      PIC X(20).
    02 CUSTADDR      PIC X(30).
    02 CUSTINFO      PIC X(42).
PROCEDURE DIVISION.
    EXEC CICS HANDLE CONDITION ERROR(FATALERR)
            NOTFOUND(NOREC)
            END-EXEC.
    MOVE INKEY TO RECKEY.
    EXEC CICS READ DATASET('CUSTMAS')
            INTO(RECDESC) LENGTH(RECLEN)
            RIDFLD(RECKEY)
            GENERIC  KEYLENGTH(3)
            GTEQ
            END-EXEC.
```

The option GENERIC indicates we wish to do a partial key search.

The option KEYLENGTH specifies the number of characters, starting at the leftmost byte, we want to search on.

The GTEQ states we wish to search for a record whose key is greater than or equal to the first three bytes of the argument associated with the

RIDFLD option. This command is useful only when desiring to search for a single record. If there is more than one record on the file, we must go into browsing mode. There are separate commands to do browsing, which is covered later in this chapter.

Next we will see how to use the Linkage Section to do generic or partial key search. All the options are the same as in the previous example except that the SET option is used in place of the INTO option.

```
WORKING-STORAGE SECTION.
01 WSWORKAREA.
    02 RECLEN        PIC S9(4) COMP VALUE +100.
    02 RECKEY        PIC X(8).
LINKAGE SECTION.
01 PTRSLST.
    02 FILLER        PIC S9(8) COMP.
    02 RECPTR        PIC S9(8) COMP.
01 RECDESC.
    02 CUSTNO        PIC X(8).
    02 CUSTNAME      PIC X(20).
    02 CUSTADDR      PIC X(30).
    02 CUSTINFO      PIC X(42).
PROCEDURE DIVISION.
    EXEC CICS HANDLE CONDITION ERROR(FATALERR)
            NOTFOUND(NOREC)
            END-EXEC.
    MOVE INKEY TO RECKEY.
    EXEC CICS READ DATASET('CUSTMAS')
            SET(RECPTR)   LENGTH(RECLEN)
            RIDFLD(RECKEY) EQUAL
            GENERIC  KEYLENGTH(3)
            GTEQ
            END-EXEC.
```

UPDATING RECORDS

So far we have seen how to read a record using a full key equal and how to do a generic search. Next we will learn how to read a record for update. When reading a record for update, it is strongly recommended to do a full key equal search.

```
EXEC CICS READ DATASET(name)
        INTO(data-area) or SET(pointer-ref)
        LENGTH(data-area)                        optional
        RIDFLD(data-area)
        EQUAL                                    optional
        UPDATE
        END-EXEC
```

The following is a detailed explanation of what happens when a read for update command is executed. Upon completion of this section, if the process appears unclear please reread this section since it is very important to understand from the view of an application programmer as well as a system analyst. The example will use a protected (LOG=YES) VSAM file.

```
DFHFCT TYPE=DATASET,DATASET=CUSTMAS,                              X
       ACCMETH=(VSAM,KSDS),                                      X
       BUFND=3,                                                   X
       BUFNI=2,                                                   X
       FILSTAT=(ENABLED,OPEN),                                    X
       LOG=YES,                                                   X
       JID=NO,                                                    X
       RECFORM=(FIXED,BLOCKED),                                   X
       SERVREQ=(GET,UPDATE,NEWREC,BROWSE,DELETE,PUT),             X
       STRNO=3

      CICS                    CICS               VSAM
    APPL PGM                  FCP

 READ UPDATE            (1)  ACQ STORAGE
                        (2)  ENQUEUE
                        (3)  VSAM GET      (4)  [REC,REC,...]  CI

     (5)
  REWRITE               (6)  VSAM PUT      (7)  [REC,REC,...]  CI
                                                    UPDATED
     (8)
  RETURN
```

The request begins in the application program and is received by the file control program. The FCP will (1) acquire storage for the record and will issue (2) an ENQUEUE which will give our task exclusive control of a SINGLE record. Next (3) the FCP will issue a VSAM get to acquire the record. At this point our task must wait for the I/O to complete and another task will get a chance to run. When VSAM gets the request it will maintain exclusive control of the control interval (4) in which our record resides. Remember a control interval in VSAM can contain many records. By giving our task exclusive control, it means no other task will be allowed to access this particular control interval with a request which leads to modification. Thus those tasks will have to wait. Any task could issue a read-only request and not wait. VSAM will pass the record back to the FCP which in turn will pass the record back to the application program. Since our task has exclusive control of a single record in CICS and an entire CI in VSAM, it is imperative to rewrite the record and terminate our task as soon as possible.

After our application program has modified the record and wishes to rewrite (5) it back to the file, it will execute the following command:

```
EXEC CICS REWRITE DATASET('CUSTMAS')
          FROM(RECDESC) LENGTH(RECLEN)
          END-EXEC
```

The option FROM indicates where the record we wish to rewrite is located.

The LENGTH option specifies how large the record is. It is possible to rewrite a different size record as long as a variable-length record has been specified in the FCT. The key of the record is not needed since CICS knows the key of the record from the previous READ/UPDATE request. Thus the key can't be changed. The request will be passed to FCP.

The FCP (6) will ask VSAM to replace the record in the control interval. Again our task must wait for the I/O to complete and other tasks will get a chance to run. VSAM (7) will replace the record, release the control interval and the FCP will release any storage associated with the record. VSAM has released exclusive control of the control interval but FCP must not release exclusive control of the record by issuing a DEQUEUE. For protected resources (LOG=YES in the FCT) the DEQUEUE is not issued until task termination or a SYNCPOINT. When our application program (8) gets control back, it can do whatever processing is needed and eventually issue a RETURN command. Figure 8-2 illustrates Working-Storage and Figure 8-3 illustrates the Linkage Section.

Notice the LENGTH option has as an argument the RECLEN label. As long as the content of this field has not changed it is fine to use since the prior READ/UPDATE has already set its value.

Notice in Figure 8-3, that zeros are moved to the label RECPTR. This is being done because FCP freed the storage where the record was originally residing. Thus when our task gets control back, the application program has an address which is no longer valid. If the application program accidentally references any labels associated with RECPTR, the result could be abending of another task, our task, or CICS. By zeroing out the RECPTR, if we accidentally reference the labels, only our task would abend and no others. This would happen because our task would be referencing an area outside of the CICS region.

Since CICS maintains exclusive control of a record and VSAM maintains exclusive control of a control interval, the application program must release this exclusive control as soon as possible. Exclusive control of the control interval is normally released with a REWRITE command. But suppose after the READ/UPDATE command has been issued, it is determined that an update should not occur. The exclusive control must be released. An efficient way of accomplishing this is by issuing the following command:

EXEC CICS UNLOCK DATASET(name) END-EXEC

We only need to specify the DATASET option. The VSAM exclusive control will be released without the I/O overhead incurred with a REWRITE command. If the Linkage Section has been used to access the record, that storage will automatically be freed. Thus the address in the BLL cell associated with the 01 record description will be invalid. We need to move zeros to the BLL cell to maintain integrity. Figure 8-4 illustrates Working-Storage.

Figure 8-5 will illustrate the Linkage Section and the BLL cell will be zeroed out.

In command CICS, it is only possible to have one outstanding READ for UPDATE for a dataset at any time in a task. When it is necessary to read another record for update from the same dataset in the same task, an intervening REWRITE /UNLOCK command is necessary to release the previous record READ for UPDATE.

Figure 8-2.

```
WORKING-STORAGE SECTION.
01 WSWORKAREA.
    02 RECLEN        PIC S9(4) COMP VALUE +100.
    02 RECKEY        PIC X(8).
01 RECDESC.
    02 CUSTNO        PIC X(8).
    02 CUSTNAME      PIC X(20).
    02 CUSTADDR      PIC X(30).
    02 CUSTINFO      PIC X(42).
PROCEDURE DIVISION.
    EXEC CICS HANDLE CONDITION ERROR(FATALERR)
            NOTFOUND(NOREC)
            END-EXEC.
    MOVE INKEY TO RECKEY.
    EXEC CICS READ DATASET('CUSTMAS')
            INTO(RECDESC) LENGTH(RECLEN)
            RIDFLD(RECKEY) EQUAL
            UPDATE
            END-EXEC
    modify the record
    EXEC CICS REWRITE DATASET('CUSTMAS')
            FROM(RECDESC)  LENGTH(RECLEN)
            END-EXEC
```

Figure 8-3.

```
WORKING-STORAGE SECTION.
01 WSWORKAREA.
    02 RECLEN        PIC S9(4) COMP VALUE +100.
    02 RECKEY        PIC X(8).
LINKAGE SECTION.
01 PTRSLST.
    02 FILLER        PIC S9(8) COMP.
    02 RECPTR        PIC S9(8) COMP.
01 RECDESC.
    02 CUSTNO        PIC X(8).
    02 CUSTNAME      PIC X(20).
    02 CUSTADDR      PIC X(30).
    02 CUSTINFO      PIC X(42).
PROCEDURE DIVISION.
    EXEC CICS HANDLE CONDITION ERROR(FATALERR)
            NOTFOUND(NOREC)
            END-EXEC.
    MOVE INKEY TO RECKEY.
    EXEC CICS READ DATASET('CUSTMAS')
            SET(RECPTR)  LENGTH(RECLEN)
            RIDFLD(RECKEY) EQUAL
            UPDATE
            END-EXEC.
    modify the record
    EXEC CICS REWRITE DATASET('CUSTMAS')
            FROM(RECDESC)  LENGTH(RECLEN)
            END-EXEC.
    MOVE ZEROS TO RECPTR.
```

Figure 8-4.

```
WORKING-STORAGE SECTION.
01 WSWORKAREA.
    02 RECLEN           PIC S9(4) COMP VALUE +100.
    02 RECKEY           PIC X(8).
01 RECDESC.
    02 CUSTNO           PIC X(8).
    02 CUSTNAME         PIC X(20).
    02 CUSTADDR         PIC X(30).
    02 CUSTINFO         PIC X(42).
PROCEDURE DIVISION.
    EXEC CICS HANDLE CONDITION ERROR(FATALERR)
            NOTFOUND(NOREC)
            END-EXEC.
    MOVE INKEY TO RECKEY.
    EXEC CICS READ DATASET('CUSTMAS')
            INTO(RECDESC) LENGTH(RECLEN)
            RIDFLD(RECKEY) EQUAL
            UPDATE
            END-EXEC.
    modify the record
    EXEC CICS UNLOCK DATASET('CUSTMAS')
            END-EXEC.
```

Figure 8-5.

```
WORKING-STORAGE SECTION.
01 WSWORKAREA.
    02 RECLEN           PIC S9(4) COMP VALUE +100.
    02 RECKEY           PIC X(8).
LINKAGE SECTION.
01 PTRSLST.
    02 FILLER           PIC S9(8) COMP.
    02 RECPTR           PIC S9(8) COMP.
01 RECDESC.
    02 CUSTNO           PIC X(8).
    02 CUSTNAME         PIC X(20).
    02 CUSTADDR         PIC X(30).
    02 CUSTINFO         PIC X(42).
PROCEDURE DIVISION.
    EXEC CICS HANDLE CONDITION ERROR(FATALERR)
            NOTFOUND(NOREC)
            END-EXEC.
    MOVE INKEY TO RECKEY.
    EXEC CICS READ DATASET('CUSTMAS')
            SET(RECPTR)   LENGTH(RECLEN)
            RIDFLD(RECKEY) EQUAL
            UPDATE
            END-EXEC.
    process the record
    EXEC CICS UNLOCK DATASET('CUSTMAS')
            END-EXEC.
    MOVE ZEROS TO RECPTR.
```

DELETING RECORDS

Perhaps there will be times when it is necessary to remove records from a file. When this need arises, the DELETE command can be used to physically remove records but only from VSAM KSDS or RRDS files.

```
EXEC CICS DELETE DATASET(name)
                  RIDFLD(data-area)               optional
                  GENERIC                         optional
                  KEYLENGTH(data-value)           optional
                  NUMREC(data-value)              optional
                  END-EXEC
```

In the first example, our program will read a record for update and examine a date field to determine whether the record should be removed. Once it has been determined that the record is eligible for deletion, it will be removed with the DELETE command. Figure 8-6 will illustrate Working-Storage.

Figure 8-6.

```
WORKING-STORAGE SECTION.
01 WSWORKAREA.
    02 RECLEN         PIC S9(4) COMP VALUE +100.
    02 RECKEY         PIC X(8).
01 RECDESC.
    02 CUSTNO         PIC X(8).
    02 CUSTNAME       PIC X(20).
    02 CUSTADDR       PIC X(30).
    02 CUSTINFO       PIC X(42).
PROCEDURE DIVISION.
    EXEC CICS HANDLE CONDITION ERROR(FATALERR)
              NOTFOUND(NOREC)
              END-EXEC.
    MOVE INKEY TO RECKEY.
    EXEC CICS READ DATASET('CUSTMAS')
              INTO(RECDESC) LENGTH(RECLEN)
              RIDFLD(RECKEY) EQUAL
              UPDATE
              END-EXEC.
    process the record
    EXEC CICS DELETE DATASET('CUSTMAS')
              END-EXEC.
NOREC.
FATALERR.
```

Figure 8-7 will illustrate the Linkage Section and the BLL cell will be zeroed out.

You will notice there was no need to specify the RIDFLD option because a prior READ for UPDATE command had already obtained the record. Exclusive control will be released. In the Linkage Section example, zeros again have been moved to maintain integrity because the storage has automatically been freed.

If we already know the record we wish to delete, is there a need to issue a READ for UPDATE first? NO! The following DELETE command could be issued to delete a single record with a full key equal to the one specified with the RIDFLD option.

```
EXEC CICS DELETE DATASET('CUSTMAS')
                  RIDFLD(RECKEY)
                  END-EXEC
```

Figure 8-7.

```
WORKING-STORAGE SECTION.
01 WSWORKAREA.
    02 RECLEN          PIC S9(4) COMP VALUE +100.
    02 RECKEY          PIC X(8).
LINKAGE SECTION.
01 PTRSLST.
    02 FILLER          PIC S9(8) COMP.
    02 RECPTR          PIC S9(8) COMP.
01 RECDESC.
    02 CUSTNO          PIC X(8).
    02 CUSTNAME        PIC X(20).
    02 CUSTADDR        PIC X(30).
    02 CUSTINFO        PIC X(42).
PROCEDURE DIVISION.
    EXEC CICS HANDLE CONDITION ERROR(FATALERR)
              NOTFOUND(NOREC)
              END-EXEC.
    MOVE INKEY TO RECKEY.
    EXEC CICS READ DATASET('CUSTMAS')
              SET(RECPTR)  LENGTH(RECLEN)
              RIDFLD(RECKEY) EQUAL
              UPDATE
              END-EXEC.
    process the record
    EXEC CICS DELETE DATASET('CUSTMAS')
              END-EXEC.
    MOVE ZEROS to RECPTR.
NOREC.
FATALERR.
```

In addition to the DATASET option, only the RIDFLD option need be specified. Its associated argument must contain the key of the record we wish to delete. This method is much more efficient but you had better be sure of the record you are removing!

Both of the previous methods illustrate ways of deleting single records. Perhaps a need will arise to remove a group of records. This method is referred to as generic or partial key deleting and is only permitted for unprotected files (LOG=NO in the FCT). In addition, there is no need for any prior read for update.

```
EXEC CICS DELETE DATASET('CUSTMAS')
          RIDFLD(RECKEY)  GENERIC  KEYLENGTH(2)
          NUMREC(RECDEL) END-EXEC
```

The GENERIC option indicates we wish to perform a partial key delete.

The option KEYLENGTH and its associated argument indicate the number of positions, starting at the leftmost byte, of the key we wish to match on. In this example, we want CICS to find every record on the file whose first 2 positions match the first 2 we have specified in the RIDFLD argument. All the records matching it will be deleted. After the operation has been completed, CICS will notify our task of the number of records deleted if we specified the NUMREC option. Of course by then it could be too late! When using this command in this manner, it is always a good idea to have a backup of the file you are working with!

ADDING RECORDS

Now that we have learned how to read, update, and delete (VSAM only) records, let's see how to add records to a file using the following command:

```
EXEC CICS WRITE DATASET(name)
               RIDFLD(data-area)
               FROM(data-area) LENGTH(data-value)
               KEYLENGTH(data-value)           optional
               MASSINSERT                      optional
               END-EXEC
```

The DATASET option indicates the file we wish to add the records to.

The RIDFLD option specifies the key of the record we wish to add.

The FROM option specifies where the record is located in our application program.

The LENGTH option indicates the size of our record.

The KEYLENGTH option is used to ensure that the key we are specifying is the same size as what is stated in the FCT. Thus this option may be useful the first few times an application program is adding records. After that it really isn't necessary. Figure 8-8 illustrates adding a record from Working-Storage.

Figure 8-8.

```
WORKING-STORAGE SECTION.
01 WSWORKAREA.
    02 RECLEN          PIC S9(4) COMP VALUE +100.
    02 RECKEY          PIC X(8).
01 RECDESC.
    02 CUSTNO          PIC X(8).
    02 CUSTNAME        PIC X(20).
    02 CUSTADDR        PIC X(30).
    02 CUSTINFO        PIC X(42).
PROCEDURE DIVISION.
    EXEC CICS HANDLE CONDITION ERROR(FATALERR)
              DUPREC(NODUPS)
              END-EXEC.
    build the record to add
    EXEC CICS WRITE DATASET('CUSTMAS')
              FROM(RECDESC) LENGTH(RECLEN)
              RIDFLD(RECKEY)
              END-EXEC
NODUPS.
FATALERR.
```

Figure 8-9 will illustrate the Linkage Section and the BLL cell will NOT be zeroed out.

There is no need to zero out the BLL cell in the Linkage Section since the application program explicitly requested the storage via the GET-MAIN command (Chapter 9). If the storage is no longer needed, a FREE-MAIN command would be issued or task termination will free the storage (Chapter 9). If we were going to add a number of records, it would only be necessary to issue the GETMAIN command once.

Figure 8-9.

```
WORKING-STORAGE SECTION.
01 WSWORKAREA.
    02 RECLEN        PIC S9(4) COMP VALUE +100.
    02 RECKEY        PIC X(8).
LINKAGE SECTION.
01 PTRSLST.
    02 FILLER        PIC S9(8) COMP.
    02 RECPTR        PIC S9(8) COMP.
01 RECDESC.
    02 CUSTNO        PIC X(8).
    02 CUSTNAME      PIC X(20).
    02 CUSTADDR      PIC X(30).
    02 CUSTINFO      PIC X(42).
PROCEDURE DIVISION.
    EXEC CICS HANDLE CONDITION ERROR(FATALERR)
              DUPREC(NODUPS)
              END-EXEC.
    EXEC CICS GETMAIN NUMBYTE(100) SET(RECPTR) END-EXEC.
    build the record to add
    EXEC CICS WRITE DATASET('CUSTMAS')
              FROM(RECDESC) LENGTH(RECLEN)
              RIDFLD(RECKEY)
              END-EXEC.
NODUPS.
FATALERR.
```

Another option MASSINSERT will allow the program to perform sequential insertion. The UNLOCK command must be issued to terminate a MASSINSERT operation. This method of inserting sequential records is efficient because I/Os are kept to a minimum, but care should be taken because this process could slow down other tasks. Before using this option, check with a system programmer.

That's all there is to adding records to files!

BROWSING

We previously learned that the FCP will only process direct access files in CICS. But we may have a need to read records sequentially. Thus it might appear that it is not possible to do this with the FCP. Do not despair! We can do browsing in CICS which simply means the act of going through a direct access file sequentially. There are separate commands to do this. The first command which we will examine will determine the starting location in the file we wish to browse.

```
EXEC CICS STARTBR DATASET(name)
                  RIDFLD(data-area)
                  KEYLENGTH(data-value)        optional
                  GENERIC                      optional
                  GTEQ or EQUAL                optional
                  END-EXEC
```

This command will cause the FCP to request VSAM to find a record on the file whose key is equal to or greater than the one specified with the RIDFLD option. When the location of the record has been found, it will be returned to the FCP and the FCP will notify the application program. The Exception Condition NOTFOUND will occur if no records can be found. Once the starting location has been found, we need to acquire the records. The command READNEXT will accomplish this.

```
EXEC CICS READNEXT DATASET(NAME)
            INTO(data-area) or SET(pointer-ref)
            RIDFLD(data-area)
            LENGTH(data-area)                optional
            KEYLENGTH(data-value)            optional
            END-EXEC
```

This command will give the application program access to the necessary record in the control interval.

When we wish to obtain the next record, another READNEXT command would be issued. Will another I/O be generated? NO! We will get the next record out of the block of records. Another I/O will occur only after all the records in the current block or control interval have been obtained. If we continue to issue the READNEXT command, eventually an ENDFILE Exception Condition will occur when we have reached the end of the file. Thus you can see that browsing can be very efficient since minimal I/O occurs. It would also seem that blocking a large number of records would be advantageous. That is very true but it could be a disadvantage if the file was also being used for updating. Why? Remember that exclusive control is maintained over a block of records except for ISAM which maintains exclusive control via a single record.

When we are finished obtaining the necessary records, it will be time to terminate the browsing operation. The command to do this is ENDBR.

```
EXEC CICS ENDBR DATASET(name) END-EXEC
```

This command will release any storage associated with the browse in addition to releasing a string in VSAM. If the Linkage Section has been used, remember to move zeros to the appropriate BLL cell. It is important to issue this command as soon as possible so that resources are not unnecessarily monopolized. Task termination will also terminate the browse operation.

That's all there is to browsing. But there are some additional features which can be used. Perhaps we are browsing a VSAM file and have the need to skip to another position in the file. This can be done using the skip-sequential feature. All this means is to skip to another higher key record in the file. See example on next page.

By merely moving another higher ascending key into the RIDFLD option argument, we are able to accomplish skip-sequential processing. Though this feature is only for VSAM files, it can be accomplished with the RESETBR command for ISAM and BDAM files. See example on next page.

Following is SKIP=SEQUENTIAL PROCESSING.

```
WORKING-STORAGE SECTION.
01 WSWORKAREA.
    02 RECLEN          PIC S9(4) COMP VALUE +100.
    02 RECKEY          PIC X(8).
01 RECDESC.
    02 CUSTNO          PIC X(8).
    02 CUSTNAME        PIC X(20).
    02 CUSTADDR        PIC X(30).
    02 CUSTINFO        PIC X(42).
PROCEDURE DIVISION.
    EXEC CICS HANDLE CONDITION ERROR(FATALERR)
              NOTFOUND(NOREC)
              END-EXEC.
    MOVE '11111111' TO RECKEY.
    EXEC CICS STARTBR DATASET('CUSTMAS')
              GENERIC   KEYLENGTH(2)
              RIDFLD(RECKEY)
              END-EXEC
    EXEC CICS READNEXT DATASET('CUSTMAS')
                       INTO(RECDESC)   LENGTH(RECLEN)
                       RIDFLD(RECKEY) KEYLENGTH(2)
                       END-EXEC.
    MOVE '88888888' TO RECKEY.
    EXEC CICS READNEXT DATASET('CUSTMAS')
                       INTO(RECDESC)    LENGTH(RECLEN)
                       RIDFLD(RECKEY)   KEYLENGTH(2)
                       END-EXEC.
NODUPS.
FATALERR.
```

Following is RESETBR PROCESSING.

```
WORKING-STORAGE SECTION.
01 WSWORKAREA.
    02 RECLEN          PIC S9(4) COMP VALUE +100.
    02 RECKEY          PIC X(8).
01 RECDESC.
    02 CUSTNO          PIC X(8).
    02 CUSTNAME        PIC X(20).
    02 CUSTADDR        PIC X(30).
    02 CUSTINFO        PIC X(42).
PROCEDURE DIVISION.
    EXEC CICS HANDLE CONDITION ERROR(FATALERR)
              NOTFOUND(NOREC)
              END-EXEC.
    MOVE '11111111' TO RECKEY.
    EXEC CICS STARTBR DATASET('CUSTMAS')
                      GENERIC   KEYLENGTH(2)
                      RIDFLD(RECKEY)
                      END-EXEC.
GET-NEXT-RECORD.
    EXEC CICS READNEXT DATASET('CUSTMAS')
                       INTO(RECDESC)   LENGTH(RECLEN)
                       RIDFLD(RECKEY) KEYLENGTH(2)
                       END-EXEC.
    MOVE '88888888' TO RECKEY.
    EXEC CICS RESETBR  DATASET('CUSTMAS')
                       INTO(RECDESC)    LENGTH(RECLEN)
                       RIDFLD(RECKEY)   KEYLENGTH(2)
                       END-EXEC.
    GO TO GET-NEXT-RECORD.
NODUPS.
FATALERR.
```

The RESETBR command will cause the current browse operation to terminate and will initiate another browse operation at the location specified via the RIDFLD option. As with the STARTBR command, a READNEXT must be issued to obtain the first record.

Another feature for VSAM files is the ability to read a file backwards. This is accomplished with the READPREV command.

```
EXEC CICS READPREV DATASET(name)
                   INTO(data-area) or SET(pointer-ref)
                   RIDFLD(data-area)
                   LENGTH(data-area)              optional
                   KEYLENGTH(data-value)          optional
                   END-EXEC.
```

All the options associated with this command are the same as those associated with the READNEXT command. The first READPREV will allow the application program to obtain the record which was pointed to by the STARTBR command. If we continue to issue the READPREV command, we will eventually get to the beginning of the file. The ENDFILE Exception Condition will occur but will really indicate that the beginning of the file has been found. ISAM and BDAM files do not currently have this feature. You may be asking yourself: "If I am reading a VSAM file using the READNEXT command, could a READPREV also be issued in the same browse operation?" The answer is YES!

```
WORKING-STORAGE SECTION.
 01 WSWORKAREA.
     02 RECLEN         PIC S9(4) COMP VALUE +100.
     02 RECKEY         PIC X(8).
 01 RECDESC.
     02 CUSTNO         PIC X(8).
     02 CUSTNAME       PIC X(20).
     02 CUSTADDR       PIC X(30).
     02 CUSTINFO       PIC X(42).
PROCEDURE DIVISION.
     EXEC CICS HANDLE CONDITION ERROR(FATALERR)
               NOTFOUND(NOREC)
               END-EXEC.
     MOVE '88888888' TO RECKEY.
     EXEC CICS STARTBR DATASET('CUSTMAS')
                  GENERIC   KEYLENGTH(2)
                  RIDFLD(RECKEY)
                  END-EXEC
     EXEC CICS READNEXT DATASET('CUSTMAS')
                  INTO(RECDESC)   LENGTH(RECLEN)
                  RIDFLD(RECKEY) KEYLENGTH(2)
                  END-EXEC.
     EXEC CICS READPREV DATASET('CUSTMAS')
                  INTO(RECDESC)   LENGTH(RECLEN)
                  RIDFLD(RECKEY)  KEYLENGTH(2)
                  END-EXEC.

 NODUPS.
 FATALERR.
```

The first time the READPREV is issued, the application program will still be pointing to the same record as was previously obtained via the

READNEXT command. Thus two READPREV commands would be necessary to obtain the first record previous to the one we are currently pointing at. This is only true when switching from READNEXT to READPREV. Keep in mind it is not possible to do skip-sequential processing in a backwards direction.

Let's examine the last feature of browsing. Perhaps we have the need to examine a direct access file sequentially and update only records with a specific date. Thus we need to do browsing and updating at the same time. Before continuing, please keep in mind that an application like this might be better suited to batch processing.

```
WORKING-STORAGE SECTION.
01 WSWORKAREA.
   02 RECLEN         PIC S9(4) COMP VALUE +100.
   02 RECKEY         PIC X(8).
01 RECDESC.
   02 CUSTNO         PIC X(8).
   02 CUSTNAME       PIC X(20).
   02 CUSTADDR       PIC X(30).
   02 CUSTDATE.
      04 CUSTMONTH   PIC XX.
      04 CUSTDAY     PIC XX.
      04 CUSTYEAR    PIC XX.
   02 CUSTSTATUS     PIC X.
   02 CUSTINFO       PIC X(42).
PROCEDURE DIVISION.
   EXEC CICS HANDLE CONDITION ERROR(FATALERR)
             NOTFOUND(NOREC)
             ENDFILE(ENDPGM)
             END-EXEC.
   MOVE '11111111' TO RECKEY.
   EXEC CICS STARTBR DATASET('CUSTMAS')
             GENERIC   KEYLENGTH(2)
             RIDFLD(RECKEY)
             END-EXEC.
GET-NEXT-RECORD.
   EXEC CICS READNEXT DATASET('CUSTMAS')
             INTO(RECDESC)   LENGTH(RECLEN)
             RIDFLD(RECKEY)  KEYLENGTH(2)
             END-EXEC.
   IF CUSTYEAR IS LESS THAN 80
      EXEC CICS READ DATASET('CUSTMAS') RIDFLD(RECKEY)
             INTO(RECDESC)   LENGTH(RECLEN)
             UPDATE   END-EXEC.
      MOVE I TO CUSTSTATUS.
      EXEC CICS REWRITE DATASET('CUSTMAS')
             FROM(RECDESC)   LENGTH(RECLEN)
             END-EXEC.
   GO TO GET-NEXT-RECORD.
ENDPGM.
   EXEC CICS RETURN END-EXEC.
NODUPS.
FATALERR.
```

When the application program has examined the date and found that the record needs to be updated, a READ for UPDATE command would be issued. Exclusive control will be applied. The record can be updated and immediately rewritten. The exclusive control will be released. After the

REWRITE command has been issued, the application program could just issue another READNEXT command.

Again please keep in mind this can be done but it is not very efficient. If the situation calls for a delete instead of a rewrite, the DELETE command could easily replace the REWRITE command.

```
WORKING-STORAGE SECTION.
01 WSWORKAREA.
    02 RECLEN          PIC S9(4) COMP VALUE +100.
    02 RECKEY          PIC X(8).
01 RECDESC.
    02 CUSTNO          PIC X(8).
    02 CUSTNAME        PIC X(20).
    02 CUSTADDR        PIC X(30).
    02 CUSTDATE.
        04 CUSTMONTH   PIC XX.
        04 CUSTDAY     PIC XX.
        04 CUSTYEAR    PIC XX.
    02 CUSTSTATUS      PIC X.
    02 CUSTINFO        PIC X(35).
PROCEDURE DIVISION.
    EXEC CICS HANDLE CONDITION ERROR(FATALERR)
                NOTFOUND(NOREC)
                ENDFILE(ENDPGM)
                END-EXEC.
    MOVE '11111111' TO RECKEY.
    EXEC CICS STARTBR DATASET('CUSTMAS')
                GENERIC  KEYLENGTH(2)
                RIDFLD(RECKEY)
                END-EXEC
GET-NEXT-RECORD.
    EXEC CICS READNEXT DATASET('CUSTMAS')
                INTO(RECDESC)  LENGTH(RECLEN)
                RIDFLD(RECKEY) KEYLENGTH(2)
                END-EXEC.
    IF CUSTYEAR IS LESS THAN 80
        EXEC CICS DELETE DATASET('CUSTMAS') RIDFLD(RECKEY)
                END-EXEC
    GO TO GET-NEXT-RECORD.
ENDPGM.
    EXEC CICS RETURN END-EXEC.
NODUPS.
FATALERR.
```

EXCEPTION CONDITIONS

DSIDERR   The DATASET name cannot be found in the file control table.

DUPKEY   Only for VSAM alternate index datasets. Indicates that more records exist with the same key. To obtain the other records a browse operation must be initiated.

DUPREC   Indicates that a record already exists on the file with the same key.

ENDFILE   Indicates that the end of file has been reached in a browse operation. When executing a READPREV command it indicates the beginning of the file has been reached.

ILLOGIC   VSAM only. Indicates a condition other than what can be determined by any Exception Condition. When this condition appears, byte one of EIBRCODE will contain the VSAM return code and byte two will contain the VSAM error code. Both codes are in hex and should be converted to decimal before looking up their meaning in the IBM VSAM manual.

INVREQ   Indicates the file operation is not specified in the file control table for the dataset.

IOERR   Indicates that an I/O error has occurred.

LENGERR   Indicates the area reserved for the input operation is not large enough to hold the record.

NOSPACE   Indicates there is not enough space in the file to contain the record.

NOTFND   Indicates that the key of the record specified can't be found.

NOTOPEN   Indicates the file is not open.

To obtain a complete listing of Exception Conditions, consult the IBM Application Programmer's Reference Manual.

EXERCISE

Let's review what we have learned.

1. What is the purpose of the file control table?
2. Explain the difference between VSAM exclusive control and CICS exclusive control when reading a record for update.
3. After a record has been rewritten from the Linkage Section, why is it a good idea to move zeros to the BLL cell associated with the record description?
4. What is the function of an UNLOCK command?
5. Describe three different methods of deleting VSAM records.
6. Define browsing.

The following is an enhancement of what our typical application program is going to do:

1. Accept input data (message).
2. Only the enter and clear keys are valid.
3. The PF1-24 and PA1-3 keys are invalid and if selected, a message will be sent back to the operator indicating an invalid key.
4. When an unformatted message has been received, Send a formatted message back to the operator so that the necessary information about the customer to be added can be gathered.
5. Edit the input message. All fields are required but only a customer name or number is needed.
   A. If OK, continue to #6.
   B. If not OK, highlight the fields that are incorrect so the operator can correct them and send back an error message.

6. Add the new customer to the file.
7. Send a message back to the operator indicating the operation has been successful.

We will code our program to accept the input message only if the operator has selected the enter or clear keys. Any other key selection will result in the following message being sent after the screen has been erased: "invalid key selection". When the clear key has been selected it will indicate that the operator desires to end the session so the following message will be sent: "session completed". There is no need to erase the screen when sending this message because when the operator presses the clear key the screen will automatically be erased. When the enter key has been chosen, the program will accept the input message which can only consist of the transaction code. At this time the label EIBCALEN will be equal to zero since no COMMAREA has been previously saved. This also indicates that it is the first time into this program and a map will be sent to the operator so data can be entered and a COMMAREA will be created at this time. Thus when we enter this program the second time the label EIBCALEN will be greater than zero indicating a map is to be received. When the data has been correctly edited, a record will be added to the customer master file. If any errors exist, a message will be sent back to the operator and the incorrect fields will be highlighted.

When a customer number has been provided, the customer master file will be searched for a key equal to the first four positions provided by the operator. When only a customer name is provided, the program will link to a subroutine, GETCNO, which will return a four-position customer key. The trailing two positions of our six-position customer key will always be zeros. Though this process may not seem very logical, please keep in mind you are learning about the capabilities of CICS at this time.

After the customer record is found, the part master file will be read and updated.

COMMENTS
1. The Exception Condition NOTFND has been established to take effect when no customer or part number can be found.
2. A check for errors is made before continuing with file accessing. This is done to eliminate the I/O involved with reading the datasets. Another check will be made after the files have been read.
3. When only a name has been provided, our program will link to the subroutine GETCNO. Since the customer name already exists in the DFHCOM-MAREA, that area will be passed. The customer number will be returned in the label CCUSTNO.
4. The size of the customer record description is moved to the label MSGLEN. A separate label could have been used.
5. The customer file (CUSTMAS) is being searched for a GENERIC/partial key equal to the first four positions of the customer key which is external to the record description.

```
        IDENTIFICATION DIVISION.
        PROGRAM-ID. COMMEXP.
        ENVIRONMENT DIVISION.
        DATA DIVISION.
        WORKING-STORAGE SECTION.
        COPY DFHAID.
        COPY ICMSET.
        COPY DFHBMSCA.
        01   WSWORKAREA.
             02 MSGLEN              PIC S9(4) COMP VALUE +25.
             02 IOAREA              PIC X(20).
             02 WSDEC128            PIC S9(4)  COMP  VALUE +128.
             02 FILLER             REDEFINES
                WSDEC128.
                04 FILLER          PIC X.
                04 WSHEX80         PIC X.
             02 WSCOMM             PIC X(32)  VALUE  LOW-VALUES.
             02 WSERRIND           PIC 9      VALUE  ZERO.
             02 WSQMRK.
                04 FILLER          PIC X      VALUE '?'.
                04 FILLER          PIC X(19)  VALUE LOW-VALUES.
             02 WSCUSTKEY          PIC X(6).
        01   CUST-RECORD.
             02 FILLER             PIC X.
             02 C-KEY              PIC X(6).
             02 FILLER             PIC X(20).
             02 C-FLAG             PIC X.
             02 FILLER             PIC X(52).
        01   PART-RECORD.
             02 FILLER             PIC X.
             02 P-KEY              PIC X(4).
             02 P-REORDER          PIC 9(5).
             02 P-AMOUNT           PIC 9(5).
             02 FILLER             PIC X(65).
        LINKAGE SECTION.
        01   DFHCOMMAREA.
             02 CCUSTNO            PIC X(4).
             02 CCUSTNM            PIC X(20).
             02 CPARTNO            PIC X(4).
             02 CQTY               PIC X(3).
             02 CQTYN              REDEFINES
                CQTY               PIC 9(3).
             02 CACTCD             PIC X.
        PROCEDURE DIVISION.
   **   IT IS A GOOD PRACTICE TO ESTABLISH A HANDLE CONDITION UPON   **
   **                    ENTRY TO A PROGRAM                          **
        EXEC CICS HANDLE CONDITION ERROR(FATALERR)
1                                  MAPFAIL(NODATA)
                                   NOTFND(NOREC)
                                   END-EXEC.
   **   THE FOLLOWING WILL DETERMINE WHICH KEY THE OPERATOR SELECTED **
        IF EIBAID = DFHENTER
           IF EIBCALEN = 32
              EXEC CICS RECEIVE MAP('ICMAP') MAPSET('ICMSET') END-EXEC
           ELSE
              EXEC CICS SEND MAP('ICMAP') MAPSET('ICMSET')
                              MAPONLY
                              ERASE    END-EXEC
              EXEC CICS RETURN
                         TRANSID(EIBTRNID)
```

```
                    COMMAREA(WSCOMM)  LENGTH(32)
                    END-EXEC
         ELSE
            IF EIBAID = DFHCLEAR
                MOVE  'SESSION COMPLETED' TO IOAREA
                EXEC CICS SEND FROM(IOAREA) LENGTH(17) END-EXEC
                EXEC CICS RETURN END-EXEC
            ELSE
                MOVE 'INVALID KEY PRESSED'  TO IOAREA
                EXEC CICS SEND FROM(IOAREA) LENGTH(19)
                         ERASE END-EXEC.
            EXEC CICS RETURN END-EXEC.
**     THE INPUT DATA WILL BE MERGED WITH THE PREVIOUSLY SAVED DATA **
       IF CUSTNOL IS GREATER THAN ZERO
           MOVE CUSTNOI TO CCUSTNO
       ELSE
           IF CUSTNOF = WSHEX80
               MOVE LOW-VALUES TO CCUSTNO.
       IF CUSTNML IS GREATER THAN ZERO
           MOVE CUSTNMI TO CCUSTNM
       ELSE
           IF CUSTNMF = WSHEX80
               MOVE LOW-VALUES TO CCUSTNM.
       IF PARTNOL IS GREATER THAN ZERO
           MOVE PARTNOI TO CPARTNO
       ELSE
           IF PARTNOF = WSHEX80
               MOVE LOW-VALUES TO CPARTNO.
       IF QTYL IS GREATER THAN ZERO
           MOVE QTYI TO CQTY
       ELSE
           IF QTYF = WSHEX80
               MOVE LOW-VALUES TO CQTY.
       IF ACTCDL IS GREATER THAN ZERO
           MOVE ACTCDI TO CACTCD
       ELSE
           IF ACTCDF = WSHEX80
               MOVE LOW-VALUES TO CACTCD.
       MOVE LOW-VALUES TO CUSTNOO CUSTNMO PARTNOO QTYO ACTCDO.
       MOVE DFHBMUNP TO CUSTNOA CUSTNMA PARTNOA QTYA.
   CONTPROCESS.
**     EDIT THE DATA WHICH NOW RESIDES IN DFHCOMMAREA              **
       IF CCUSTNO = LOW-VALUES AND CCUSTNM = LOW-VALUES
           MOVE WSQMRK TO CUSTNOO
           MOVE  -1    TO CUSTNOL
           MOVE   1    TO WSERRIND
           MOVE DFHBMBRY TO CUSTNOA.
       IF CPARTNO = LOW-VALUES
           MOVE WSQMRK TO PARTNO
           MOVE  -1   TO PARTNOL
           MOVE   1   TO WSERRIND
           MOVE DFHBMBRY TO PARTNOA.
       IF CQTY = LOW-VALUES
           MOVE WSQMRK TO QTYO
           MOVE  -1    TO QTYL
           MOVE   1    TO WSERRIND
           MOVE DFHBMBRY TO QTYA
       ELSE
           IF CQTY IS NOT NUMERIC
               MOVE -1 TO QTYL
```

```
                    MOVE 1   TO WSERRIND
                    MOVE DFHBMBRY TO QTYA.
            IF CACTCD = LOW-VALUES
                MOVE WSQMRK TO ACTCDO
                MOVE  -1    TO ACTCDL
                MOVE   1    TO WSERRIND
                MOVE DFHBMBRY TO ACTCDA.
            IF WSERRIND = ZERO
2               NEXT SENTENCE
            ELSE
                GO TO MOVE-ERROR-MSG.
            IF CCUSTNO = LOW-VALUES
                EXEC CICS LINK PROGRAM('GETCNO')
3                          COMMAREA(DFHCOMMAREA)
                           LENGTH(EIBCALEN)
                           END-EXEC.
        MOVE CCUSTNO TO WSCUSTKEY.
     READ-CUSTOMER-FILE.
4       MOVE +80  TO  MSGLEN.
        EXEC CICS READ DATASET('CUSTMAS')
5                    RIDFLD(WSCUSTKEY)
                     INTO(CUST-RECORD)  LENGTH(MSGLEN)
                     GENERIC           KEYLENGTH(4)
                     END-EXEC.
     READ-PART-FILE.
6       MOVE +80  TO  MSGLEN.
        EXEC CICS READ DATASET('PARTMAS')
7                    RIDFLD(CPARTNO)
                     INTO(PART-RECORD)  LENGTH(MSGLEN)
                     UPDATE
                     END-EXEC.
        IF WSERRIND = ZERO
            ADD-RECORD.
     MOVE-ERROR-MSG.
        MOVE 'ERRORS HIGHLIGHTED    PLEASE CORRECT AND RESUBMIT' TO
            ERRMSGO.
     SEND-DATAONLY-MAP.
        EXEC CICS SEND MAP('ICMAP') MAPSET('ICMSET')
                     DATAONLY
                     CURSOR        END-EXEC.
        EXEC CICS RETURN
                 TRANSID(EIBTRNID)
                 COMMAREA(DFHCOMMAREA)
                 LENGTH(EIBCALEN)
                 END-EXEC.
     ADD-RECORD.
        IF CACTCD = 'A'
8           ADD CQTYN TO P-AMOUNT
        ELSE
            SUBTRACT CQTYN FROM P-AMOUNT.
        EXEC CICS REWRITE DATASET('PARTMAS')
9                    FROM(PART-RECORD)  LENGTH(MSGLEN)
            END-EXEC.
  **   THE COMMAREA WILL BE REFRESHED                       **
        MOVE LOW-VALUES TO DFHCOMMAREA.
        MOVE -1 TO CUSTNOL.
        MOVE 'UPDATE SUCCESSFUL' TO ERRMSGO.
10      EXEC CICS SEND MAP('ICMAP') MAPSET('ICMSET')
                     ERASEAUP
                     CURSOR
```

```
                    DATAONLY
                    END-EXEC.
11      EXEC CICS RETURN
                    TRANSID(EIBTRNID)
                    COMMAREA(DFHCOMMAREA)
                    LENGTH(EIBCALEN)
                    END-EXEC.
    NOREC.
        IF EIBRSRCE = 'CUSTMAS'
12          MOVE -1 TO CUSTNOL
            MOVE 1 TO WSERRIND
            MOVE DFHBMBRY TO CUSTNOA
            MOVE CCUSTNO TO CUSTNOO
            GO TO READ-PART-FILE
        ELSE
            MOVE -1 TO PARTNOL
            MOVE DFHBMBRY TO PARTNOA
            GO TO SEND-ERROR-MSG.
    NODATA.
        MOVE LOW-VALUES TO ICMAPO.
        IF DFHCOMMAREA = LOW-VALUES
            MOVE 'NO DATA ENTERED' TO ERRMSGO
            MOVE -1    TO CUSTNOL.
        GO TO SEND-DATAONLY-MAP.
    FATALERR.
 **    THE FOLLOWING WILL PROCESS ANY EXCEPTION CONDITIONS          **
        EXEC CICS ABEND ABCODE('CMEX') END-EXEC.
        GOBACK.
```

6. Again, we are establishing the size of our record description. This is similiar to comment #3.

7. The part number file (PARTMAS) is being read for update using the key (CPARTNO) in the DFHCOMMAREA.

8. The necessary changes to the part record are made.

9. The part number record is being written back to the file.

10. The screen will be erased, all the attributes will be reset to their original settings, the cursor will be placed in the customer number field, and the message will be sent to the screen.

11. The COMMAREA is refreshed and the operator can begin processing the next customer.

12. This is a common routine to be used for determining which file generated the NOTFND condition. The label EIBRSRCE contains the name of the dataset and can thus be tested. This type of processing is preferred over separate HANDLE CONDITION commands because it involves less overhead. In Chapter 13, we will see another technique which will cause less branching in the program.

Storage Control

So far in our program processing, there has not been a need for the application program to acquire any storage areas since the proper CICS management module has obtained the storage on behalf of our task. We could summarize things this way: in general, all application programs do input and/or output operations to files and terminals. These operations can be done in the Working-Storage or Linkage Sections of application programs. If all operations are performed in the Working-Storage Section, there would be no need to dynamically acquire storage while our program is processing because the storage will be acquired during program initialization by CICS.

When input operations are performed using the Linkage Section, the storage is acquired on behalf of the application program by the various management modules and then the address is returned to the application program. Again there is no need for the application program to acquire storage. Output operations can also be performed using the Linkage Section. Any area in the Linkage Section can be used as long as a valid address exists for the area. For instance, an area which was previously used for an input operation could be used for an output operation.

ACQUIRING STORAGE

But there will be instances when no input area exists or the input area is not large enough. When this happens, the application program must acquire its own storage. The way to do this is by issuing the following command:

```
EXEC CICS GETMAIN LENGTH(data-value)
                  SET(pointer-ref)
                  INITIMG(data-area)                optional
                  END-EXEC
```

The LENGTH option indicates the number of bytes (size of area) we need.

The SET option contains the BLL cell where we want the address of the acquired storage area returned.

The INITIMG option will initialize the obtained area to the one-byte hex configuration specified in the argument associated with this option. Generally it is not a good idea to use this option for the following reasons:

1. The initialization process is slow and time-consuming.
2. Usually once an area has been obtained, data is moved to it, so it really would appear to be redundant effort.

The typical time this command is used is when adding records to a file using the Linkage Section. Generally no prior input operation has occurred. A storage area must be obtained and the record can be assembled in the obtained area and written to a file. Figure 9-1 illustrates this method of adding a record.

In Figure 9-1, two 100-byte records are being added to the file. Notice that after the first has been added, there is no need to issue another GETMAIN command. This is because our application program explicitly requested the storage by issuing the GETMAIN command. Previously we learned that if we issued a READ for UPDATE with the SET option followed by a REWRITE, the obtained area was automatically freed. This is because our application program was not the explicit requester. In that case FCP was, so FCP will also free the storage. We could summarize all this by simply stating: whatever program explicitly requests the storage (GETMAIN) is responsible to release that storage.

We have seen how to obtain the storage. Let's see how to release it. The FREEMAIN command is used to release a storage area previously obtained via a GETMAIN command.

```
EXEC CICS FREEMAIN DATA (data-area) END-EXEC
```

The DATA option should contain the name of the 01 level to be freed and not the BLL cell name. Figure 9-2 contains the FREEMAIN command after the second record has been added.

Figure 9-1.

```
WORKING-STORAGE SECTION.
01   WSWORKAREA.
     02 RECLEN                  PIC S9(4) COMP VALUE +100.
     02 RECKEY                  PIC X(8).
     02 RECOUNT                 PIC 9              VALUE 0.
LINKAGE SECTION.
01   PTRSLST.
     02 FILLER                  PIC S9(8) COMP.
     02 RECPTR                  PIC S9(8) COMP.
01   RECDESC.
     02 CUSTNO                  PIC X(8).
     02 CUSTNAME                PIC X(20).
     02 CUSTADDR                PIC X(30).
     02 CUSTINFO                PIC X(42).
PROCEDURE DIVISION.
     EXEC CICS HANDLE CONDITION ERROR(FATALERR)
                                DUPREC(NODUPS)
                                END-EXEC.
     EXEC CICS GETMAIN LENGTH(100) SET(RECPTR) END-EXEC.
BUILD-RECORD.
     build the record to add
     EXEC CICS WRITE DATASET('CUSTMAS')
                     FROM(RECPTR)   LENGTH(RECLEN)
                     RIDFLD(RECKEY)
                     END-EXEC.
     IF RECOUNT IS LESS THAN 2
        GO TO BUILD-RECORD.
     EXEC CICS RETURN END-EXEC.
NODUPS.
FATALERR.
```

Notice in Figure 9-2 that after the area has been freed, zeros are moved to the BLL cell associated with the area. As previously stated this is a good idea to help maintain the integrity of our CICS system.

Although it is always a good idea to FREEMAIN the area when it is no longer needed, if we forget to release the storage it will automatically be done at task termination. Thus this storage will normally exist until task termination.

Suppose we issue a GETMAIN and there is no storage available. The default is to have our task wait until storage becomes available. Usually this is a very safe default to take unless your CICS system typically goes short on storage. Then you may not want to take the default. This is an area that would be unique to each installation and any corrective action should be discussed with the system programmer.

EXCEPTION CONDITION

NOSTG   Indicates the requested storage is not available. Default action is to suspend the task until storage becomes available.

To obtain a complete listing of Exception Conditions, consult the IBM Application Programmer's Reference Manual.

Figure 9-2.

```
WORKING-STORAGE SECTION.
01   WSWORKAREA.
       02 RECLEN                  PIC S9(4)  COMP VALUE +100.
       02 RECKEY                  PIC X(8).
       02 RECOUNT                 PIC 9            VALUE 0.
LINKAGE SECTION.
01   PTRSLST.
       02 FILLER                  PIC S9(8)  COMP.
       02 RECPTR                  PIC S9(8)  COMP.
01   RECDESC.
       02 CUSTNO                  PIC X(8).
       02 CUSTNAME                PIC X(20).
       02 CUSTADDR                PIC X(30).
       02 CUSTINFO                PIC X(42).
PROCEDURE DIVISION.
     EXEC CICS HANDLE CONDITION ERROR(FATALERR)
                                DUPREC(NODUPS)
                                END-EXEC.
     EXEC CICS GETMAIN LENGTH(100) SET(RECPTR) END-EXEC.
BUILD-RECORD.
     build the record to add
     EXEC CICS WRITE DATASET('CUSTMAS')
                       FROM(RECPTR)   LENGTH(RECLEN)
                       RIDFLD(RECKEY)
                       END-EXEC.
     IF RECOUNT IS LESS THAN 2
          GO TO BUILD-RECORD.
     EXEC CICS FREEMAIN DATA(RECDESC) END-EXEC.
     MOVE ZEROS TO RECPTR.
     EXEC CICS RETURN END-EXEC.
NODUPS.
FATALERR.
```

EXERCISE

Let's review what we have learned.

1. Define the purpose of the storage control program.
2. Why is the idea of initializing acquired storage not a good idea?
3. After a FREEMAIN command has been executed, why should zeros be moved to the BLL cell associated with the area?

10 Temporary Storage

In Chapter 7, Basic Mapping Support, we learned to save data beyond task termination through the use of the COMMAREA option. This was done in an effort to cut down on data transmission thereby improving response time. Unfortunately, the COMMAREA cannot be recovered in the event of abnormal task termination or CICS abnormal termination. This can present a problem if we need to recover saved data. Perhaps you are wondering why it would be necessary to save data beyond task termination. In our example of the Happy Seed Company we know that we need to collect information about the customer in addition to collecting the information about the products which the customer wishes to order. A problem will arise if an abend occurs. The customer and product information would be lost.

The facility to use to avoid this situation is temporary storage. It is an area that will exist beyond task termination. Figure 10-1 illustrates auxiliary temporary storage.

You will notice that auxiliary temporary storage is just a separate disk (VSAM) file. Thus it is recoverable in the event of an abend. Whenever accessing auxiliary temporary storage an I/O will occur. It is recommended for storing large amounts of data, large amounts generally meaning any size greater than 200 bytes, or if it is necessary to recover data in the event of a task or CICS system abend.

Figure 10-1.

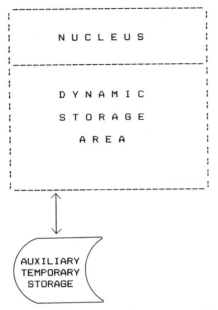

Figure 10-2 illustrates main temporary storage which uses the dynamic storage area.

Main temporary storage is good to use when needing quick access to data (no I/O) and not needing any recovery, since main temporary storage is not a recoverable area (it resides in memory). Care should be exercised when using main storage because all tasks are processed in main storage. We might cause CICS performance to degrade by using too much main storage thereby leaving insufficient storage for other tasks to process.

Whenever application programs store information in temporary storage the information is stored as variable-length records. These records subsequently are stored in queues. Thus a temporary storage queue can contain one or more records with all records being of variable length. These queues are given l-8 character names. There is no need to predefine these queues in any particular table.

As you can see from Figure 10-2 main and auxiliary temporary storage can have many queues. The maximum is a function of the number of bytes allocated to these areas. Some people even view these temporary storage queues as minifiles. We just stated that the queue names are not predefined in any table. That is not completely true! If you would like the queue to be recoverable in the event of an abend, its 1-8 character name or prefix must be stored in the temporary storage table (TST). This also means that the queue must reside in auxiliary temporary storage. Thus the TST is used primarily for recovery purposes.

Let's observe a typical application and how it would use temporary storage. Using again the Happy Seed Company we have an order entry department which handles customers all day long. We know that it is possi-

Figure 10-2.

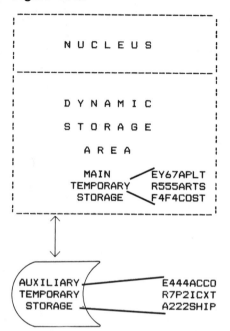

ble for a number of customers to call at the same time and place orders. In this situation it is very likely that three (3) operators at three different terminals could be using the same transaction. We also know that the same application program would be called since all operators are using the same transaction.

The sequence of events would be:

1. Collect customer information and store in temporary storage queue.
2. Collect product information and store in the same temporary storage queue.
3. Add records to the customer master file by reading the temporary storage queue.
4. Delete the temporary storage queue when finished adding records.

WRITING TEMPORARY STORAGE

To write records to temporary storage we need to issue the following command:

```
EXEC CICS WRITEQ TS QUEUE(name)
                FROM(data-area)
                LENGTH(data-value)
                MAIN or AUXILIARY          optional
                ITEM(data-area)           optional
                END-EXEC
```

The QUEUE option specifies the name of the queue in which we wish to have the records stored.

The FROM option indicates the location of the record in our application program we wish to write.

The LENGTH option indicates the size of the record.

The MAIN option indicates the data is to be written to main storage (no I/O occurs).

The AUXILIARY option, which is the default, indicates the data is to be written to auxiliary storage (I/O occurs).

The ITEM option will contain the number of the record just written to the queue. Thus, the temporary storage program informs our application program of the record number. We can NEVER specify it when writing new records to the queue. It will be ignored if specified. The first record in the queue will be number one, the second number two, etc. Think of these queues as being similar to an entry sequence dataset. Figure 10-3 illustrates adding records to a temporary storage queue.

Figure 10-3.

```
WORKING-STORAGE SECTION.
01   WSWORKAREA.
     02 RECLEN                PIC S9(4) COMP VALUE +100.
     02 RECOUNT               PIC 9          VALUE 1.
01   WORKAREA.
     02 TSQNAME.
        02 TSTERMID           PIC X(4).
        02 FILLER             PIC X(4)       VALUE 'OE01'.
01   TSRECD.
     02 CUSTNO                PIC X(8).
     02 CUSTNAME              PIC X(20).
     02 CUSTADDR              PIC X(30).
     02 CUSTINFO              PIC X(42).
PROCEDURE DIVISION.
     EXEC CICS HANDLE CONDITION ERROR(FATALERR)
                               END-EXEC.

     MOVE EIBTRMID TO TSTRMID.
BUILD-RECORD.
     build the record to add
     EXEC CICS WRITEQ TS QUEUE(TSQNAME)
                         FROM(TSRECD)   LENGTH(RECLEN)
                         END-EXEC.
     IF RECOUNT IS LESS THAN 2
        GO TO BUILD-RECORD.
     EXEC CICS RETURN END-EXEC.
FATALERR.
```

In Figure 10-3 notice how the queue name argument was created. Why was it done this way?

We previously stated that each operator could be processing a different customer at the same time. Thus each operator would be using the same transaction and thereby the same program. If the queue name was not created dynamically (at task execution) all the records for all the customers would be written to the same queue. Imagine the chaos created!

To avoid this, we want each queue to be unique to an operator/terminal so only that operator's data goes to the appropriate queue. This can be accomplished by using the label EIBTRMID and any four-character code. We know that the EIBTRMID label is filled in prior to our program getting control. The four-character code could be one applicable to a specific application. The combination used is not as important as the concept of each customer's data in its own queue. The method chosen here will work given the proper application.

That's all there is to writing a record to a temporary storage queue. AUXILIARY does not have to be specified since it is a default. If you wish to write to main storage then the MAIN option must be specified.

Keep in mind that records written to a queue cannot be split between main storage and auxiliary storage. All records for a queue must go to auxiliary storage or main storage but not both.

READING TEMPORARY STORAGE

Going back to the Happy Seed Company again, suppose the operator has collected all the information from the customer and prior to creating the order on a master file, the operator performs a cross balance routine. The results of the routine do not balance. At this time the operator decides to review what was previously keyed in to try and find the error. Now the temporary storage queue must be read with the following command:

```
EXEC CICS READQ TS QUEUE(name)
                 INTO(data-area) or SET(pointer-ref)
                 LENGTH(data-area)
                 NEXT or ITEM(data-area)              optional
                 END-EXEC
```

The QUEUE option specifies the name of the queue we wish to read.

The INTO option indicates where the record is to be placed.

The SET option specifies where the record address of the area containing the temporary storage record.

The LENGTH option indicates the size of the receiving area.

The NEXT option, which is the default, indicates to the temporary storage program to give the next available record in the queue.

The ITEM option specifies the specific record desired.

The NEXT and ITEM options are mutually exclusive.

There is no need to specify MAIN or AUXILIARY because the temporary storage program keeps track of the location of the queues.

The SET, LENGTH, and QUEUE options are the same as we previously learned. Since the records in the queue are variable length be sure when using the INTO option that an area large enough for the largest record has been reserved. Whenever a record is read from a queue a pointer to the next available record in the queue is kept. Thus, whenever the NEXT option has been specified we automatically get the next available record. This may seem like a good option but it could lead to problems.

Suppose in our application we have ten (10) records in a queue and have issued the READ command seven (7) times to perhaps review what is in the queue. The internal pointer for the queue is pointing at number eight. But at this time the operator decides everything is correct and wishes to add the information to a master file. Logically we would want the application program to begin sequentially reading the queue starting with the first record. But, if the READQ TS command is issued with the NEXT option we will get number eight (8) instead of number one (1) and bypass the first seven (7) records.

To avoid this situation, it is usually better to issue the READQ TS command with the ITEM option instead of the NEXT option. Figure 10-4 illustrates sequentially reading a temporary storage queue with the ITEM option.

Figure 10-4.

```
WORKING-STORAGE SECTION.
01   WSWORKAREA.
     02 RECLEN                    PIC S9(4) COMP VALUE +100.
     02 RECOUNT                   PIC 99         VALUE 1.
01   WORKAREA.
     02 TSQNAME.
        02 TSTERMID               PIC X(4).
        02 FILLER                 PIC X(4)       VALUE 'OE01'.
01   TSRECD.
     02 CUSTNO                    PIC X(8).
     02 CUSTNAME                  PIC X(20).
     02 CUSTADDR                  PIC X(30).
     02 CUSTINFO                  PIC X(42).
PROCEDURE DIVISION.
     EXEC CICS HANDLE CONDITION ERROR(FATALERR)
                                ITEMERR(ENDPGM)
                                END-EXEC.
     MOVE EIBTRMID TO TSTRMID.
READ-RECORD.
     EXEC CICS READQ TS QUEUE(TSQNAME)
                    INTO(TSRECD)   LENGTH(RECLEN)
                    ITEM(RECOUNT)
                    END-EXEC.
     process temporary storage record
     IF RECOUNT IS LESS THAN 9
        ADD 1 TO RECOUNT
        GO TO READ-RECORD.
ENDPGM.
     EXEC CICS RETURN END-EXEC.
FATALERR.
```

Let's see how to process the temporary storage queue sequentially using the Linkage Section.

```
WORKING-STORAGE SECTION.
01   WSWORKAREA.
     02 RECLEN                    PIC S9(4) COMP VALUE +100.
     02 RECOUNT                   PIC 99         VALUE 1.
01   WORKAREA.
     02 TSQNAME.
        02 TSTERMID               PIC X(4).
        02 FILLER                 PIC X(4)       VALUE 'OE01'.
LINKAGE SECTION.
01   PTRSLST.
     02 FILLER                    PIC S9(8) COMP.
     02 TSPTR                     PIC S9(8) COMP.
01   TSRECD.
     02 CUSTNO                    PIC X(8).
     02 CUSTNAME                  PIC X(20).
     02 CUSTADDR                  PIC X(30).
     02 CUSTINFO                  PIC X(42).
PROCEDURE DIVISION.
     EXEC CICS HANDLE CONDITION ERROR(FATALERR)
```

```
                                         ITEMERR(ENDPGM)
                                         END-EXEC.
        MOVE EIBTRMID TO TSTRMID.
    READ-RECORD.
        EXEC CICS READQ TS QUEUE(TSQNAME)
                            SET(TSPTR)  LENGTH(RECLEN)
                            ITEM(RECOUNT)
                            END-EXEC.
        process temporary storage record
        IF RECOUNT IS LESS THAN 9
            ADD 1 TO RECOUNT
            GO TO READ-RECORD.
    ENDPGM.
        EXEC CICS RETURN END-EXEC.
    FATALERR.
```

Since we wanted to process the queue sequentially we initialized the ITEM argument (RECOUNT) to one (1) and read the first record. The temporary storage record information was processed. Then, we checked to see if all the records had been read via an IF statement and if not, one was added to the ITEM argument and we read the next one. This will force the queue to be processed sequentially. If we had a queue which needed to be processed this way, but we never knew how many records there would be, is there a way of knowing when we reach the end of the queue? Sure! We use the Exception Condition ITEMERR. Since queues are like entry sequence datasets whenever the item number we specify cannot be found in our sequential search it actually means we have reached the end. Figure 10-5 illustrates this concept.

Back to the operator at Happy Seed Company. When the record causing the imbalance has been found, it must be updated with the correct information. The command needed to replace the record in a queue is the same WRITEQ TS command but with the two (2) additional options of REWRITE and ITEM.

```
        EXEC CICS WRITEQ TS QUEUE(name)
                         INTO(data-area) or SET(pointer-ref)
                         LENGTH(data-value)
                         REWRITE                        optional
                         ITEM(data-value)               optional
                         END-EXEC
```

Figure 10-5.

```
WORKING-STORAGE SECTION.
01   WSWORKAREA.
     02 RECLEN                   PIC S9(4) COMP VALUE +100.
     02 RECOUNT                  PIC 99         VALUE 1.
01   WORKAREA.
     02 TSQNAME.
        02 TSTERMID              PIC X(4).
        02 FILLER                PIC X(4)       VALUE 'OE01'.
01   TSRECD.
     02 CUSTNO                   PIC X(8).
     02 CUSTNAME                 PIC X(20).
     02 CUSTADDR                 PIC X(30).
     02 CUSTINFO                 PIC X(42).
PROCEDURE DIVISION.
     EXEC CICS HANDLE CONDITION ERROR(FATALERR)
                                ITEMERR(ENDPGM)
                                END-EXEC.
     MOVE EIBTRMID TO TSTRMID.
READ-RECORD.
     EXEC CICS READQ TS QUEUE(TSQNAME)
                        INTO(TSRECD)  LENGTH(RECLEN)
                        ITEM(RECOUNT)
                        END-EXEC.
```

```
         process temporary storage record
      GO TO READ-RECORD.
ENDPGM.
      EXEC CICS RETURN END-EXEC.
FATALERR.
```

The REWRITE option indicates that we wish to replace an already existing record.

The ITEM option specifies the number of the record we wish to replace.

This command does not require a prior READQ TS command. If the application program already knows the record format, with the appropriate data and its item number, only the WRITEQ TS command need be issued. If we do not know all the information then a prior READQ TS command would have to be issued. Figure 10-6 illustrates the use of both the READQ TS and the WRITEQ TS commands.

Figure 10-7 illustrates the updating of a temporary storage record without a prior READQ TS command.

Figure 10-6.

```
WORKING-STORAGE SECTION.
01   WSWORKAREA.
     02 RECLEN                PIC S9(4) COMP VALUE +100.
     02 RECOUNT               PIC 99         VALUE 1.
01   WORKAREA.
     02 TSQNAME.
        02 TSTERMID           PIC X(4).
        02 FILLER             PIC X(4)       VALUE 'OE01'.
01   TSRECD.
     02 CUSTNO                PIC X(8).
     02 CUSTNAME              PIC X(20).
     02 CUSTADDR              PIC X(30).
     02 CUSTINFO              PIC X(42).
PROCEDURE DIVISION.
     EXEC CICS HANDLE CONDITION ERROR(FATALERR)
                                ITEMERR(ENDPGM)
                                END-EXEC.
     MOVE EIBTRMID TO TSTRMID.
READ-RECORD.
     EXEC CICS READQ TS QUEUE(TSQNAME)
                        INTO(TSRECD)  LENGTH(RECLEN)
                        ITEM(RECOUNT)
                        END-EXEC.
        process temporary storage record
     EXEC CICS WRITEQ TS QUEUE(TSQNAME)
                         FROM(TSRECD)   LENGTH(RECLEN)
                         REWRITE        ITEM(RECOUNT)
                         END-EXEC.
ENDPGM.
     EXEC CICS RETURN END-EXEC.
FATALERR.
```

Figure 10-7.

```
WORKING-STORAGE SECTION.
01   WSWORKAREA.
     02 RECLEN                PIC S9(4) COMP VALUE +100.
     02 RECOUNT               PIC 99         VALUE 1.
01   WORKAREA.
     02 TSQNAME.
        02 TSTERMID           PIC X(4).
        02 FILLER             PIC X(4)       VALUE 'OE01'.
01   TSRECD.
     02 CUSTNO                PIC X(8).
     02 CUSTNAME              PIC X(20).
     02 CUSTADDR              PIC X(30).
     02 CUSTINFO              PIC X(42).
```

```
PROCEDURE DIVISION.
    EXEC CICS HANDLE CONDITION ERROR(FATALERR)
                                 ITEMERR(ENDPGM)
                              END-EXEC.
    MOVE EIBTRMID TO TSTRMID.
READ-RECORD.
    process temporary storage record
    EXEC CICS WRITEQ TS QUEUE(TSQNAME)
                        FROM(TSRECD)   LENGTH(RECLEN)
                        ITEM(RECOUNT)
                     END-EXEC.
ENDPGM.
    EXEC CICS RETURN END-EXEC.
FATALERR.
```

DELETING TEMPORARY STORAGE

After the queue has been processed, the queue should be deleted because it is no longer needed. The following command will delete an entire queue:

EXEC CICS DELETEQ TS QUEUE(name) END-EXEC

If queues which are no longer needed are not deleted, problems can arise. Eventually we can run out of temporary storage and when this happens any tasks requiring temporary storage will be suspended. When a task is suspended the response to the operator will be delayed causing user dissatisfaction. In some situations tasks will be abended. Thus it is a good idea to be sure to delete any temporary storage queues which are no longer needed.

That is all there is to it! Keep in mind that all the records will be deleted. Perhaps you are thinking, "Is there a way to delete single records within a queue?" The answer is no! Either all the records are deleted or they all stay. A way to simulate a deleted record would be to rewrite the record in the queue with an indicator stating that the record has been deleted. Currently this is the only way to do it.

EXCEPTION CONDITIONS

INVREQ   Occurs when writing a record with a length of zero or writing a record with a length which exceeds the control interval size specified for auxiliary temporary storage.

IOERR   Indicates that an I/O error has occurred.

ITEMERR   Indicates that the item number cannot be found on a READQ TS command whether stated (ITEM) or implied (NEXT). This Exception Condition can occur with the WRITEQ TS command when the REWRITE and ITEM options have been specified.

LENGERR   Indicates the area reserved for the input operation is not large enough to hold the record.

NOSPACE   Indicates there is not enough space to store the record. The default action is to suspend the task until storage becomes available.

QIDERR   Indicates the name specified with the QUEUE option can't be found in MAIN or AUXILIARY storage.

To obtain a complete listing of Exception Conditions, consult the IBM Application Programmer's Reference Manual.

EXERCISE

Let's review what we have learned.

1. What is the function of the temporary storage program?
2. What is the purpose of the temporary storage table?
3. Describe the difference between main and auxiliary temporary storage.
4. What is a temporary storage queue?
5. A - What is the function of the ITEM option when adding a temporary storage record?

   B - What is the function of the ITEM option when rewriting a temporary storage record?
6. What is the difference between the NEXT and ITEM options when reading temporary storage records?

In our example of the Happy Seed Company, it was stated that a message would be sent to the shipping department after the customer information had been obtained. Using the same program we have been working on, let's write an auxiliary temporary storage record containing the customer number and name, the part number, and quantity. The temporary storage queue name will be 'OE01SHIP' and it will not be a unique queue because we want to collect the information from all operators until 5 records have been written to the queue. At that time a transaction (SHIV) will be initiated at the shipping department printer (Chapter 11).

SOURCE PROGRAM LISTING

```
        IDENTIFICATION DIVISION.
        PROGRAM-ID. COMMEXP.
        ENVIRONMENT DIVISION.
        DATA DIVISION.
        WORKING-STORAGE SECTION.
        COPY DFHAID.
        COPY ICMSET.
        COPY DFHBMSCA.
        01  WSWORKAREA.
            02 MSGLEN            PIC S9(4) COMP VALUE +25.
            02 IOAREA            PIC X(20).
            02 WSDEC128          PIC S9(4)   COMP  VALUE +128.
            02 FILLER            REDEFINES
               WSDEC128.
               04 FILLER         PIC X.
               04 WSHEX80        PIC X.
            02 WSCOMM            PIC X(32)   VALUE  LOW-VALUES.
            02 WSERRIND          PIC 9       VALUE  ZERO.
            02 WSQMRK.
               04 FILLER         PIC X       VALUE '?'.
               04 FILLER         PIC X(19)   VALUE LOW-VALUES.
            02 WSCUSTKEY         PIC X(6).
        01  CUST-RECORD.
            02 FILLER            PIC X.
            02 C-KEY             PIC X(6).
            02 FILLER            PIC X(20).
            02 C-FLAG            PIC X.
            02 FILLER            PIC X(52).
        01  PART-RECORD.
            02 FILLER            PIC X.
            02 P-KEY             PIC X(4).
            02 P-REORDER         PIC 9(5).
            02 P-AMOUNT          PIC 9(5).
            02 FILLER            PIC X(65).
```

```
      LINKAGE SECTION.
      01  DFHCOMMAREA.
          02  CCUSTNO            PIC X(4).
          02  CCUSTNM            PIC X(20).
          02  CPARTNO            PIC X(4).
          02  CQTY              PIC X(3).
          02  CQTYN             REDEFINES
              CQTY              PIC 9(3).
          02  CACTCD            PIC X.
      PROCEDURE DIVISION.
   **     IT IS A GOOD PRACTICE TO ESTABLISH A HANDLE CONDITION UPON   **
   **                     ENTRY TO A PROGRAM                           **
          EXEC CICS HANDLE CONDITION ERROR(FATALERR)
                                     MAPFAIL(NODATA)
                                     NOTFND(NOREC)
                                     END-EXEC.
   **     THE FOLLOWING WILL DETERMINE WHICH KEY THE OPERATOR SELECTED **
          IF EIBAID = DFHENTER
             IF EIBCALEN = 32
                EXEC CICS RECEIVE MAP('ICMAP') MAPSET('ICMSET') END-EXEC
             ELSE
                EXEC CICS SEND MAP('ICMAP') MAPSET('ICMSET')
                               MAPONLY
                               ERASE    END-EXEC
             EXEC CICS RETURN
                          TRANSID(EIBTRNID)
                          COMMAREA(WSCOMM)   LENGTH(32)
                          END-EXEC
          ELSE
             IF EIBAID = DFHCLEAR
                MOVE  'SESSION COMPLETED' TO IOAREA
                EXEC CICS SEND FROM(IOAREA) LENGTH(17) END-EXEC
                EXEC CICS RETURN END-EXEC
             ELSE
                MOVE 'INVALID KEY PRESSED'  TO IOAREA
                EXEC CICS SEND FROM(IOAREA) LENGTH(19)
                               ERASE END-EXEC
             EXEC CICS RETURN END-EXEC.
   **     THE INPUT DATA WILL BE MERGED WITH THE PREVIOUSLY SAVED DATA **
          IF CUSTNOL IS GREATER THAN ZERO
             MOVE CUSTNOI TO CCUSTNO
          ELSE
             IF CUSTNOF = WSHEX80
                MOVE LOW-VALUES TO CCUSTNO.
          IF CUSTNML IS GREATER THAN ZERO
             MOVE CUSTNMI TO CCUSTNM
          ELSE
             IF CUSTNMF = WSHEX80
                MOVE LOW-VALUES TO CCUSTNM.
          IF PARTNOL IS GREATER THAN ZERO
             MOVE PARTNOI TO CPARTNO
          ELSE
             IF PARTNOF = WSHEX80
                MOVE LOW-VALUES TO CPARTNO.
          IF QTYL IS GREATER THAN ZERO
             MOVE QTYI TO CQTY
          ELSE
             IF QTYF = WSHEX80
                MOVE LOW-VALUES TO CQTY.
          IF ACTCDL IS GREATER THAN ZERO
             MOVE ACTCDI TO CACTCD
          ELSE
             IF ACTCDF = WSHEX80
                MOVE LOW-VALUES TO CACTCD.
          MOVE LOW-VALUES TO CUSTNOO CUSTNMO PARTNOO QTYO ACTCDO.
          MOVE DFHBMUNP TO CUSTNOA CUSTNMA PARTNOA QTYA.
      CONTPROCESS.
```

```
**    EDIT THE DATA WHICH NOW RESIDES IN DFHCOMMAREA               **
    IF CCUSTNO = LOW VALUES AND CCUSTNM = LOW-VALUES
        MOVE WSQMRK TO CUSTNOO
        MOVE  -1     TO CUSTNOL
        MOVE   1     TO WSERRIND
        MOVE DFHBMBRY TO CUSTNOA.
    IF CPARTNO = LOW-VALUES
        MOVE WSQMRK TO PARTNO
        MOVE  -1   TO PARTNOL
        MOVE   1   TO WSERRIND
        MOVE DFHBMBRY TO PARTNOA.
    IF CQTY = LOW-VALUES
        MOVE WSQMRK TO QTYO
        MOVE  -1     TO QTYL
        MOVE   1     TO WSERRIND
        MOVE DFHBMBRY TO QTYA.
    IF CACTCD = LOW-VALUES
        MOVE WSQMRK TO ACTCDO
        MOVE  -1     TO ACTCDL
        MOVE   1     TO WSERRIND
        MOVE DFHBMBRY TO ACTCDA.
    IF WSERRIND = ZERO
        NEXT SENTENCE
    ELSE
        GO TO MOVE-ERROR-MSG.
    IF CCUSTNO = LOW-VALUES
        EXEC CICS LINK PROGRAM('GETCNO')
                       COMMAREA(DFHCOMMAREA)
                       LENGTH(EIBCALEN)
                       END-EXEC.
    MOVE CCUSTNO TO WSCUSTKEY.
READ-CUSTOMER-FILE.
    MOVE +80  TO  MSGLEN.
    EXEC CICS READ DATASET('CUSTMAS')
                   RIDFLD(WSCUSTKEY)
                   INTO(CUST-RECORD)   LENGTH(MSGLEN)
                   GENERIC             KEYLENGTH(4)
                   END-EXEC.
READ-PART-FILE.
    MOVE +80  TO  MSGLEN.
    EXEC CICS READ DATASET('PARTMAS')
                   RIDFLD(CPARTNO)
                   INTO(PART-RECORD)   LENGTH(MSGLEN)
                   UPDATE
                   END-EXEC.
    IF WSERRIND = ZERO
        GO TO ADD-RECORD.
MOVE-ERROR-MSG.
    MOVE 'ERRORS HIGHLIGHTED    PLEASE CORRECT AND RESUBMIT' TO
         ERRMSGO.
SEND-DATAONLY-MAP.
    EXEC CICS SEND MAP('ICMAP') MAPSET('ICMSET')
                   DATAONLY
                   CURSOR        END-EXEC.
    EXEC CICS RETURN
             TRANSID(EIBTRNID)
             COMMAREA(DFHCOMMAREA)
             LENGTH(EIBCALEN)
             END-EXEC.
ADD-RECORD.
    IF CACTCD = 'A'
        ADD CQTYN TO P-AMOUNT
    ELSE
        SUBTRACT CQTYN FROM P-AMOUNT.
    EXEC CICS REWRITE DATASET('PARTMAS')
                      FROM(PART-RECORD)  LENGTH(MSGLEN)
                      END-EXEC.
```

```
1       EXEC CICS WRITEQ TS QUEUE('OEO1SHIP')
                          FROM(DFHCOMMAREA)
                          LENGTH(31)
                          END-EXEC.
     MOVE -1 TO CUSTNOL.
     MOVE 'UPDATE SUCCESSFUL' TO ERRMSGO.
     MOVE LOW-VALUES TO DFHCOMMAREA.
     EXEC CICS SEND MAP('ICMAP') MAPSET('ICMSET')
                      ERASEAUP
                      CURSOR
                      DATAONLY
                      END-EXEC.
     EXEC CICS RETURN
                  TRANSID(EIBTRNID)
                  COMMAREA(DFHCOMMAREA)
                  LENGTH(EIBCALEN)
                  END-EXEC.
 NOREC.
     IF EIBRSRCE = 'CUSTMAS'
         MOVE -1 TO CUSTNOL
         MOVE 1 TO WSERRIND
         MOVE DFHBMBRY TO CUSTNOA
         MOVE CCUSTNO TO CUSTNOO
         GO TO READ-PART-FILE
     ELSE
         MOVE -1 TO PARTNOL
         MOVE DFHBMBRY TO PARTNOA
         GO TO MOVE-ERROR-MSG.
 NODATA.
     MOVE LOW-VALUES TO ICMAPO.
     IF DFHCOMMAREA = LOW-VALUES
         MOVE 'NO DATA ENTERED' TO ERRMSGO
         MOVE -1    TO CUSTNOL.
     GO TO SEND-DATAONLY-MAP.
 FATALERR.
**   THE FOLLOWING WILL PROCESS ANY EXCEPTION CONDITIONS
     EXEC CICS ABEND ABCODE('CMEX') END-EXEC.
     GOBACK.
```

COMMENTS

No Exception Conditions unique to temporary storage (i.e., IOERR, INVREQ, NOSPACE) have been established because the chances of them occurring are minimal. The Exception Condition ERROR can be used to trap these situations when they do occur.

1. There is no need to dynamically (at task execution time) create the queue name because we wanted other tasks to store data in the same queue. Since we have the necessary information for the temporary storage record in the DFHCOMMAREA, there is no need to build the record in a separate area because it can be written from where it already resides. A good programming technique is to examine how the data will be used. As can be seen in this example by proper area layout (i.e., DFHCOMMAREA), four MOVE statements were eliminated in addition to the extra storage needed to define a temporary storage record. The savings may be small but considering that a transaction can be executed thousands of times a day, the savings do add up. There is no need to specify AUXILIARY because that is the default.

11 Transient Data

The transient data program (TDP) of CICS provides a generalized queuing facility. The data will be stored in transient data queues. Figure 11-1 illustrates the first type of transient data queue.

The extrapartition datasets (Figure 11-1) are sequential datasets managed by QSAM. They are used to pass information from CICS to another batch region/partition. They can also be used to pass information from a batch region/partition to CICS. Figure 11-2 illustrates this concept.

Extrapartition datasets can be opened by CICS for input or output. In addition, the records can be written to or read from these QSAM datasets. Individual records cannot be updated or physically deleted within CICS. The extrapartition datasets are defined in the destination control table (DCT) in Figure 11-3.

When would an extrapartition dataset be required? Perhaps we have an application which will process thousands of updating transactions per day. Since updating online incurs more overhead it may be impossible to process everything in one day. We could though, collect the data (queue it) to an extrapartition transient data queue. After all the information has been collected we could initiate a batch job which would read this extrapartition queue and update our master file. This would give the online system more time in which to process other transactions.

Another feature of transient data is the intrapartition dataset, Figure 11-4.

Figure 11-1.

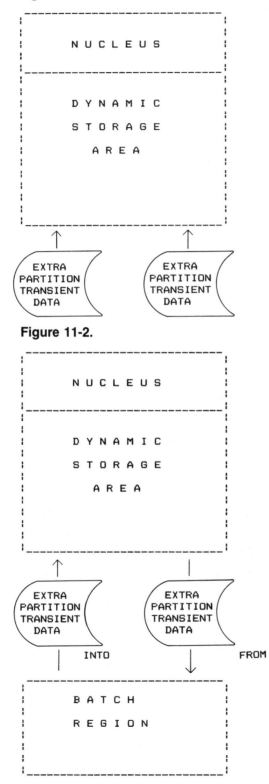

Figure 11-2.

Figure 11-3.

```
DFHDCT  TYPE=EXTRA,
        DESTID=E999,
        DSCNAME=STATS,    This parameter points to the DDNAME
        OPEN=INITIAL          in the JCL.
```

Figure 11-4.

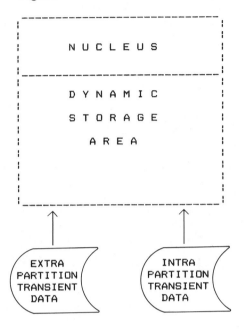

Intrapartition transient data is for use only within the CICS system to pass information between tasks. These intrapartition queues can contain one or more records. Again, individual records can be written to or read from but cannot be updated or physically deleted. Even though these queues are organized as direct access datasets, records can only be processed sequentially.

Why should we use intrapartition transient data? Going back to the Happy Seed Company example, it was stated that a message was sent to the shipping department but no indication was given as to how the message was delivered. Through the use of intrapartition transient data we could have a transaction automatically initiated at the shipping department without human intervention (automatic task initiation or ATI). How is this done? We place the proper information in the destination control table. Figure 11-5 illustrates a typical intrapartition destination control table entry. It will be used to show how a transaction can be internally initiated. By eliminating the human element less can go wrong!

Figure 11-5.

```
DFHDCT    TYPE=INTRA,
          DESTID=E444,
          DESTFAC=TERMINAL,
          TRANSID=SHIV,
          TRIGLEV=1
```

In our example the operator collected information about the customer order and a message was sent back to the operator indicating a successful update. Following that we need to write a record to DESTID E444. When the transient data record is written, the TDP will check the trigger level (TRIGLEV) to determine if it is time to initiate a transaction. Since the trigger level contains a 1 and the queue contains 1 (or more) records, it means it is time to initiate a transaction. The DCT parameter TRANSID indicates that the transaction to initiate is SHIV. Since the transaction is to run at the shipping department printer, its term id has to be stated in the DCT as the DESTID. Once the transaction SHIV is initiated, the program will read the transient data queue (E444) and send the necessary shipping document to the printer (E444). Thus we are able to accomplish work with no human intervention!

Notice in the prior example that the term id at which the task will be initiated is the same as the dest id. This is called a direct destination. Suppose our company implements new naming conventions and all printer identifications in the terminal control table must now start with the letter P. Since our programs are currently using a printer with an identification of E444, it would appear that the programs would require modifications. This could be a major undertaking. Fortunately, we can change our original entry (Figure 11-5) from DESTID = E444 to DESTID = P444 and create an indirect (alias) destination in the DCT (Figure 11-6). The following entries would be require.

Figure 11-6.

```
DFHDCT    TYPE=INTRA,              DFHDCT    TYPE=INDIRECT,
          DESTID=P444,                      DESTID=E444,
          DESTFAC=TERMINAL,                 INDDEST=P444
          TRANSID=SHIV,
          TRIGLEV=1
```

The INDDEST operand specifies the name of the actual destination which in our example is the printer P444. In this way only the destination control table would require reassembly, while our application is still writing to DESTID E444. Thus an indirect destination is another means of pointing to a direct destination.

The trigger level parameter (TRIGLEV) in the DCT indicates how many records are to be written to a particular destination before initiating a task. Once the task has been initiated, the task would read the transient data queue beginning with the first record and continuing in a forward direction only. Depending on the options specified in the DCT, it may be

---

necessary to delete the transient data records after they have been processed. Since it is possible to confuse the temporary storage and transient data facilities let us compare them to see how much they differ.

TEMPORARY STORAGE	TRANSIENT DATA
1. Direct access	1. Sequential access
2. Update capability	2. No update capability
3. No automatic task initiation	3. Automatic task initiation
4. No predefinition of queues	4. Predefinition of queues (DCT)

WRITING TRANSIENT DATA

Thus you can observe the two facilities accomplish different functions. To write records to transient data queues the following command would be issued:

```
EXEC CICS WRITEQ TD QUEUE(name)
                FROM(data-area)
                LENGTH(data-value)           optional
                END-EXEC
```

The QUEUE option indicates the name of the queue where we want the record to be written. It can be a 1-4 character name and must be in the DCT. Figure 11-5 is repeated to illustrate the QUEUE name.

```
DFHDCT TYPE = INTRA,
        DESTID = E444,              This is the QUEUE name.
        DESTFAC = TERMINAL,
        TRANSID = SHIV,
        TRIGLEV = 1
```

The FROM option indicates where in our application program the record to be written resides.

The LENGTH option specifies the size of our record to be written. For extrapartition queues the LENGTH option is not required because the records are fixed length.

It is not necessary to specify whether the queue is intrapartition or extrapartition since the TDP can obtain this information from the destination control table.

The following is an example of writing a 100-byte record to intrapartition queue E444.

In this example, the NOSPACE Exception Condition has been established. This condition can occur because the intrapartition transient data area is usually not allocated a great amount of space and is not a very volatile area. Thus when the condition arises an abend will be generated with the appropriate abend code.

```
      WORKING-STORAGE SECTION.
      01  WSWORKAREA.
          02  RECLEN                  PIC S9(4) COMP VALUE +100.
      01  TDRECD.
          02  CUSTNO        PIC X(8).
          02  CUSTNAME      PIC X(20).
          02  CUSTADDR      PIC X(30).
          02  CUSTINFO      PIC X(42).
      PROCEDURE DIVISION.
          EXEC CICS HANDLE CONDITION ERROR(FATALERR)
                                     NOSPACE(NOSPACERR)
                                     END-EXEC.
      WRITE-RECORD.
          build transient data record
          EXEC CICS WRITEQ TD QUEUE('E444')
                              FROM(TDRECD)  LENGTH(RECLEN)
                              END-EXEC.
      ENDPGM.
          EXEC CICS RETURN END-EXEC.
      NOSPACERR.
          EXEC CICS ABEND ABCODE('NOSP') END-EXEC.
      FATALERR.
```

READING TRANSIENT DATA

When it is time to process the transient data queue the following command would be issued:

```
EXEC CICS READQ TD QUEUE(name)
                INTO(data-area) or SET(pointer-ref)
                LENGTH(data-area)                        optional
                END-EXEC
```

The QUEUE option specifies the 1-4 character name of the queue in the DCT we wish to read.

The INTO option specifies where we want the record returned in our application program.

The SET option specifies where we want the address of the record returned in our application program. The SET and INTO options are mutually exclusive.

The LENGTH option, when used with the INTO option indicates how large of an area we have reserved in our application program for the record. When the LENGTH option is used with the SET option, the LENGTH option will indicate to our application program the size of the record. Notice with the READ command we cannot specify which record we want to read. Since we are dealing with sequential queues we can only read them in a forward direction one after the other. Thus it is impossible to read directly a specific record within a transient data queue. The following is an example of a program reading an intrapartition destination queue. To read an extrapartition queue there would be no change.

Notice in our example we go back and continue reading the queue. When the QZERO Exception Condition occurs we know we have reached the end of the queue.

```
WORKING-STORAGE SECTION.
01  WSWORKAREA.
    02 RECLEN                    PIC S9(4) COMP VALUE +100.
01  TDRECD.
    02 CUSTNO               PIC X(8).
    02 CUSTNAME             PIC X(20).
    02 CUSTADDR             PIC X(30).
    02 CUSTINFO             PIC X(42).
PROCEDURE DIVISION.
    EXEC CICS HANDLE CONDITION ERROR(FATALERR)
                              QZERO(ENDPGM)
                              END-EXEC.
READ-RECORD.
    EXEC CICS READQ TD QUEUE('E444')
                   INTO(TDRECD)   LENGTH(RECLEN)
                   END-EXEC.
    process transient data record
    GO TO READ-RECORD.
ENDPGM.
    EXEC CICS RETURN END-EXEC.
FATALERR.
```

DELETING TRANSIENT DATA

After we have read all the records within our intrapartition transient data queue, depending on the options specified in the DCT, it may be necessary to delete the queue. Again it is a good idea to delete any queues which are no longer needed. The command to delete the queue is:

```
EXEC CICS DELETEQ TD QUEUE(name)
         END-EXEC.
```

The QUEUE option specifies the 1-4 character name of the queue in the DCT we wish to delete.

In the following example, after all the records have been processed, the queue will be deleted prior to task termination.

The QUEUE option indicates the name of the queue we wish to delete. When this command is issued the entire queue will be deleted. We cannot delete a single record within a queue. The entire queue stays or the entire queue is deleted.

```
WORKING-STORAGE SECTION.
01  WSWORKAREA.
    02 RECLEN                    PIC S9(4) COMP VALUE +100.
01  TDRECD.
    02 CUSTNO               PIC X(8).
    02 CUSTNAME             PIC X(20).
    02 CUSTADDR             PIC X(30).
    02 CUSTINFO             PIC X(42).
PROCEDURE DIVISION.
    EXEC CICS HANDLE CONDITION ERROR(FATALERR)
                              QZERO(DELTQ)
                              END-EXEC.
```

```
READ-RECORD.
    EXEC CICS READQ TD QUEUE('E444')
                    INTO(TDRECD)   LENGTH(RECLEN)
                    END-EXEC.
    process transient data record
    GO TO READ-RECORD.
DELTQ.
    EXEC CICS DELETEQ TD QUEUE('E444') END-EXEC.
ENDPGM.
    EXEC CICS RETURN END-EXEC.
FATALERR.
```

EXCEPTION CONDITIONS

IOERR	Indicates that an I/O error has occurred.
LENGERR	Indicates the area we have reserved in our application program is not large enough to hold the record which we are trying to read. The length specified on an output operation is greater than the maximum specified for the queue in the DCT. An incorrect LENGTH has been specified for a fixed-length record.
NOSPACE	Indicates there is no more space to write our transient data records.
NOTOPEN	Indicates that the destination is not open.
QBUSY	Indicates that the queue we are trying to read is currently being written to or deleted. When this Exception Condition occurs the default action is to make the task issuing the READQ TD command wait until the QUEUE is no longer busy.
QIDERR	Indicates the QUEUE name cannot be found in the destination control table.
QZERO	Indicates there are no more records to read in the queue.

The default action for all the previous Exception Conditions will be abnormal task termination except as noted for the QBUSY Exception Condition.

To obtain a complete listing of Exception Conditions, consult the IBM Application Programmer's Reference Manual.

EXERCISE

Let's review what we have learned about transient data.

1. What is the function of the transient data program?
2. What is the purpose of the destination control table?
3. What is the difference between extrapartition and intrapartition transient data?
4. Describe automatic task initiation.
5. Explain the difference between a direct destination and an indirect (alias) destination.
6. Explain the difference between temporary storage and transient data.

We will now proceed with inserting the necessary code in our application program to write a record to a transient data queue after five records have been written to the temporary storage queue. The following will be in entry in the DCT:

```
DFHDCT TYPE = INTRA,
       DESTID = E444,
       DESTFAC = TERMINAL,
       TRANSID = SHIV,
       TRIGLEV = 1
```

The DESTID E444 is the transient data queue name for program COMMEXP but will be the term id (printer) for transaction SHIV. This is an example of a direct destination. When transaction SHIV is initiated, it will invoke program TRANSDAT which will read the transient data queue (E444) to obtain the name of the temporary storage queue (OE01SHIP). The program, TRANSDAT, will read the entire temporary storage queue and when finished both the transient and temporary storage queues will be deleted.

Let's see how both programs COMMEXP and TRANSDAT would be coded. Since our order entry program COMMEXP will be used again, only the necessary areas needed to illustrate this concept will be shown.

SOURCE LISTING PROGRAM

```
IDENTIFICATION DIVISION.
PROGRAM-ID. COMMEXP.
ENVIRONMENT DIVISION.
DATA DIVISION.
WORKING-STORAGE SECTION.
01   WSWORKAREA.
     02 TSITEM  PIC S9(4) COMP.
     02 TSQNAME PIC X(8)
               VALUE 'OE01SHIP'.



LINKAGE SECTION.
01   DFHCOMMAREA.
     02 CCUSTNO      PIC X(4).
     02 CCUSTNM      PIC X(20).
     02 CPARTNO      PIC X(4).
     02 CQTY         PIC X(3).
     02 CQTYN        REDEFINES
        CQTY         PIC 9(3).
     02 CACTCD       PIC X.
PROCEDURE DIVISION.
     EXEC CICS HANDLE CONDITION
               ERROR(FATALERR)
1              NOSPACE(FATALERR)
               MAPFAIL(NODATA)
               NOTFND(NOREC)
               END-EXEC.
ADD-RECORD.
     EXEC CICS REWRITE
```

COMMENTS

1. The Exception Condition NOSPACE has been established to take effect when the space reserved for transient data has been exhausted.

2. The temporary storage record is being written from the DFHCOMMAREA with a length of 31. The ITEM option has been specified so it can be checked later in the program.

3. A check is being made to determine if five records have been written to temporary storage.

4. The transient data record is being written and it contains the name of the temporary storage queue.

5. After the map is sent the task will terminate.

```
                    DATASET ('PARTMAS')
                    FROM (PART-RECORD)
                    LENGTH (MSGLEN)
                    END-EXEC.
 2     EXEC CICS WRITEQ TS
                    QUEUE (TSQNAME)
                    FROM (DFHCOMMAREA)
                    LENGTH (31)
                    ITEM (TSITEM)
                    END-EXEC.
 3     IF TSITEM = 5
 4         EXEC CICS WRITEQ TD
                    QUEUE ('E444')
                    FROM (TSQNAME)
                    LENGTH (8)
                    END-EXEC.
 5     EXEC CICS RETURN END-EXEC.


SOURCE PROGRAM LISTING

IDENTIFICATION DIVISION.
PROGRAM-ID. TRANSDAT.
ENVIRONMENT DIVISION.
DATA DIVISION.
WORKING-STORAGE SECTION.
01 WSWORKAREA.
    02 TSDQLEN PIC S9(4)
           COMP    VALUE +8.
01 TDREC.
    02 TDTSQ      PIC X(8).
01 TSREC.
    02 TSCUSTNO  PIC X(4).
    02 TSCUSTNM  PIC X(20).
    02 TSPARTNO  PIC X(4).
    02 TSQTY     PIC XXX.
  PROCEDURE DIVISION.
     EXEC CICS HANDLE CONDITION
                    ERROR (FATALERR)
 1                  ITEMERR (DELTSQ)
                    END-EXEC.
 2     EXEC CICS READQ TD
                    QUEUE ('E444')
                    INTO (TDREC)
                    LENGTH (TSDQLEN)
                    END-EXEC.
 3     MOVE 31 TO TSDQLEN.
  READ-TS-Q.
 4     EXEC CICS READQ TS
                    QUEUE (TDTSQ)
                    INTO (TSREC)
                    LENGTH (TSDQLEN)
                    ITEM (TSITEM)
                    END-EXEC.
     process the ts record data
 5     ADD 1 TO TSITEM.
 6     GO TO READ-TS-Q.
  DELTSQ.
 7     EXEC CICS DELETEQ TS
                    QUEUE (TDTSQ)
                    END-EXEC.
```

COMMENTS

1. The Exception Condition ITEMERR has been established to take effect after all the records in the temporary storage queue have been read.

2. The transient data queue is being read to acquire the name of the temporary storage queue to read. This technique would be good to use when the temporary storage queue names change but the required processing is the same.

3. The label will now be used for reading temporary storage. If the records we were reading were all of different lengths then we would need to establish the correct size after every READQ TS command.

4. The temporary storage records are being read and we are using the ITEM option to ensure that the queue is processed sequentially.

5. One is added to the record counter. There is no need to check any counter for five since we are using the ITEMERR Exception Condition. It would be fine to check a counter instead of using the ITEMERR method.

6. Another temporary storage record will be acquired.

7. The temporary storage queue will be deleted after all the records in it have been processed.

```
8    EXEC CICS DELETEQ TD
             QUEUE('E444')
             END-EXEC.
9    EXEC CICS RETURN END-EXEC.
```

8. The transient data queue will all be deleted prior to task termination.

9. The program will eventually terminate.

 **Interval Control**

The interval control program (ICP) of CICS manages all time-related functions. With it, we are able to do the following major functions: inquire about the time of day and date, delay processing of a task, and initiate a task with no human intervention. There is no particular table associated with interval control. The ICP is able to accomplish these functions by use of a time of day clock maintained by the CICS system which operates on a 24:00:00 hour basis.

ACQUIRING THE CURRENT TIME

To acquire the current time of day and date, the following command would be issued:

EXEC CICS ASKTIME END-EXEC

The EIBTIME and EIBDATE fields in the EIB will be updated. This command is preferred over the COBOL current time and current date routines. Why would we need to get a time more current than when our task started, or a more current date than today? In many installations the CICS production system is available twenty-four (24) hours a day. Thus, if a task was initiated at 23:59:58 and finishes after midnight, the time and date would be different. This is very important if the task is doing time/date stamping of records.

TIME DELAY

Through the use of interval control, we have the ability to delay a task. Perhaps you are wondering about delaying a task when all along it has been stressed to give the best response time possible. There may be an application which does online printing using special forms. Before the application starts to print the actual data, it would send a message stating what forms should be mounted and aligned. While the forms are being mounted, the task would need to be delayed. Another reason for delaying a task would be if we were doing terminal samplings. In this example the task would not be attached to a terminal but would need to sample the network every 5 minutes. Once the sample has been taken, the task must be delayed another 5 minutes. These are just two of the various reasons for delaying a task.

To delay processing of a task the following command would be issued:

```
EXEC CICS DELAY
         INTERVAL(hhmmss) or INTERVAL(0) or TIME(hhmmss)    optional
         REQID(name)                                        optional
         END-EXEC
```

The INTERVAL and TIME options are mutually exclusive. When the interval option has been specified it simply means to delay the task for a specific period of time. The default is INTERVAL(0). The argument HHMMSS can be specified as a decimal value NOT enclosed in quotes (e.g., 121005) or as a previously defined data name with an assigned value (e.g., PIC S9(7) COMP-3 VALUE +121005).

Figure 12-1.

```
EXEC CICS DELAY
          INTERVAL(1000)
          END-EXEC
```

In Figure 12-1 the ten minutes specified with the interval option will be added to the current time. Thus, if the current time is 9 A.M. and the DELAY command is issued, the ten minutes will be added to 9 A.M. and at 9:10 A.M. the task will resume processing at the next sequential instruction following the DELAY command in the application program.

In Figure 12-2 the TIME option was chosen. If the current time is 9 A.M. and the DELAY command is issued the task will resume execution at 11 A.M at the next sequential instruction following the DELAY command in the application program. Thus the TIME option specifies the delaying of a task until a specific time of day.

When the argument specifies HHMMSS any value from 0-99 hours can be specified. Any value from 0-59 can be specified for minutes and any

Figure 12-2.

```
EXEC CICS DELAY
        TIME(110000)
        REQID('SHIVPRNT')
        END-EXEC
```

value from 0-59 can be specified for seconds. Do not be misled by the 99 hours value. Since it is possible for CICS to be operational twenty-four (24) hours a day, whenever midnight passes, a time adjustment program is run and it will simply subtract twenty-four (24) hours from any outstanding interval control request.

What happens if a TIME option argument is specified and the time has already passed (e.g., it is 9 A.M. and the DELAY command was issued with a TIME option argument of 7 A.M.)? When the ICP gets the request it will determine the expiration time. If the expiration time is the same or up to and including six (6) hours prior to the current clock time, the time is considered to be expired and the function will proceed.

CANCEL A REQUEST

Suppose our task was delayed for two (2) hours and there was a need in one (1) hour to cancel the delay. Is this possible? Of course, by issuing the following command:

```
EXEC CICS CANCEL
        REQID(name)                              optional
        TRANSID(name)                            optional
        END-EXEC
```

The REQID option specifies the request identification, consisting of 1-8 characters, that is to be canceled. If we need to cancel the DELAY in Figure 12-2 we would code the CANCEL command as follows:

```
EXEC CICS CANCEL REQID ('SHIVPRNT') END-EXEC
```

The TRANSID option specifies the transaction to cancel. When this command is used in conjunction with the delay command the time must not have expired.

The CANCEL command can also be used with the POST and START commands.

START A TASK

We learned in the previous chapter that it was possible with transient data to initiate a task without human intervention based on the accumulation of records. Now we will see another way to initiate a task without human intervention based only on time. To initiate a task based on time we would issue the following command:

```
EXEC CICS START
        TRANSID(name)
        INTERVAL(hhmmss) or INTERVAL(0) or TIME(hhmmss)    optional
        REQID(name)                                        optional
        TERMID(name)                                        optional
        FROM(data-area) LENGTH(data-value)                 optional
        END-EXEC
```

The TRANSID option specifies the transaction which is to be initiated. This transaction must be stated in the program control table (PCT).

The INTERVAL and TIME options are mutually exclusive. The INTERVAL option specifies a task is to be started within a certain period of time. The default is INTERVAL(0). The TIME option indicates a task is to be started at a specific period of time.

The TERMID option specifies the name of the terminal where this task is to be started.

The REQID option specifies the request id which would be needed if we wish to cancel this outstanding START as long as the time has not expired.

The FROM and LENGTH options specify the data and its size that we are passing to the starting task.

If we wish to start a task in two (2) hours at terminal E456 and we wish to pass data fifteen (15) bytes long we would issue the following START command:

```
EXEC CICS START
        TRANSID('SHIV')
        INTERVAL(20000)
        FROM(WSPASSINFO) LENGTH(15)
        TERMID(E456)
        REQID('SHIVPRNT')
        END-EXEC
```

The data that we are passing to the starting task can be any area in our program to which we have addressability. The REQID option will allow us to cancel with the CANCEL command this start request if within two (2) hours we find a need to cancel the request.

Since many tasks could issue the START command for the same terminal, trans id, and time, it is possible to have more than one START request waiting to be initiated at a specific time. When the time has expired only the first interval control request (START) will be initiated. CICS allows only one task to be active at a terminal at any point in time. After the task has terminated the next task (START) will be initiated.

RETRIEVE DATA

If we are attempting to start transaction SHIV at terminal E456 and we are passing data to it, the starting task must have a way to retrieve that data. The command to retrieve data would be the following:

```
EXEC CICS RETRIEVE
          INTO(data-area) or SET(pointer-ref)
          LENGTH(data-area)
          END-EXEC
```

The INTO and SET options are mutually exclusive. The INTO option indicates the area in our application program we have reserved for the data. The SET option indicates where we would like the address of the data returned.

The LENGTH option indicates the size of the area we have reserved when using the INTO option. The LENGTH will indicate the size of the actual area being passed when used with the SET option.

We learned before that multiple STARTS could be issued for a terminal with the same term id, trans id, and time. Suppose data was passed with each START. Once the first task has been initiated, it must retrieve the data being passed and after it has processed the data, you would think it should issue a RETURN command to terminate the task. This would be okay but if there were four more STARTS differing only in the data being passed, CICS would have to go through all the overhead of initiating four more tasks. To eliminate some of this overhead, the task which was initiated first should issue multiple RETRIEVE commands until the Exception Condition ENDDATA occurs. At this time we know we have retrieved and processed all the necessary data but without the overhead of initiating four additional tasks.

NOTIFICATION

It is possible to have CICS notify our task when a specific period of time has elapsed. To do this, we would issue the following command:

```
EXEC CICS POST
          INTERVAL(hhmmss) or INTERVAL(0) or TIME(hhmmss)     optional
          SET(POINTER-REF)
          REQID(NAME)                                         optional
          END-EXEC
```

The INTERVAL option indicates that our task will be notified when a specific period of time has elapsed. The default is an INTERVAL(0).

The TIME option indicates that our task will be notified at a specific time.

The SET option argument will contain the address of the acquired event control block (ECB). The ECB is a four-byte area initialized to low-values when acquired. After the time has elapsed, the ECB is posted (i.e, it is changed from all low-values to hex '40008000').

It is also possible in CICS to wait for an event to occur. To do this the following command would be issued:

EXEC CICS WAIT EVENT ECADDR(pointer-ref) END-EXEC

The ECADDR option indicates the area where CICS is to search to see if the event has occurred (i.e., the pointer-ref from the EXEC CICS POST SET(POINTER-REF).

There may be times when it is necessary in an application program to delay response time to the user. Why would you want to do this? If this is a new user and a brand new application and a brand new CICS environment and we do not slow down response time, the initial response time to the user will be very quick. It will be quick because there are no other applications or tasks competing for the same resources. As time goes on and more applications come online, the response time will gradually degrade. Eventually the user is going to complain that the response time is getting very poor. A way to avoid this is by conditioning the user to a busy system. This can be accomplished by using the POST and WAIT commands. In Figure 12-3 we will see how this is done.

Figure 12-3.

```
        WORKING-STORAGE SECTION.
        01  WSWORKAREA.
            02 RECLEN              PIC S9(4) COMP VALUE +100.
            02 RECOUNT             PIC 99         VALUE 1.
        COPY ICMSET.
        LINKAGE SECTION.
        01  PTRSLST.
            02 FILLER             PIC S9(8) COMP.
            02 ECBPTR             PIC S9(8) COMP.
        01  ECBAREA.
            02 FILLER             PIC X(4).
        PROCEDURE DIVISION.
            EXEC CICS HANDLE CONDITION ERROR(FATALERR)
                                  END-EXEC.
        READ-RECORD.
   1        EXEC CICS RECEIVE MAP('ICMAP')  MAPSET('ICMSET')
                                  END-EXEC.
   2        EXEC CICS POST INTERVAL(2) SET(ECBPTR) END-EXEC.
            process the input map data
            before sending the map out, check to determine if the time
            has expired
   3        IF ECBAREA NOT = LOW-VALUES
                GO TO SEND-MAP.
   4        EXEC CICS WAIT EVENT ECADDR(ECBPTR) END-EXEC.
        SEND-MAP.
            EXEC CICS SEND MAP('ICMAP')  MAPSET('ICMSET')
                       DATAONLY  CURSOR  END-EXEC.
        ENDPGM.
            EXEC CICS RETURN END-EXEC.
        FATALERR.
```

1. The RECEIVE command is receiving a map which contains data which was entered by the operator. Once we have received the map we will now ask CICS to notify us when two seconds have elapsed.

2. This will be accomplished with the POST command. When the POST command is issued CICS will acquire a four-byte event control block and the address of that event control block will be returned in the label ECBPTR. We will immediately get control back and continue processing. When the processing has been completed, and let's say we have some errors on the screen, before we send the map containing the incorrect data back to the operator, we want to be sure that two seconds have elapsed.

3. We can do this by checking the ECBAREA to determine if it has been posted. If the area contains low-values, it simply means that two seconds have not elapsed. Thus the area has not been POSTED.

4. WAIT on an event within CICS (i.e., time elapsing). When an event has occurred, the event control block will be POSTed to nonlow-values, our program will get control at the next sequential instruction, which in this case happens to be a SEND MAP.

If, when we check our event control block area (#3) and we find that it does not equal low-values, it means that the time has elapsed. Thus, we can go and send our MAP out immediately without issuing the WAIT command. As you can see this is a way to delay response time to the user. Before using this option, it is highly recommended to check with a system programmer first.

EXCEPTION CONDITIONS

ENDDATA	Indicates that there is no more data to retrieve.
EXPIRED	Indicates the time specified in a POST, START, or DELAY command has expired.
INVREQ	Indicates that the interval control command is not valid.
INVTSREQ	Indicates that temporary storage is not supported.
IOERR	Indicates an I/O error has occurred.
LENGERR	Indicates that the area reserved in our program is not large enough for the data.
NOTFND	Indicates the request identifier specified in a CANCEL command cannot be found. When this Exception Condition occurs with the RETRIEVE command, it indicates that no data has been passed to the starting task.
TERMIDERR	Indicates that the terminal has not been specified in the terminal control table.
TRANSIDERR	Indicates that the transaction has not been specified in the program control table.

The default action for all the above with the exception of EXPIRED is abnormal task termination. To obtain a complete listing of Exception Conditions, consult the IBM Application Programmer's Reference Manual.

EXERCISE

Let's review what we have learned.

1. What is the function of the interval control program?
2. What is the purpose of the START command?
3. Describe three ways to initiate a task.
4. What is the function of a POST command?
5. Describe a method of controlling response time.

In our prior example using the transient data facility of CICS (Chapter 11), we saw how a transaction could be initiated without human intervention. When setting up the transient data facility, it was necessary to have the correct entries stored in the DCT. With interval control, there is no specific interval control table to be concerned with. This saves time and maintenance. In the following example, the same two programs will be used, only program COMMEXP will issue a START command instead of the transient data command. Therefore the second program, TRANSDAT, will not read transient data.

SOURCE LISTING PROGRAM

```
IDENTIFICATION DIVISION.
PROGRAM-ID. COMMEXP.
ENVIRONMENT DIVISION.
DATA DIVISION.
WORKING-STORAGE SECTION.
01   WSWORKAREA.
     02 TSITEM  PIC S9(4) COMP.
     02 TSQNAME PIC X(8)
             VALUE 'OE01SHIP'.




LINKAGE SECTION.
01   DFHCOMMAREA.
     02 CCUSTNO      PIC X(4).
     02 CCUSTNM      PIC X(20).
     02 CPARTNO      PIC X(4).
     02 CQTY         PIC X(3).
     02 CQTYN        REDEFINES
        CQTY         PIC 9(3).
     02 CACTCD       PIC X.
PROCEDURE DIVISION.
     EXEC CICS HANDLE CONDITION
               ERROR(FATALERR)
1              MAPFAIL(NODATA)
               NOTFND(NOREC)
               END-EXEC.

ADD-RECORD.
     EXEC CICS REWRITE
```

COMMENTS

1. No special Exception Conditions have been established for the interval control START command.

2. The temporary storage record is being written from the DFHCOMMAREA with a length of 31. The ITEM option has been specified so it can be checked later in the program.

3. A check is being made to determine if five records have been written to temporary storage.

4. The interval control START command is being issued for terminal E444 and transaction SHIV. The INTERVAL(0) option indicates to initiate the transaction immediately.

5. After the map is sent the task will terminate.

```
                    DATASET('PARTMAS')
                    FROM(PART-RECORD)
                    LENGTH(MSGLEN)
                    END-EXEC.
2    EXEC CICS WRITEQ TS
                    QUEUE(TSQNAME)
                    FROM(DFHCOMMAREA)
                    LENGTH(31)
                    ITEM(TSITEM)
                    END-EXEC.
3    IF TSITEM = 5
4       EXEC CICS START
                    INTERVAL(0)
                    TERMID('E444')
                    TRANSID('SHIV')
                    FROM(TSQNAME)
                    LENGTH(8)
                    END-EXEC.
5    EXEC CICS RETURN END-EXEC.
```

SOURCE PROGRAM LISTING

```
    IDENTIFICATION DIVISION.
    PROGRAM-ID. TRANSDAT.
    ENVIRONMENT DIVISION.
    DATA DIVISION.
    WORKING-STORAGE SECTION.
    01   WSWORKAREA.
         02 ICTSLEN PIC S9(4)
            COMP      VALUE +8.
    01   ICDATA.
         02 ICTSQ    PIC X(8).
    01   TSREC.
         02 TSCUSTNO PIC X(4).
         02 TSCUSTNM PIC X(20).
         02 TSPARTNO PIC X(4).
         02 TSQTY    PIC XXX.
    PROCEDURE DIVISION.
         EXEC CICS HANDLE CONDITION
                    ERROR(FATALERR)
1                   ITEMERR(DELTSQ)
                    END-EXEC.
2        EXEC CICS RETRIEVE
                    INTO(ICDATA)
                    LENGTH(ICTSLEN)
                    END-EXEC.

3        MOVE 31 TO ICTSLEN.
     READ-TS-Q.
4        EXEC CICS READQ TS
                    QUEUE(ICTSQ)
                    INTO(TSREC)
                    LENGTH(ICTSLEN)
                    ITEM(TSITEM)
                    END-EXEC.
         process the ts record data
5        ADD 1 TO TSITEM.
6        GO TO READ-TS-Q.
     DELTSQ.
7        EXEC CICS DELETEQ TS
```

COMMENTS

1. The Exception Condition ITEMERR has been established to take effect after all the records in the temporary queue have been read.

2. The data passed via the interval control START command is being retrieved.

3. The label will now be used for reading temporary storage. If the records we were reading were all of different lengths then we would need to establish the correct size after every READQ TS command.

4. The temporary storage records are proessed using the ITEM option to ensure that the queue is processed sequentially.

5. One is added to the record counter. There is no need to check any counter for five since we are using the ITEMERR Exception Condition. It would be fine to check a counter instead of using the ITEMERR method.

6. Another temporary storage record will be acquired.

7. The temporary storage queue will be deleted after all the records in it have been processed. There is no need to delete the area passed via interval con-

```
              QUEUE(TDTSQ)
              END-EXEC.
8    EXEC CICS RETURN
              END-EXEC.
```

trol since it will be deleted at task termination.

8. The program will eventually terminate.

13 Additional Features

PAGE BUILDING

We will examine two additional functions of basic mapping support, page building and message routing. A discussion of these two functions was delayed until now because they require the services and understanding of other CICS facilities.

In many instances, there will be a need to create a transaction which will display all the customers with the same last name. When the operator enters a very common last name (e.g., Jones, Smith, etc.), it is very possible to have more customers than can be displayed at one time on the screen. Once the operator views the first group of customers, it may be necessary to acquire another group of customers. In addition, the operator would like to have to press only the enter key to get the next group. BMS provides this facility through the concept of page building.

To illustrate this concept, let's assume we have a customer file which is keyed by customer last name and the dimensions of the terminals we will be using are 24 lines long by 80 characters (columns) wide. In addition, the top two lines of every screen will contain constant title information and the bottom two lines will contain constant instructional information. Each of the remaining twenty lines on the screen will contain information about each customer. The following is an example of the screen:

```
1                          CUSTOMER INQUIRY
2      NAME                    ADDRESS              ORDER NUMBER
3       :                        :                      :
:       :                        :                      :
        :                        :                      :
22      :                        :                      :
23                     MORE CUSTOMERS TO FOLLOW
24                     PRESS ENTER TO CONTINUE


       Let's define the actual map set to be used.


   CUSTMAP   DFHMSD TYPE=&DSECT,TERM=3270,TIOAPFX=YES,LANG=COBOL,  x
                    MODE=INOUT,STORAGE=AUTO                         x
                    CTRL=FREEKB,                                    x
                    EXTATT=YES
1 CUSTDTL   DFHMDI SIZE=(01,80)
  CUSTNAM   DFHMDF POS=(01,02),LENGTH=20
  CUSTADR   DFHMDF POS=(01,28),LENGTH=20
  ORDRNO    DFHMDF POS=(01,54),LENGTH=10
2 CUSTHDR   DFHMDI SIZE=(02,80),LINE=1,COLUMN=1,HEADER=YES
            DFHMDF POS=(01,29),LENGTH=16,INITIAL='CUSTOMER INQUIRY'
            DFHMDF POS=(02,10),LENGTH=04,INITIAL='NAME'
            DFHMDF POS=(02,39),LENGTH=07,INITIAL='ADDRESS'
            DFHMDF POS=(02,55),LENGTH=12,INITIAL='ORDER NUMBER'
3 CUSTTRL   DFHMDI SIZE=(02,80),LINE=23,COLUMN=1
4 MSGLINE   DFHMDF POS=(23,04),LENGTH=25,                          x
               INITIAL='MORE CUSTOMERS TO FOLLOW'
            DFHMDF POS=(24,04),LENGTH=25,                          x
               INITIAL='PRESS ENTER TO CONTINUE'
            DFHMSD TYPE=FINAL
```

We will examine only those statements which have not previously been explained. The mapset (CUSTMAP) is composed of three maps.

1. The first map is defined as one line long and since the LINE and COLUMN options have been omitted, it means the map should be written to the next available completely empty line. The necessary data fields have been defined with the DFHMDF macros.

2. The second of three maps is defined as a header (HEADER=YES) because it will appear at the top of every screen. In addition, the constant information to appear has also been specified via the DFHMDF macros.

3. The third map is defined as a trailer (TRAILER=YES) because it appears at the bottom of every page. The necessary constant information has been supplied via the DFHMDF macros.

4. A literal will be moved to this field when no more records can be found.

When the screen is built it will contain the CUSTHDR map, 20 CUSTDTL maps, and the CUSTTRL map. Since our terminal screen in this example is 24 x 80, it means that it is possible to place 22 maps on a single terminal screen! The terms page and screen are interchangeable for this discussion.

The application program will accept the unformatted message which contains the transaction and customer name (i.e., INQI, JONES). The

tomer file will be read until no more records with the same name are found. In the process, it will be building the necessary pages (screens) in storage. Prior to task termination, it will send out the first page (screen) built. Thus the operator will receive no response until all the pages have been built.

```
SOURCE PROGRAM LISTING

     IDENTIFICATION DIVISION.
     PROGRAM-ID. PAGEBULD.
     ENVIRONMENT DIVISION.
     DATA DIVISION.
     WORKING-STORAGE SECTION.
     COPY DFHAID.
     COPY CUSTMAP.
     01  WSWORKAREA.
         02 MSGLEN              PIC S9(4) COMP VALUE +25.
         02 IOAREA.
            04 FILLER           PIC X(5).
            04 INCUSTNAME        PIC X(20).
            04 FILLER            PIC X.
            04 OUTMSG            PIC X(17).
     01  CUST-RECORD.
         02 CUSTNAME            PIC X(20).
         02 CUSTADDR            PIC X(20).
         02 CUSTORDRNO          PIC X(10).
     PROCEDURE DIVISION.
     **  IT IS A GOOD PRACTICE TO ESTABLISH A HANDLE CONDITION UPON  **
     **                    ENTRY TO A PROGRAM                        **
         EXEC CICS HANDLE CONDITION ERROR(FATALERR)
1                                    OVERFLOW(SEND-TRAILER)
                                     NOTFND(NOREC)
                                     ENDFILE(END-TASK)
                                     LENGERR(BEGIN-BROWSE)
                                     END-EXEC.
     ** THE FOLLOWING WILL DETERMINE WHICH KEY THE OPERATOR SELECTED **
2        IF EIBAID = DFHENTER
             EXEC CICS RECEIVE INTO(IOAREA) LENGTH(MSGLEN) END-EXEC
         ELSE
             MOVE 'INVALID KEY PRESSED'  TO IOAREA
             EXEC CICS SEND FROM(IOAREA) LENGTH(19)
                     ERASE END-EXEC
         EXEC CICS RETURN END-EXEC.
     BEGIN-BROWSE.
     ** THE BROWSE OPERATION WILL BE INITIATED SEARCHING FOR A FULL  **
     **       KEY EQUAL TO THE ENTERED BY THE OPERATOR               **
3        EXEC CICS STARTBR DATASET('CUSTMAS')
                       RIDFLD(INCUSTNAME) EQUAL END-EXEC.
     **         THE HEADER MAP WILL BE SENT                          **
4        EXEC CICS SEND MAP('CUSTHDR') MAPSET('CUSTMAP')
                   ACCUM PAGING
                   MAPONLY ERASE END-EXEC.
     READ-AND-BUILD-OUTPUT.
     ** THE DETAIL MAP WILL BE BUILT WHILE BROWSING THE CUSTOMER FILE **
5        MOVE +50 TO MSGLEN
6        EXEC CICS READNEXT DATASET('CUSTMAS') INTO(CUST-RECORD)
                   LENGTH(MSGLEN) RIDFLD(INCUSTNAME) END-EXEC.
7        IF INCUSTNAME IS NOT EQUAL TO CUSTNAME
             MOVE 'NO MORE RECORDS EXIST' TO MSGLINEO
             EXEC CICS ENDBR DATASET('CUSTMAS') END-EXEC
```

```
                GO TO END-TASK.
 8       MOVE CUSTNAME    TO   CUSTNAM.
         MOVE CUSTADDR    TO   CUSTADR.
         MOVE CUSTORDRNO TO ORDRNO.
 9       EXEC CICS SEND MAP('CUSTDTL') MAPSET('CUSTMAP')
                  ACCUM PAGING END-EXEC.
         GO TO READ-AND-BUILD-OUTPUT.
     SEND-TRAILER.
     **            THE TRAILER MAP WILL BE SENT                    **
10       EXEC CICS SEND MAP('CUSTTRL') MAPSET('CUSTMAP')
                  ACCUM PAGING MAPONLY END-EXEC.
     ** A NEW PAGE WILL BE CREATED REQUIRING ANOTHER HEADER MAP     **
     **          TO BE BUILT. A NEW COUNT WILL AUTOMATICALLY        **
     **                      BE RESUMED                             **
11       EXEC CICS SEND MAP('CUSTHDR') MAPSET('CUSTMAP')
                  ACCUM PAGING
                  MAPONLY ERASE END-EXEC.
     ** SINCE THE DETAIL MAP WHICH CAUSED THE OVERFLOW CONDITION HAS **
     **          NOT BE SENT, IT WILL BE DONE NOW                   **
12       EXEC CICS SEND MAP('CUSTDTL') MAPSET('CUSTMAP')
                  ACCUM PAGING END-EXEC.
13       GO TO READ-AND-BUILD-OUTPUT.
     END-TASK.
     ** THE TRAILER MAP WILL BE SENT TO COMPLETE THE LAST PAGE      **
14       EXEC CICS SEND MAP('CUSTTRL') MAPSET('CUSTMAP')
                  ACCUM PAGING MAPONLY END-EXEC.
15       EXEC CICS SEND PAGE END-EXEC.
16       EXEC CICS RETURN END-EXEC.
     NOREC.
17       MOVE 'RECORD NOT FOUND' TO OUTMSG.
18       EXEC CICS SEND FROM(IOAREA) LENGTH(43) ERASE END-EXEC.
19       EXEC CICS RETURN END-EXEC.
     FATALERR.
     **  THE FOLLOWING WILL PROCESS ANY EXCEPTION CONDITIONS        **
         EXEC CICS ABEND ABCODE('PGBD') END-EXEC.
         GOBACK.
```

COMMENTS

1. The Exception Condition OVERFLOW will occur when the number of lines in the map being sent plus the number of lines in the largest trailer map in the mapset (if any trailer maps exists) exceed the number of lines remaining in the current page being built.

   The Exception Condition NOTFND will occur if the record specified in the STARTBR command can't be found. The Exception Condition ENDFILE will occur if the end of the file has been reached while issuing the READ-NEXT command.

   The Exception Condition LENGERR has been established in the event the operator enters more than 25 characters. Since the program requires less than 25 characters, truncation will occur if more characters are entered and the task will continue to process normally.

2. A check is made to determine which key the operator pressed.

3. The browse operation is initiated searching for a key EQUAL to the one specified with the RIDFLD option.

4. The heading is created for the first page to be built. The ACCUM option indicates this is one of several commands to build a page.

The PAGING option indicates that the pages being built are to be stored in auxiliary temporary storage and NOT sent immediately to the terminal.

5. The size of the CUST-RECORD is established. This is done on every read because the records are variable length and we are only concerned with the first 50 bytes.

6. The customer file will be browsed.

7. A check is made to determine if the names have changed. When they do change, the browsing operation will be terminated. This is very important especially when working with VSAM files because a string needs to be released.

8. The detail map line is created.

9. The detail map is sent. Since the first SEND MAP command included the ACCUM and PAGING options, subsequent commands must also include them. If omitted, an INVREQ Exception Condition will result.

10. The trailer map is sent when the OVERFLOW Exception Condition occurs. Once the trailer map is sent, a page has been completely built.

11. The header map is sent again to start the building of another page and BMS line counting will start from the beginning.

12. The detail line which caused the OVERFLOW condition is now sent.

13. The program will return to reading the next record.

14. Since no more pages need to be built, the trailer map will be sent to complete the page being built.

15. The first page of the message set just built will be sent.

16. The program terminates.

17. A message will be sent when the NOTFND Exception Condition occurs on the STARTBR command.

18. The message is sent to the terminal after the screen has been erased. As you will notice the original input is sent back along with the message. This helps the operator to know which name could not be found.

19. The program terminates.

After the first page has been displayed, the operator can request additional pages via paging commands which must be defined by the system programmer. In many installations, these paging commands are not available because of the overhead created by page building.

It would appear that page building is easy and straightforward. No one can disagree with that! But we should consider whether it is better to code a program that is easy and very inefficient or to spend some extra time in coding and develop a program that is very efficient. Let's examine the program and see why it is not very efficient.

We know that I/O is very slow and that every time a program issues a command, the task has the potential to lose control. In our program, we never know how many records will exist for a given customer name. Names that are common will usually increase in number causing additional I/O. In addition to the I/O, the program is issuing many BMS commands. Since the pages are stored in auxiliary temporary storage, this causes additional I/O.

The initial response time to the user will be rather slow and the following requests will be much quicker because the pages are already built. This uneven response time usually causes user dissatisfaction. Even if we make the user aware of this and they feel it is okay, other tasks will be impacted by this program since we are sharing resources in CICS. In addition, it is possible for the operator to find the necessary information on the first or second page and never view the following pages that had been built and saved. For these reasons great care should be exercised when using the page building concept.

Let's examine another way to provide the operator with the paging capability but at the same time improve on the efficiency of the program. We will begin by redefining the mapset previously created without changing the contents displayed to the operator. The mapset will contain only one map. Following is the modified mapset.

```
   CUSTMAP   DFHMSD TYPE=&DSECT,TERM=3270,TIOAPFX=YES,LANG=COBOL, x
                    MODE=INOUT,                                    x
                    CTRL=FREEKB,                                   x
                    EXTATT=YES
1  CUSTMAP   DFHMDI SIZE=(24,80),LINE=1,COLUMN=1
2            DFHMDF POS=(01,29),LENGTH=16,INITIAL='CUSTOMER INQUIRY'
             DFHMDF POS=(02,10),LENGTH=04,INITIAL='NAME'
             DFHMDF POS=(02,46),LENGTH=07,INITIAL='ADDRESS'
             DFHMDF POS=(02,63),LENGTH=12,INITIAL='ORDER NUMBER'
3  CUSTDTL   DFHMDF POS=(03,01),LENGTH=79,OCCURS=20
4  MSGLINE   DFHMDF POS=(23,04),LENGTH=25,                        x
                    INITIAL='MORE CUSTOMERS TO FOLLOW'
             DFHMDF POS=(24,04),LENGTH=25,                        x
                    INITIAL='PRESS ENTER TO CONTINUE'
             DFHMSD TYPE=FINAL
```

We will examine only those statements which have not previously been explained.

1. The map is defined as 24 lines long by 80 columns wide.
2. The constants which were previously stored in a separate header map are now part of the single map. This eliminates the need for the header map.
3. The detail map is eliminated by defining a detail line which will occur 20 times.
4. The trailer map has been eliminated by including the constants in the single map.

The necessary changes to the program will now be examined.

```
SOURCE PROGRAM LISTING

IDENTIFICATION DIVISION.
PROGRAM-ID. PGEBLDII.
ENVIRONMENT DIVISION.
DATA DIVISION.
WORKING-STORAGE SECTION.
COPY DFHAID.
COPY CUSTMAP.
01  WSWORKAREA.
```

```
          02 MSGLEN                 PIC S9(4) COMP VALUE +25.
  1       02 LINESUB                PIC S9(4) COMP VALUE +1.
          02 IOAREA.
             04 FILLER              PIC X(5).
             04 INCUSTNAME          PIC X(20).
             04 FILLER              PIC X.
             04 OUTMSG              PIC X(17).
  2       02 WSCUSTDTL.
             04 CUSTNAM             PIC X(20).
             04 FILLER              PIC X(8)    VALUE SPACES.
             04 CUSTADR             PIC X(20).
             04 FILLER              PIC X(4)    VALUE SPACES.
             04 ORDRNO              PIC X(10).
      01 CUST-RECORD.
          02 CUSTNAME               PIC X(20).
          02 CUSTADDR               PIC X(20).
          02 CUSTORDRNO             PIC X(10).
      LINKAGE SECTION.
      01 DFHCOMMAREA.
  3       02 CCUSTKEY               PIC X(20).
      PROCEDURE DIVISION.
      **   IT IS A GOOD PRACTICE TO ESTABLISH A HANDLE CONDITION UPON   **
      **                    ENTRY TO A PROGRAM                          **
          EXEC CICS HANDLE CONDITION ERROR(FATALERR)
  4                               NOTFND(NOREC)
                                  ENDFILE(END-TASK)
                                  LENGERR(BEGIN-BROWSE)
                                  END-EXEC.
      **   THE FOLLOWING WILL DETERMINE WHICH KEY THE OPERATOR SELECTED **
  5       IF EIBAID = DFHENTER
             IF EIBCALEN = 20
                GO TO BEGIN-BROWSE
             ELSE
                MOVE CCUSTKEY TO INCUSTNAME
          ELSE
             MOVE 'INVALID KEY PRESSED'  TO IOAREA
             EXEC CICS SEND FROM(IOAREA) LENGTH(19)
                       ERASE END-EXEC
          EXEC CICS RETURN END-EXEC.
      BEGIN-BROWSE.
      ** THE BROWSE OPERATION WILL BE INITIATED SEARCHING FOR A FULL    **
      **       KEY EQUAL TO THE ENTERED BY THE OPERATOR                 **
          EXEC CICS STARTBR DATASET('CUSTMAS')
                    RIDFLD(INCUSTNAME) EQUAL END-EXEC.
      READ-AND-BUILD-OUTPUT.
      ** THE DETAIL MAP WILL BE BUILT WHILE BROWSING THE CUSTOMER FILE **
          EXEC CICS READNEXT DATASET('CUSTMAS') INTO(CUST-RECORD)
          MOVE +50 TO MSGLEN.
                    LENGTH(MSGLEN) RIDFLD(INCUSTNAME) END-EXEC.
          IF INCUSTNAME IS NOT EQUAL TO CUSTNAME
             MOVE 'NO MORE RECORDS EXIST' TO MSGLINEO
             EXEC CICS ENDBR DATASET('CUSTMAS') END-EXEC
             GO TO END-TASK.
  6       MOVE CUSTNAME    TO  CUSTNAM.
          MOVE CUSTADDR    TO  CUSTADR.
          MOVE CUSTORDRNO TO ORDRNO.
  7       MOVE WSCUSTDTL TO CUSTDTL (LINESUB).
  8       IF LINESUB IS LESS THAN 19
             ADD 1 TO LINESUB
             GO TO READ-AND-BUILD-OUTPUT.
```

```
 9      EXEC CICS SEND MAP('CUSTMAP')
               ERASE END-EXEC.
10      EXEC CICS RETURN TRANSID(EIBTRNID)
               COMMAREA(INCUSTNAME)
               LENGTH(20)
               END-EXEC.
   NOREC.
       MOVE 'RECORD NOT FOUND' TO OUTMSG.
       EXEC CICS SEND FROM(IOAREA) LENGTH(43) ERASE END-EXEC.
       EXEC CICS RETURN END-EXEC.
   FATALERR.
   **  THE FOLLOWING WILL PROCESS ANY EXCEPTION CONDITIONS        **
       EXEC CICS ABEND ABCODE('PGBD') END-EXEC.
       GOBACK.
```

COMMENTS

1. A line counter has been created because the program will do its own line counting instead of having BMS check for the Exception Condition OVER-FLOW.

2. Single detail lines will be built in this area and then moved to the actual map.

3. A DFHCOMMAREA is required to save the key of the next record to be displayed if the operator requests another page.

4. The OVERFLOW Exception Condition has been removed.

5. A check is made to determine if the enter key has been pressed. In addition, the EIBCALEN is checked to determine if the operator is requesting another page.

6. The detail line is being created.

7. The Working-Storage detail is being moved to the correct occurrence within the map.

8. A check is made to determine if 20 detail lines have been created.

9. If 20 lines have been created, the map will be sent to the terminal.

10. The program terminates and saves the next record key.

The program will process only 20 records per task and if the operator requires another page, the necessary information can be obtained from the DFHCOMMAREA. This will smooth out the response time because each request will process the same amount of records. Fortunately, the I/O of reading the customer file has been substantially reduced. In addition, there is only one SEND MAP command which will reduce the number of times our task potentially could lose control. The program is much more efficient and all that was required was a little extra programming effort!

If the operator had a need to page backwards, is there a way to provide for it? An easy way to provide for this would be by writing the map to a temporary storage queue prior to sending the map to the operator. When the operator requests the prior page, the program would only have to read the temporary storage queue instead of rereading the customer master file! In this way, we have satisfied the user need and made the program efficient without the use of BMS page building!

MESSAGE ROUTING

We will examine an additional function of basic mapping support, message routing. Message routing provides the ability to develop broadcasting and message switching applications. This allows applications to build and send messages to different BMS supported terminals throughout the CICS network. The messages are built (stored in temporary storage) and sent based on time (interval control) to the proper terminals and/or signed on operators. Since the messages are stored in auxiliary temporary storage, it is possible to provide recovery as long as the correct entries are made in the temporary storage table. As you can see, this is a very powerful function requiring the services of various CICS facilities and can generate considerable overhead. With this in mind, care should be exercised when using this function.

To initiate message routing, we would issue the following command:

```
EXEC CICS ROUTE
        INTERVAL(hhmmss) or INTERVAL(0) or TIME(hhmmss)     optional
        ERRTERM(name)                                        optional
        TITLE(data-area)                                     optional
        LIST(data-area)                                      optional
        OPCLASS(data-area)                                   optional
        REQID(name)                                          optional
        END-EXEC
```

This command will initiate building of the messages by first checking if the terminals specified are valid (in the terminal control table) and, if operators have been specified, are they signed on and have the correct operator classes. After the command has been executed, it is the responsibility of the application program to check the return status codes of the ROUTE to determine how successful it was.

Before proceeding any further, let's take a logical view of the order of execution of the commands in an application program.

```
SOURCE LISTING
WORKING-STORAGE SECTION.
PROCEDURE DIVISION.
   EXEC CICS HANDLE CONDITION ERROR ......  END-EXEC

   EXEC CICS ROUTE ......  END-EXEC.

   check to determine the status of the ROUTE command

   EXEC CICS SEND MAP ACCUM PAGING.... END-EXEC.

   EXEC CICS SEND PAGE ... END-EXEC.

   EXEC CICS RETURN END-EXEC.
```

The ROUTE command will establish the routing environment only. The SEND MAP ACCUM command will create the actual message to be sent. The SEND PAGE command will complete building of the messages and send them to their destinations. With this in mind, let's examine the options of the ROUTE command.

The INTERVAL option indicates the interval of time after which the messages should be sent. The default is INTERVAL(0) indicating the messages should be sent as soon as possible.

The TIME option indicates a specific time of day when the messages should be delivered. When both options are omitted, the default is to deliver them as soon as possible.

The ERRTERM option specifies the terminal to notify if the message is deleted because it can't be delivered within the allocated time. When this option is omitted, the originating terminal will receive the notification.

The TITLE option allows a title to be assigned to the actual message. This title is only displayed upon request and not as part of the actual message. The format of the title is:

```
¦ ¦ ¦    DAILY STATUS REPORT¦
----------------------------
  A              B
```

A is a two-byte length field.

B is the actual title field which can contain up to 62 characters.

The length field indicates the length of the title including the two-byte length field.

The LIST and OPCLASS options specify the terminals and/or operators to which the message should be delivered. Since this can be confusing, let's examine them one at a time.

The LIST option argument (data-area) points to a list of 16-byte entries. The 16-byte entries are usually contiguous. It is possible to have noncontiguous entries but they must all be chained together. Whether contiguous or not, the last entry must end with a two-byte binary halfword initialized to minus 1 (-1), i.e., PIC S9(4) COMP VALUE -1. Each entry has the following format:

```
¦ TERMID ¦ LDC (VTAM) ¦ OPERID ¦ STAT FLAG ¦ BLANKS ¦
------------------------------------------------------
    4          2          3          1          6
```

The TERMID specifies the terminal id or logical unit id. This is a four-byte field and should contain any trailing spaces. When not used, it should contain spaces.

The LDC two-character mnemonic is for certain logical units (VTAM ONLY). Otherwise it should contain spaces.

The OPERID specifies the three-character operator identification. Otherwise it should contain spaces.

The one-byte STAT FLAG indicates how successful the route was for this particular entry. The status flag values are:

X'80'   Entry has been excluded. Another flag will be on in the status flag byte indicating why the entry was excluded.

X'40'   Indicates the terminal id can't be found in the terminal control table.

X'20' The the terminal is not supported by BMS.

X'10' The operator specified is not signed on. One of the following will cause this condition:
The TERMID and OPERID were specified and the operator was not signed on at the terminal.
Only the OPERID was specified and the operator was not signed on to any terminal.
A TERMID only was specified in the entry but the operator signed on at the terminal did not have any of the specified security classes (OPCLASS).

X'08' The operator was signed on to a terminal not supported by BMS.

X'04' The LDC mnemonic is not in the terminal control table.

The OPCLASS specifies that the message should go to all terminals which have an operator of this class signed on.

When OPCLASS and LIST are omitted, all terminals will receive the message.

When only the LIST option is specified, the message will be delivered as specified in each ENTRY.

When only OPCLASS has been specified, the message will be sent to the terminals having an operator signed on with at least one of the specified operator class codes.

When the LIST and OPCLASS are used together, the following happens:

Entries containing an OPERID, will ignore the OPCLASS option.

Entries containing no OPERID, will have the OPCLASS take effect but only for those terminals specified in the LIST option.

The REQID option can be used when message recovery is desirable. Recovery will only take effect if the PAGING option has been specified on the output command and the task has been logically completed.

```
SOURCE PROGRAM LISTING

IDENTIFICATION DIVISION.
PROGRAM-ID. ROUTEEXP.
ENVIRONMENT DIVISION.
DATA DIVISION.
WORKING-STORAGE SECTION.
COPY ROUTEMP.
01   WSWORKAREA.
     02 WSABCODE          PIC X(4)       VALUE 'ROUT'.
01   ROUTE-LIST.
     02 TERMID            PIC X(4)       VALUE 'E654'.
     02 LDCCODE           PIC X(2)       VALUE  SPACES.
     02 OPERID            PIC X(3)       VALUE  SPACES.
     02 STATUS-FLAG       PIC X.
     02 FILLER            PIC X(4)       VALUE  SPACES.
     02 FILLER            PIC S9(4) COMP VALUE  -1.
PROCEDURE DIVISION.
** IT IS A GOOD PRACTICE TO ESTABLISH A HANDLE CONDITION UPON **
**                  ENTRY TO A PROGRAM                        **
     EXEC CICS HANDLE CONDITION ERROR(FATALERR)
                                 END-EXEC.
```

```
      BEGIN-ROUTE.
  **        THE ROUTE  OPERATION WILL BE INITIATED              **
  1     EXEC CICS ROUTE TIME(120000)
                   LIST(ROUTE-LIST)
                   END-EXEC.
  2     IF STATUS-FLAG IS NOT EQUAL TO LOW-VALUES
           MOVE 'RTFL' TO WSABCODE
           GO TO FATALERR.
  3     EXEC CICS SEND MAP('MSGMAP') MAPSET('ROUTEMP')
                   ACCUM PAGING MAPONLY END-EXEC.
  4     EXEC CICS SEND PAGE END-EXEC.
  5     EXEC CICS RETURN END-EXEC.
      FATALERR.
  **   THE FOLLOWING WILL PROCESS ANY EXCEPTION CONDITIONS       **
  6     EXEC CICS ABEND ABCODE(WSABCODE) END-EXEC.
        GOBACK.
```

COMMENTS

1. No special Exception Conditions have been established.

2. The STATUS-FLAG is checked to determine if the ROUTE command was successful. If it was not, a literal is moved to WSABCODE to indicate where the dump occurred. The abend logic path will be taken.

3. The message is being sent with the proper options.

4. The SEND PAGE command is issued to initiate the routing of the message.

5. The program terminates.

6. The abend logic will be invoked if any exceptional conditions occur.

The following are additional basic mapping Exception Conditions.

IGREQID	Indicates the prefix specified in the REQID is different from the previously established REQID.
INVERRTERM	The terminal specified in the ROUTE command is invalid or not supported by BMS.
INVLDC	Indicates an invalid LDC mnemonic.
INVREQ	Indicates the disposition of the routed message has been changed.
OVERFLOW	Indicates the current map plus the largest trailer map in the mapset will not fit on the remaining lines on the page. The default action is to ignore the condition.
RTEFAIL	Indicates the message being routed is only for the terminal that initiated the transaction. The default action is to give control back to the program at the instruction following the ROUTE command.
RTESOME	Indicates that some of the terminals specified in the ROUTE command will not receive the message. The default is to give control back to the program at the instruction following the ROUTE command.
TSIOERR	Indicates an I/O error with temporary storage.

To obtain a complete listing of Exception Conditions, consult the IBM Application Programmer's Reference Manual.

ACCESSING SYSTEM AREAS

When we went through the task initiation process, system areas (i.e., CSA, CWA, TWA) were mentioned. The following command would be issued to reference the areas:

```
EXEC CICS ADDRESS CSA(pointer-ref)          optional
                  CWA(pointer-ref)          optional
                  TWA(pointer-ref)          optional
                  TCTUA(pointer-ref)        optional
                  END-EXEC
```

The option CSA allows accessing of the common system area which contains the addresses of management modules, tables, and other necessary CICS system information. Unless absolutely necessary, it is recommended to avoid accessing this area. If a program accidentally destroys data in the CSA it might cause CICS to abend.

The CWA allows accessing of the common work area which contains installation defined data. This area is appended to the CSA and only one copy exists just like the CSA. It is the user's responsibility to maintain integrity of the CWA.

The option TWA allows accessing of the transaction work area which is appended to the TCA and exists for the life of each task. Its size is stated in the program control table for each transaction. This area can be used to store data or perform data manipulations during task execution. It can also be used to pass information between programs in a task. Any data stored in this area will be lost upon task termination because the area exists only for the life of the task.

The TCTUA option allows accessing of the user portion of the terminal control table terminal entry (TCTTE). The size is stated in the terminal control table. This area exists for the life of CICS and it is the user's responsibility to maintain this area.

These are the only areas which can be accessed via the ADDRESS command. Since no exception conditions exist with this command, how can we be certain that the command returned a valid address? By checking the argument (i.e., pointer-ref) for hex 'FF000000'. This would indicate that the area does not exist and any subsequent referencing of that area could lead to unpredictable results, i.e., task or system termination. Let's see how to use the ADDRESS command.

```
SOURCE PROGRAM LISTING

IDENTIFICATION DIVISION.
PROGRAM-ID. ADDRPGM.
ENVIRONMENT DIVISION.
DATA DIVISION.
WORKING-STORAGE SECTION.
01   WSWORKAREA.
     02 WS-NO-ADDRESS.
          04 FILLER          PIC X          VALUE HIGH-VALUES.
          04 FILLER          PIC X(3)        VALUE LOW-VALUES.
LINKAGE SECTION.
01   PTRSLST.
```

```
            02 FILLER              PIC S9(8)      COMP.
            02 TWAPTR              PIC S9(8)      COMP.
       01  TWAAREA.
            02 TWADATA             PIC X(10).
     PROCEDURE DIVISION.
  1       EXEC CICS ADDRESS TWA(TWAPTR)
                    END-EXEC.
  2       IF TWAPTR = WS-NO-ADDRESS
               GO TO TERMINATE-TASK.
  3       continue processing
                        :
                        :
  4 TERMINATE-TASK.
```

COMMENTS

1. The ADDRESS command is issued to gain access to the TWA.
2. A check is made to determine the presence of a valid address. If a valid address does not exist, the task will be terminated.
3. When a valid address exists, normal processing will continue.
4. The task termination logic.

The CSA option should always return an address because, without the CSA, CICS could not run!

Once a valid address has been obtained, we must be sure that the area associated with the dsect is of sufficient size. The following command will accomplish this.

```
      EXEC CICS ASSIGN CWALENG(data-area)          optional
                       TWALENG(data-area)          optional
                       TCTUALENG(data-area)        optional
                       END-EXEC
```

The argument data-area will contain the size of the area after the command has been executed and should be defined as an S9(4) COMP field.

The CWALENG option will obtain the size of the common work area.

The TWALENG will obtain the size of the transaction work area.

The TCTUA option will obtain the size of the terminal control table user area.

There is no CSA option because it is a fixed-length area.

Let's see how this command would be used in our prior example.

```
     SOURCE PROGRAM LISTING

     IDENTIFICATION DIVISION.
     PROGRAM-ID. ADDRPGM.
     ENVIRONMENT DIVISION.
     DATA DIVISION.
     WORKING-STORAGE SECTION.
     01  WSWORKAREA.
          02 TWAL               PIC S9(4)      COMP.
     LINKAGE SECTION.
     01  PTRSLST.
          02 FILLER             PIC S9(8)      COMP.
          02 TWAPTR             PIC S9(8)      COMP.
```

```
01   TWAAREA.
     02 TWADATA              PIC X(10).
  PROCEDURE DIVISION.
1       EXEC CICS ASSIGN TWALENG(TWAL)
                END-EXEC.
2       IF TWAL IS LESS THAN 10
           GO TO TERMINATE-TASK.
3       EXEC CICS ADDRESS TWA(TWAPTR)
                END-EXEC.
     continue processing
                  :
                  :
4 TERMINATE-TASK.
```

COMMENTS

1. The ASSIGN command is issued first because it is useless to obtain an address if the area is not of the correct size to start with.

2. The TWAL label is checked to determine if the area is as large as our dsect (TWAAREA). This will insure correct addressability. If the area is not large enough, the task will be terminated.

3. The ADDRESS command is issued only for an area of the correct size and this eliminates the need of checking for a valid address since one must exist if the area is of sufficient size!

4. The task termination logic.

DUMP CONTROL

Even though part of the programming process is to try and eliminate any errors that might occur while processing, often the best laid plans go astray. When things are not going according to plan, we need a method of determining what is going wrong. The dump control program (DCP) of CICS will dump certain areas of main storage to one of two dump data sets: A or B. To obtain a print out of the dumped areas, the program DFHDUP, which is a CICS dump utility, can be executed in a separate region. To dump storage the following command would be issued:

```
EXEC CICS DUMP DUMPCODE(name)
              FROM(data-area) LENGTH(data-value)    optional
              TASK                                   optional
              STORAGE                                optional
              PROGRAM                                optional
              TERMINAL                               optional
              TABLES                                 optional
              COMPLETE                               optional
              PCT PPT SIT TCT FCT DCT                optional
              END-EXEC
```

With this command we are able to obtain main storage areas associated with our task and/or any of the CICS tables. The tables can only be obtained if so stated during the CICS gen. The DUMP command when executed in an application program will dump the requested areas and will allow the task to continue processing at the next sequential instruction following the DUMP command. Do not confuse the DUMP command with the ABEND command which we learned previously actually terminates the task. The DUMP command will not generate any message at the user terminal.

The DUMPCODE option will allow us to specify a four-character name which will be printed at the top of our dump. Since the ABEND codes produced by the various CICS management modules all begin with the letter A, it is a good idea to have the ABEND codes issued by our application programs not begin with the letter A. This will avoid confusion.

The STORAGE option will dump the following areas:

TCA and if applicable the TWA

Common system area including the common work area

Trace table if it is active

General registers

TCTTE if applicable

Any transaction storage areas

The PROGRAM option will DUMP the following areas:

STORAGE option areas with the exception of transaction storage

Program storage areas and any register save areas.

The TERMINAL option will DUMP the following areas:

STORAGE option areas with the exception of transaction storage

Any applicable terminal input/output areas.

The TASK option will DUMP the following areas:

STORAGE option areas

PROGRAM option areas

TERMINAL option areas

TASK is the default.

If we want any of the particular tables we would just specify the particular TABLE option. If we desire to have all the tables instead of specifying each individual table we could just use the keyword TABLES. If we want all of the above, we would have to state the option COMPLETE.

Let's see several ways of coding this particular command. Perhaps we are performing several calculations in an application program and getting incorrect results. We need a way to look at the intermediate results to determine what is going wrong. The way to do this is by issuing the following command:

```
EXEC CICS DUMP DUMPCODE(name)
          FROM(data-area) LENGTH(data-area)
          END-EXEC
```

This command will only dump the areas specified with the FROM and LENGTH option.

Perhaps we cannot get enough information by using only the FROM and LENGTH option. We need the storage, program, and terminal areas. The way to obtain all three areas would be to issue the following command:

EXEC CICS DUMP DUMPCODE(name) TASK END-EXEC

This command will dump all the areas associated with our particular task but we will not obtain any tables. The TASK option is the default and is not required.

If we desire to obtain the file control table and the program control table we would code the following command:

```
EXEC CICS DUMP DUMPCODE(name)
            FCT PCT
            END-EXEC
```

If we desire to obtain all the tables we would code the following command:

```
EXEC CICS DUMP DUMPCODE(name)
            TABLES
            END-EXEC
```

If we desire to obtain all the tables and all the areas associated with our task we could code the following command:

```
EXEC CICS DUMP DUMPCODE(name)
            COMPLETE
            END-EXEC
```

That is all there is to obtaining areas within our task. There are no Exception Conditions with the DUMP control command.

ERROR CONDITION PROCESSING

Previously we learned and saw illustrated that a HANDLE CONDITION creates a go to environment. But suppose in our program we wanted to get control back in our program after the execution of a command without creating a go to environment. Is it possible? Yes, through the use of an IGNORE command which we learned about in Chapter 4 but did not see illustrated. Let's see how this can be done by extracting selected portions from the application program we previously coded.

COMMENTS

1. The HANDLE CONDITION command is issued but without the NOTFND condition.

2. The IGNORE command is issued with the NOTFND condition. No paragraph label is stated because this command means to give our program control back at the next sequential executable instruction following the command

```
      PROCEDURE DIVISION.
1         EXEC CICS HANDLE CONDITION ERROR(FATALERR) END-EXEC.
2         EXEC CICS IGNORE NOTFND END-EXEC.
                        :
                        :
      READ-CUSTOMER-FILE.
          MOVE +80 TO MSGLEN.
3         EXEC CICS READ DATASET('CUSTMAS')
                         RIDFLD(WSCUSTKEY)
                         INTO(CUST-RECORD)    LENGTH(MSGLEN)
                         GENERIC              KEYLENGTH(4)
                         END-EXEC.
4         IF EIBRCODE IS NOT EQUAL TO LOW-VALUES
                  error record processing.
      READ-PART-FILE.
          MOVE +80 TO MSGLEN.
5         EXEC CICS READ DATASET('PARTMAS')
                         RIDFLD(CPARTNO)
                         INTO(PART-RECORD)    LENGTH(MSGLEN)
                         UPDATE
                         END-EXEC.
6         IF EIBRCODE IS NOT EQUAL TO LOW-VALUES
                  error record processing.
          continue with processing.
```

that caused that condition. It stays in effect until changed by a HANDLE
CONDITION specifying a NOTFND condition.

3. The READ command remains unchanged.

4. Control is returned to our program when a record is found and not found.
    We need a way to distinguish between the two situations. Whenever a com-
    mand has been successfully processed, the EIBRCODE field will contain low-
    values. Thus in our example by checking for non-low-values we can deter-
    mine if a record has not been found.

    This technique helps to avoid branching to different routines and then
    branching back to our original logic as we did in our previously coded pro-
    gram.

5. The READ command remains unchanged.

6. The checking of the EIBRCODE field would be the same as #4.

Another method can be used to determine the results of the execution of a
command. This would be through the use of the NOHANDLE option.
This option is coded as part of the actual command and means it is the
responsibility of the application program to determine the results of the
execution of the command. Let's see how this is accomplished by again
extracting portions of our program.

```
      WORKING-STORAGE SECTION.
      01  WSWORKAREA.
1         02  WS-HEX81           PIC S9(4) COMP VALUE +129.
          02  FILLER             REDEFINES
              WS-HEX81.
              04  FILLER         PIC X.
              04  WSNOTFOUND     PIC X.
2         02  WSEIBRCODE.
              04  WSBYTEZERO     PIC X.
              04  FILLER         PIC X(5).
```

```
         PROCEDURE DIVISION.
3                  :
                   :
                   :
                   :
         READ-CUSTOMER-FILE.
             MOVE +80 TO MSGLEN.
4            EXEC CICS READ DATASET('CUSTMAS')
                            RIDFLD(WSCUSTKEY)
                            INTO(CUST-RECORD)    LENGTH(MSGLEN)
                            GENERIC              KEYLENGTH(4)
                            NOHANDLE
                            END-EXEC.
             MOVE EIBRCODE TO WSEIBRCODE.
5            IF EIBRCODE IS EQUAL TO LOW-VALUES
                 NEXT SENTENCE
             ELSE
6               MOVE EIBRCODE TO WSEIBRCODE
7               IF WSBYTEZERO = WSNOTFOUND
                   error record processing
                ELSE
8                  GO TO FATALERR.
```

COMMENTS

1. The value for a NOTFND is established. How was it determined that a hex 81 indicated a NOTFND condition? By using Figure 4-4 we know that a READ command has a code of 06 02. Proceeding to Figure 4-5 we use the value of byte zero of the EIBFN code (06) and find that when byte zero of the EIBRCODE contains a hex 81 a NOTFND condition exists.

2. A field has been set aside to test byte zero of the EIBRCODE field.

3. No HANDLE CONDITION or IGNORE command has been issued.

4. The READ command includes the NOHANDLE option. This means to give our program control back at the next sequential executable instruction regardless of the results of the command.

5. A return code of low-values indicates a successful execution and processing will continue.

6. The EIBRCODE field is moved to WSEIBRCODE so byte zero can be tested.

7. A check is made for a NOTFND condition and the appropriate error processing will be done.

8. Any other return codes will cause the logic to go to FATALERR.

This method eliminates the issuing of HANDLE CONDITION and IGNORE commands and is thus more efficient. But it also requires the checking of return codes in hex which isn't always easy in COBOL. One way to solve the hex checking problem would be by creating a common copy member containing all possible hex values which any program could use.

Both methods work and the final decision is up to you but remember to keep maintenance in mind.

You may be wondering: is it possible to mix them all in one program? The answer is yes and the NOHANDLE option has top priority followed by the IGNORE command and lastly the HANDLE CONDITION command.

Suppose in our program we did not want to issue an ABEND command in the FATALERR paragraph but instead wished to transfer control to a common error program. Is it possible? Yes and let's see how to accomplish this again by extracting and using our previous program.

```
      WORKING-STORAGE SECTION.
      01  WSWORKAREA.
1         02 WSERRINFO.
             04 WSEIBFN          PIC XX.
             04 WSEIBRCODE        PIC X(6).
      PROCEDURE DIVISION.
                      ¦
                      ¦
                      ¦
                      ¦
      FATALERR.
2         MOVE EIBFN TO WSEIBFN.
          MOVE EIBRCODE TO WSEIBRCODE.
3         EXEC CICS XCTL PROGRAM('ERRORPGM')
                         COMMAREA(WSERRINFO)
                         LENGTH(8)
                         END-EXEC.
```

COMMENTS

1. An area has been established to hold the information to pass to the error program.

2. The necessary information is moved out of the executive interface block. This is done because the fields are updated whenever a command is issued and if the fields were not moved the error program would receive the wrong information.

3. Control is passed to the error program along with the necessary error information.

ADVANCED TECHNIQUES

The following program will accept a transaction with or without data from an unformatted screen. The unformatted data stream may appear in any of the following formats:

```
TRANSACTION
TRANSACTION,SELECTION
TRANSACTION,SELECTION,CUSTOMER NUMBER
```

When only a transaction is entered, the program will display a menu selection screen. If the operator already knows what selection to make, it can be entered along with the transaction code. If a customer number is required for the selection, it can also be entered. The selection and customer number must be separated by commas. If the data following the transaction is correct, control will be transferred to the appropriate program. If not correct, the menu selection screen will be displayed. The clear key will allow the operator to cancel out of the session. The enter key will be used to enter data. All other key selections will be invalid and a message will

be sent back to the operator indicating the problem. The following is the
format of the menu selection screen:

```
                1           2           3           4           5           6 ......
     123456789012345678901234567890123456789012345678901234567890123456 7
01
02                                 #   MENU SELECTION
03
04                                 #1. CUSTOMER DISPLAY      *
05
06                                 #2. CUSTOMER UPDATE       *
07
08                                 #3. CUSTOMER DELETE       *
09
10                                 #4. CUSTOMER ADD
11
12
13
14
15
16                                 #* CUSTOMER NUMBER REQUIRED
17
18
19
20            #SELECTION:# #      #CUSTOMER NUMBER:#         #
21
22   #PRESS CLEAR TO END SESSION
23   #
24
```

```
     MENUS     DFHMSD TYPE=&DSECT,TERM=3270,TIOAPFX=YES,                       x
                       LANG=COBOL,                                              x
                       MODE=INOUT,                                              x
                       CTRL=FREEKB,                                             x
                       EXTATT=YES
     MENUM     DFHMDI SIZE=(24,80),LINE=1,COLUMN=1
               DFHMDF POS=(02,29),LENGTH=17,INITIAL='  MENU SELECTION'
               DFHMDF POS=(04,29),LENGTH=23,INITIAL='1. CUSTOMER DISPLAY   *'
               DFHMDF POS=(06,29),LENGTH=23,INITIAL='2. CUSTOMER UPDATE    *'
               DFHMDF POS=(08,29),LENGTH=23,INITIAL='3. CUSTOMER DELETE    *'
               DFHMDF POS=(10,29),LENGTH=15,INITIAL='4. CUSTOMER ADD'
               DFHMDF POS=(16,29),LENGTH=27,                                    x
                      INITIAL='* CUSTOMER NUMBER REQUIRED'
               DFHMDF POS=(20,18),LENGTH=09,INITIAL='SELECTION'
     SELECT    DFHMDF POS=(20,29),LENGTH=01,ATTRB=UNPROT
               DFHMDF POS=(20,31),LENGTH=01
               DFHMDF POS=(20,37),LENGTH=16,INITIAL='CUSTOMER NUMBER:'
     CUSTNO    DFHMDF POS=(20,54),LENGTH=06,ATTRB=UNPROT
               DFHMDF POS=(20,61),LENGTH=01
               DFHMDF POS=(22,04),LENGTH=26,                                    x
                      INITIAL='PRESS CLEAR TO END SESSION'
     ERRMSG    DFHMDF POS=(23,04),LENGTH=76
               DFHMSD TYPE=FINAL
```

The name of the mapset is MENUS and is defined in the processing
program table (PPT). The map name is MENUM and is not kept track of in
any CICS table. This mapset needs no explanation since it does not contain
anything different from our previous mapset except initial titles.

SOURCE PROGRAM LISTING

```
         IDENTIFICATION DIVISION.
         PROGRAM-ID. MENUEXP.
         ENVIRONMENT DIVISION.
         DATA DIVISION.
         WORKING-STORAGE SECTION.
         COPY DFHAID.
1        COPY MENUS.
         COPY DFHBMSCA.
         01  WSWORKAREA.
2            02  WSIOAREA.
                 04  WSIOTRANSID      PIC X(4).
                 04  FILLER           PIC X.
                 04  WSIOSELECT       PIC X.
                 04  WSIOSELECTNUM    REDEFINES
                     WSIOSELECT       PIC 9.
                 04  FILLER           PIC X.
                 04  WSIOCUSTNO       PIC X(6).
             02  WSMSGLEN             PIC S9(4)   COMP VALUE +13.
             02  WSDEC128             PIC S9(4)   COMP  VALUE +128.
             02  FILLER               REDEFINES
                 WSDEC128.
                 04  FILLER           PIC X.
                 04  WSHEX80          PIC X.
             02  WSQMARK.
                 04  FILLER           PIC X       VALUE '?'.
                 04  FILLER           PIC X(5)    VALUE LOW-VALUES.
3            02  WS-PROGRAMS.
                 04  FILLER           PIC X(8)    VALUE 'DISPPGM'.
                 04  FILLER           PIC X(8)    VALUE 'UPDTPGM'.
                 04  FILLER           PIC X(8)    VALUE 'DELTPGM'.
                 04  FILLER           PIC X(8)    VALUE 'ADDPGM'.
             02  WS-INDIVPGM          REDEFINES
                                      OCCURS 4 TIMES PIC X(8).
         LINKAGE SECTION.
         01  DFHCOMMAREA.
             02  DFHINDICATOR         PIC X.
         PROCEDURE DIVISION.
     **      IT IS A GOOD PRACTICE TO ESTABLISH A HANDLE CONDITION UPON    **
     **                      ENTRY TO A PROGRAM                            **
         EXEC CICS HANDLE CONDITION ERROR(FATALERR)
4                                    MAPFAIL(EDIT-MAP-DATA)
                                     END-EXEC.
     **      THE FOLLOWING WILL DETERMINE WHICH KEY THE OPERATOR SELECTED  **
     **      THE EIBCALEN LABEL WILL BE USED TO DETERMINE IF IT IS THE     **
     **      FIRST TIME INTO THE PROGRAM                                   **
         IF EIBAID = DFHENTER
5            IF EIBCALEN = ZERO
                 GO TO EDIT-UNFORMATTED-DATA-STREAM
             ELSE
                 GO TO RECEIVE-FORMATTED-DATA-STREAM
         ELSE
6            IF EIBAID = DFHCLEAR
                 MOVE 'SESSION COMPLETED' TO WSIOAREA
                 EXEC CICS SEND FROM(WSIOAREA) LENGTH(17) END-EXEC
                 EXEC CICS RETURN END-EXEC
             ELSE
7                MOVE 'INVALID KEY PRESSED' TO WSIOAREA
                 EXEC CICS SEND FROM(WSIOAREA) LENGTH(19)
                          ERASE END-EXEC
                 EXEC CICS RETURN END-EXEC.
```

```
        EDIT-UNFORMATTED-DATA-STREAM.
8           EXEC CICS RECEIVE INTO(WSIOAREA) LENGTH(WSMSGLEN)
                    NOHANDLE
                    END-EXEC.
            IF WSIOSELECT = '4'
                GO TO TRANSFER-CONTROL
            ELSE
                IF WSIOSELECT IS GREATER THAN '1' AND LESS THAN '4'
                    IF WSIOCUSTNO IS NUMERIC
                        GO TO TRANSFER-CONTROL.
9       SEND-MENU-MAP.
                EXEC CICS SEND MAP('MENUM') MAPSET('MENUS')
                        ERASE MAPONLY END-EXEC
                EXEC CICS RETURN TRANSID(EIBTRNID)
                        COMMAREA(WSIOTRANSID)  LENGTH(1) END-EXEC.
10      TRANSFER-CONTROL.
            EXEC CICS XCTL PROGRAM(WS-INDIVPGM(WSIOSELECTNUM))
                COMMAREA(WSIOCUSTNO)  LENGTH(6) END-EXEC.
11      RECEIVE-FORMATTED-DATA-STREAM.
            EXEC CICS RECEIVE MAP('MENUM') MAPSET('MENUS') END-EXEC.
        EDIT-MAP-DATA.
        **   THE INPUT DATA WILL BE NOW BE EDITTED                    **
            IF SELECTL = ZEROS
                MOVE WSQMARK TO SELECTO
                MOVE  -1     TO SELECTL
                MOVE   1     TO WSERRIND
                MOVE DFHBMBRY TO SELECTA
            ELSE
                IF SELECTI IS LESS THAN ZERO OR GREATER THAN '4'
                    MOVE  -1  TO SELECTL
                    MOVE   1  TO WSERRIND
                    MOVE DFHBMBRY TO SELECTA
                ELSE
                    MOVE DFHBMFSE TO SELECTA.
            IF CUSTNOL = ZEROS
                MOVE WSQMARK  TO CUSTNOO
                MOVE  -1      TO CUSTNOL
                MOVE   1      TO WSERRIND
                MOVE DFHBMBRY TO CUSTNOA
            ELSE
                IF CUSTNOI NOT NUMERIC
                    MOVE  -1  TO CUSTNOL
                    MOVE   1  TO WSERRIND
                    MOVE DFHBMBRY TO CUSTNOA
                ELSE
                    MOVE DFHBMFSE TO CUSTNOA.
            IF WSERRIND = ZERO
                MOVE SELECTI TO WSIOSELECT
                MOVE CUSTNOI TO WSIOCUSTNO
                GO TO TRANSFER-CONTROL.
            MOVE 'ERRORS HIGHLIGHTED    PLEASE CORRECT AND RESUBMIT' TO
                ERRMSGO.
12      SEND-DATAONLY-MAP.
            EXEC CICS SEND MAP('MENUM') MAPSET('MENUS')
                        DATAONLY CURSOR         END-EXEC.
            EXEC CICS RETURN TRANSID(EIBTRNID)
                    COMMAREA(DFHCOMMAREA)  LENGTH(EIBCALEN) END-EXEC.
13      FATALERR.
        **   THE FOLLOWING WILL PROCESS ANY EXCEPTION CONDITIONS      **
            EXEC CICS ABEND ABCODE('CMEX') END-EXEC.
            GOBACK.
```

COMMENTS

1. The MENUS mapset is copied into the program.

2. An input area is provided to interpret the unformatted input data stream. An area large enough to contain only the necessary maximum number of characters has been provided. All other characters will be truncated.

3. A program table has been established and redefined so it can be referenced via a subscript. This method also allows for future programs to be added without major program modifications.

4. The Exception Condition MAPFAIL has been established along with a catchall ERROR Exception Condition. When a MAPFAIL occurs, the program will continue processing as if no MAPFAIL Exception Condition occurred. This is being done since there is a very small amount of data being processed and the chance of a MAPFAIL is minimal.

5. Since we previously stated that the enter key was the only valid input key, we also need to know if we have an unformatted data stream or a formatted data stream. The EIBCALEN label is used for this purpose. Only after this program sends out the MENUMAP and issues a RETURN with a TRANSID and COMMAREA will the EIBCALEN label be greater than zero.

6. When the CLEAR key is pressed, the appropriate message will be sent.

7. Any other key will produce an error message. In some applications other types of actions may be taken but it all depends on the application design.

8. The unformatted data stream is received and processed. The NOHANDLE option has been inserted into the command. Thus if more than 13 characters are transmitted, they will be truncated and normal processing will continue. This is being done because the program only requires a maximum of 13 characters and to send an error message to the operator is unnecessary.

9. The MENUMAP is sent when only the transaction is keyed in or the data following the transaction is invalid. The invalid data could be displayed here but again that is a function of the application design. A one-byte area is saved to act as an indicator that a map is currently displayed. Any area of the program could be used and the contents of the area is not important.

10. Control is transferred to the appropriate program. A subscript has been used in the command and as stated previously this allows for future modifications with minor program changes.

11. The formatted data stream is received and processed. The data will be sent back to the operator when errors exist. This seems to conflict with what we previously learned about transmitting a minimal number of characters! This method has been chosen because VERY little data is required and the chance for error is MINOR. This method should not be used on screens with large amounts of data and where the chance for error is great.

12. The errors are sent back to the operator. A COMMAREA of one byte is created to act as an indicator that a map is currently displayed.

13. If an unexpected error occurs the task will abend with a transaction dump.

That's all there is to it!

CICS COMMANDS

Following is a list of the most frequently used commands. Brackets [ ]
indicate the enclosed identifiers are optional.

EXCEPTIONAL CONDITIONS

1. HANDLE CONDITION   condition [(label)]
   [condition [(label)]] . . .

2. IGNORE CONDITION   condition
   [condition] . . .

ACCESS TO SYSTEM INFORMATION

1. ADDRESS   option(pointer-ref)
   [option(pointer-ref)]. . .

    Options: CSA,CWA,TCTUA,TWA

2. ASSIGN   option(data-area)
   [option(data-area)]. . .

Exceptional conditions:INVREQ

Options:

Storage Area Lengths	CWALENG,	TCTUALENG,	TWALENG	
2980 Values	NUMTAB,	STATIONID,	TELLERID	
BMS Values	DESTCOUNT,	LDCMNEM,	LDCNUM,	PAGENUM,
Batch Data Interchange Values	DESTID,	DESTIDLENG		
3270 Screen Size	SCRNHT,	SCRNWD		
Other	ABCODE,	APPLID,	COLOR,	DELMITER,
	EXTDS,	FACILITY,	FCI,	HILIGHT,
	OPCLASS,	OPID,	OPSECURITY	PRINSYSID,
	PS,	RESTART,	SIGDATA,	STARTCODE,
	SYSID,	TERMCODE,	UNATTEND,	VALIDATION

FILE CONTROL

1. READ   DATASET(name)
   SET(pointer-ref) or INTO(data-area)
   [LENGTH(data-area)]
   RIDFLD(data-area)
   [KEYLENGTH(data-value) [GENERIC]]
   [SYSID(name)]
   [SEGSET(name) or SEGSETALL]
   [RBA or RRN]   (VSAM only)
   [DEBKEY or DEBREC]   (blocked DAM only)
   [GTEQ or *EQUAL*]   (VSAM only)
   [UPDATE]

    Exceptional conditions: DSIDERR, DUPKEY, ILLOGIC (VSAM only),
   INVREQ,
   IOERR, ISCINVREQ, LENGERR, NOTFND,
   NOTOPEN,
   SEGIDERR,SYSIDERR

2. WRITE DATASET(name)
FROM(data-area)
[LENGTH(data-value)]
RIDFLD(data-area)
[KEYLENGTH(data-value)]
[SYSID(name)]
[RBA OR RRN]   (VSAM only)
[MASSINSERT]   (VSAM only)
[SEGSETALL]

Exceptional conditions: DSIDERR, DUPREC, ILLOGIC (VSAM only),
IOERR
ISCINVREQ, LENGERR, NOSPACE,
NOTOPEN, SYSIDERR

3. REWRITE DATASET(name)
FROM(data-area)
[LENGTH(data-value)]
[SYSID(name)]
[SEGSETALL]

  Exceptional conditions: DSIDERR, ILLOGIC (VSAM
only), INVREQ, IOERR,
ISCINVREQ, LENGERR,
NOSPACE, NOTOPEN,
SYSIDERR

4. DELETE DATASET(name)   (VSAM only)
[RIDFLD(data-area)]   (mandatory with GENERIC)
[KEYLENGTH(data-value)] (mandatory with GENERIC)
[GENERIC [NUMREC(data-area)]]
[SYSID(name)]
[RBA or RRN]

Exceptional conditions: DSIDERR, ILLOGIC (VSAM only), IOERR, ISCI-
NVREQ,
NOTFND, NOTOPEN, SYSIDERR

5. UNLOCK DATASET(name)
[SYSID(name)]

Exceptional conditions: DSIDERR, ILLOGIC (VSAM only), IOERR, ISCI-
NVREQ,
NOTOPEN, SYSIDERR

6. STARTBR DATASET(name)
RIDFLD(data-area)
[KEYLENGTH(data-value) [GENERIC]]
REQID(data-value)
[SYSID(name)]
[RBA or RRN]   (VSAM only)
[DEBKEY or DEBREC] (blocked DAM only)
[*GTEQ* or EQUAL]   (VSAM only)

Exceptional conditions: DSIDERR, ILLOGIC (VSAM only), INVREQ,
IOERR,

ISCINVREQ, NOTFND, NOTOPEN, SYS-
IDERR

7. READNEXT   DATASET(name)
SET(pointer-ref) or INTO(data-area)
[LENGTH(data-area)]
RIDFLD(data-area)
[KEYLENGTH(data-value)]
REQID(data-value)
[SYSID(name)]
[SEGSET(name) or SEGSETALL]
[RBA or RRN]   (VSAM only)

Exceptional conditions: DSIDERR, DUPKEY, ENDFILE, ILLOGIC
(VSAM only),
INVREQ, IOERR, ISCINVREQ, LENGERR,
NOTFND,
NOTOPEN, SEGIDERR, SYSIDERR

8. READPREV   DATASET(name)   (VSAM only)
SET(pointer-ref) or INTO(data-area)
[LENGTH(data-area)]
RIDFLD(data-area)
[KEYLENGTH(data-value)]
REQID(data-value)
[SYSID(name)]
[SEGSET(name) or SEGSETALL]
[RBA or RRN]

Exceptional conditions: DSIDERR, DUPKEY, ENDFILE, ILLOGIC,
INVREQ,
IOERR, ISCINVREQ, LENGERR, NOTFND,
NOTOPEN,
SEGIDERR, SYSIDERR

9. RESETBR   DATASET(name)
RIDFLD(data-area)
[KEYLENGTH(data-value) [GENERIC]]
REQID(data-value)
[SYSID(name)]
[*GTEQ* or EQUAL]   (VSAM only)
[RBA or RRN]   (VSAM only)

Exceptional conditions: ILLOGIC (VSAM only), INVREQ, IOERR, ISCI-
NVREQ,
NOTFND, NOTOPEN, SYSIDERR

10. ENDBR   DATASET(name)
REQID(data-value)
[SYSID(name)]

Exceptional conditions: ILLOGIC (VSAM only), INVREQ, ISCINVREQ,
SYSIDERR

TERMINAL CONTROL

1. STANDARD CICS/VS TERMINAL SUPPORT (BTAM OR TCAM)

   a. RECEIVE   INTO(data-area) or SET(pointer-ref)
                      LENGTH(data-area)

    Exceptional conditions: LENGERR

   b. SEND   FROM(data-area)
              LENGTH(data-value)
              [DEST(name)]
              [WAIT]

   c. CONVERSE   FROM(data-area)
                  FROMLENGTH(data-value)
                  INTO(data-area) or SET(pointer-ref)
                  TOLENGTH(data-area)
                  [DEST(name)]

    Exceptional conditions: LENGERR

   d. ISSUE RESET

   e. ISSUE DISCONNECT

2. LUTYPE4 LOGICAL UNIT

   a. RECEIVE   INTO(data-area) or SET(pointer-ref)
                      LENGTH(data-area)

    Exceptional conditions: EOC, EODS, INBFMH, LENGERR, SIGNAL

   b. SEND   FROM(data-area)
              LENGTH(data-value)
               [WAIT]
              [INVITE or LAST]
              [CNOTCOMPL or DEFRESP]
              [FMH]

    Exceptional conditions: IGREQCD, SIGNAL

   c. CONVERSE   FROM(data-area)
                  FROMLENGTH(data-value)
                  [INTO(data-area) or SET(pointer-ref)]
                  [TOLENGTH(data-area)]
                  [DEFRESP]
                  [FMH]

    Exceptional conditions: EOC, EODS, IGREQCD, INBFMH, LENGERR, SIGNAL

   d. FREE   [SESSION(name)]

    Exceptional conditions: INVREQ, NOTALLOC, SESSIONERR

   e. WAIT   SIGNAL

    Exceptional condition: SIGNAL

   f. ISSUE DISCONNECT

    Exceptional condition: SIGNAL

3. LUTYPE6 LOGICAL UNIT

    a. RECEIVE   [SESSION(name)]
                        INTO(data-area) or SET(pointer-ref)
                        LENGTH(data-area)

    Exceptional conditions: INBFMH, NOTALLOC, LENGERR, SES-
SIONERR, SIGNAL

    b. SEND   [SESSION(name)]
              [WAIT]
              [INVITE or LAST]
              [ATTACHID(name)]
              [FROM(name)]
              LENGTH(name)
              [FMH]
              [DEFRESP]

    Exceptional conditions: CBIDERR, NOTALLOC, SESSIONERR, SIG-
NAL

    c. CONVERSE   [SESSION(name)]
                      [ATTACHID(name)]
                      [FROM(name)]
                      FROMLENGTH(name)
                      [INTO(data-area) or SET(pointer-ref)]
                      [TOLENGTH(data-area)]
                      [FMH]
                      [DEFRESP]

    Exceptional conditions: CBIDERR, INBFMH, LENGERR, NOTA-
                                        LLOC,
                                        SESSIONERR, SIGNAL

    d. ALLOCATE   SYSID(name) or SESSION(name)
                      [PROFILE(name)]

    Exceptional conditions: CBIDERR, INVREQ, SESSBUSY, SES-
                                        SIONERR,
                                        SYSBUSY, SYSIDERR

    e. BUILD   ATTACH
              [ATTACHID(name)]
              [PROCESS(name)][RESOURCE(name)]
              [RPROCESS(name)][RRESOURCE(name)]
              [QUEUE(name)][IUTYPE(name)]
              [DATASTR(name)][RECFM(name)]

    f. EXTRACT   ATTACH
                  [ATTACHID(name) or SESSION(data-area)]
                  [PROCESS(data-area)][RESOURCE(data-area)]
                  [RPROCESS(data-area)][RRESOURCE(data-area)]
                  [QUEUE(data-area)][IUTYPE(data-area)]
                  [DATASTR(data-area)][RECFM(data-area)]

    Exceptional conditions: CBIDERR, INVREQ, NOTALLOC, SES-
SIONERR

---

g. EXTRACT   TCT
                  NETNAME(name)
                  SYSID(data-area) or TERMID(data-area)

    Exceptional condition: INVREQ

h. FREE   [SESSION(name)]

    Exceptional conditions: INVREQ, NOTALLOC, SESSIONERR

i. POINT   [SESSION(name)]

    Exceptional conditions: NOTALLOC, SESSIONERR

j. WAIT   SIGNAL

k. WAIT   TERMINAL [SESSION(name)]

    Exceptional conditions: NOTALLOC, SESSIONERR, SIGNAL

l. ISSUE   DISCONNECT [SESSION(name)]

    Exceptional conditions: NOTALLOC, SESSIONERR

m. ISSUE   SIGNAL [SESSION(name)]

    Exceptional conditions: NOTALLOC

4. 3270 INFORMATION DISPLAY SYSTEM (BTAM OR TCAM)

    a. HANDLE   AID option[(label)]
                       [option[(label)]]...

       Options: PA1,PA2,PA3,PF1 through PF24, CLEAR, ENTER, LIGHT-PEN,
                      OPERID, ANYKEY

    b. RECEIVE   INTO(data-area) or SET(pointer-ref)
                       LENGTH(data-area)
                       [ASIS]
                       [BUFFER]   (not TCAM)

    Exceptional condition: LENGERR

    c. SEND   FROM(data-area)
                LENGTH(data-value)
                [DEST(name)]   (TCAM only)
                [WAIT]
                [STRFIELD or [[ERASE][CTLCHAR(data-value)]]]

    d. CONVERSE   FROM(data-area)
                      FROMLENGTH(data-value)
                     [INTO(data-area) or SET(pointer-ref)]
                     [TOLENGTH(data-area)]
                     [STRFIELD or [[ERASE][CTLCHAR(data-value)]]]

    Exceptional condition: LENGERR

    e. ISSUE PRINT   (not TCAM)

    f. ISSUE COPY   TERMID(name)   (not TCAM)
                   [CTLCHAR(data-value)]
                   [WAIT]

    Exceptional condition: TERMIDERR

    g. ISSUE ERASEAUP [WAIT]

    h. ISSUE RESET

i. ISSUE DISCONNECT

5. 3270 IN 2260 COMPATIBILITY MODE (BTAM)

    a. RECEIVE   INTO(data-area) or SET(pointer-ref)
                       LENGTH(data-area)
                       [LEAVEKB]

      Exceptional condition: LENGERR

    b. SEND   FROM(data-area)
               LENGTH(data-value)
               [LINEADR(data-value)]
               [WAIT]
               [ERASE]
               [LEAVEKB]

    c. CONVERSE   FROM(data-area)
                    FROMLENGTH(data-value)
                    [INTO(data-area) or SET(pointer-ref)]
                    [TOLENGTH(data-area)]
                    [LINEADDR(data-value)]
                    [ERASE]

      Exceptional condition: LENGERR

    d. ISSUE DISCONNECT

6. 3270 LOGICAL UNIT

    a. RECEIVE   INTO(data-area) or SET(pointer-ref)
                       LENGTH(data-area)
                       [ASIS]
                       [BUFFER]

      Exceptional condition: LENGERR

    b. SEND   FROM(data-area)
               LENGTH(data-value)
                [WAIT]
                [INVITE or LAST]
                [STRFIELD or [[ERASE][CTLCHAR(data-value)]]]

    c. CONVERSE   FROM(data-area)
                      FROMLENGTH(data-value)
                    [INTO(data-area) or SET(pointer-ref)]
                    [STRFIELD or [[ERASE][CTLCHAR(data-value)]]]
                    [TOLENGTH(data-area)]
                    [DEFRESP]

      Exceptional condition: LENGERR

    d. FREE   [SESSION(name)]

      Exceptional conditions: INVREQ, NOTALLOC, SESSIONERR

    e. ISSUE PRINT

    f. ISSUE COPY   TERMID(name)
                      [CTLCHAR(data-value)]
                      [WAIT]

      Exceptional condition: TERMIDERR

g. ISSUE ERASEAUP [WAIT]

h. ISSUE DISCONNECT

7. 3270 SCS PRINTER LOGICAL UNIT

   a. SEND   FROM(data-area)
                 LENGTH(data-value)
                 [DEST(name)]
                 [WAIT]
                 [INVITE or LAST]
                 [CNOTCOMPL or DEFRESP]
                 [DEFRESP]

   b. FREE   [SESSION(name)]

      Exceptional conditions: INVREQ, NOTALLOC, SESSIONERR

   c. ISSUE DISCONNECT

8. 3270-DISPLAY LOGICAL UNIT (LUTYPE2)

   a. RECEIVE   INTO(data-area) or SET(pointer-ref)
                  LENGTH(data-area)
                  [ASIS]
                  [BUFFER]

      Exceptional condition: LENGERR

   b. SEND   FROM(data-area)
                 LENGTH(data-value)
                 [DEST(name)]
                 [WAIT]
                 [STRFIELD or [[ERASE][CTLCHAR(data-value)]]]
                 [INVITE or LAST]
                 [DEFRESP]

   c. CONVERSE   FROM(data-area)
                  FROMLENGTH(data-value)
                  [INTO(data-area) or SET(pointer-ref)]
                  [TOLENGTH(data-area)]
                  [STRFIELD or [[ERASE][CTLCHAR(data-value)]]]
                  [DEST(name)]
                  [DEFRESP]

      Exceptional condition: LENGERR

   d. FREE   [SESSION(name)]

      Exceptional conditions: INVREQ, NOTALLOC, SESSIONERR

   e. ISSUE PRINT

   f. ISSUE ERASEAUP [WAIT]

   g. ISSUE DISCONNECT

9. 3270-PRINTER LOGICAL UNIT (LUTYPE3)

   a. RECEIVE   INTO(data-area) or SET(pointer-ref)
                  LENGTH(data-area)
                  [ASIS]
                  [BUFFER]

      Exceptional condition: LENGERR

b. SEND   FROM(data-area)
               LENGTH(data-value)
               [DEST(name)]
               [WAIT]
               [STRFIELD or [[ERASE][CTLCHAR(data-value)]]]]
               [INVITE or LAST]
               [DEFRESP]

c. CONVERSE   FROM(data-area)
               FROMLENGTH(data-value)
               [INTO(data-area) or SET(pointer-ref)]
               [TOLENGTH(data-area)]
               [STRFIELD or [[ERASE][CTLCHAR(data-value)]]]]
               [DEST(name)]
               [DEFRESP]

Exceptional condition: LENGERR

d. FREE   [SESSION(name)]

Exceptional conditions: INVREQ, NOTALLOC, SESSIONERR

e. ISSUE PRINT

f. ISSUE ERASEAUP [WAIT]

g. ISSUE DISCONNECT

10. 3270 SCS PRINTER LOGICAL UNIT

a. SEND   FROM(data-area)
               LENGTH(data-value)
               [DEST(name)]
               [WAIT]
               [INCITE or LAST]
               [CNOTCOMPL or DEFRESP]
               [DEFRESP]

b. FREE   [SESSION(name)]

Exceptional conditions: INVREQ, NOTALLOC, SESSIONERR

c. ISSUE DISCONNECT

BASIC MAPPING SUPPORT (BMS)

1. RECEIVE   MAP(name)
               [SET(pointer-ref) or INTO(data-value)]
               [MAPSET(name)]
               [FROM(data-area)LENGTH(data-value) or TERMINAL[ASIS]]

Exceptional conditions: EOC, EODS, INVMPSZ, MAPFAIL, RDATT

2. SEND   MAP(name)
               FROM(data-area) [DATAONLY] or MAPONLY
               [LENGTH(data-value)]
               [MAPSET(name)]
               [FMHPARM]   LUs only
               [REQID(name)]
               [LDC(name)]   LUs only

```
                    [CURSOR[(data-value)]]
                    [SET(pointer-ref) or PAGING or TERMINAL[WAIT]]
                    [ACCUM]
                    [ERASE or ERASEAUP]
                    [PRINT]
                    [FREEKB]
                    [ALARM]
                    [FRSET]
                    [L40 or L64 or L80 or HONEOM]
                    [NLEOM]
                    [LAST]                                      LUs only
      Exceptional conditions:    IGREQCD, IGREQID, INVLDC, INVMPSZ,
                                 INVREQ,
                                 OVERFLOW, RETPAGE, TSIOERR, WRBRK

 3. SEND TEXT       FROM(data-area)
                    LENGTH(data-value)
                    [FMHPARM]                                   LUs only
                    [REQID(name)]
                    [LDC(name)]                                 LUs only
                    [CURSOR[(data-value)]]
                    [SET(pointer-ref) or PAGING or TERMINAL[WAIT]]
                    [HEADER(data-area)]
                    [TRAILER(data-area)]
                    [JUSTIFY(data-value) or JUSTFIRST or JUSTLAST]
                    [ACCUM or NOEDIT]
                    [ERASE]
                    [PRINT]
                    [FREEKB]
                    [ALARM]
                    [L40 or L64 or L80 or HONEOM]
                    [NLEOM]
                    [LAST]                                      LUs only
                    Exceptional conditions:    IGREQCD,  IGREQID,
                                               INVLDC,   INVREQ,
                                               RETPAGE,
                                               TSIOERR, WRBRK

 4. SEND PAGE       [[[TRANSID(name)] or RELEASE] or RETAIN]
                    [TRAILER(data-area)]
                    [FMHPARM(name)]                             LUs only
                    [AUTOPAGE[CURRENT or ALL] or NOAUTOPAGE]
                    [OPERPURGE]
                    [LAST]                                      LUs only
                    Exceptional conditions:    IGREQCD, IGREQID,
                    INVREQ, RETPAGE,
                    TSIOERR, WRBRK

 5. PURGE MESSAGE
      Exceptional conditions:    TSIOERR
```

6. ROUTE   [INTERVAL(hhmmss) or INTERVAL(0) or TIME(hhmmss)]
                 [ERRTERM[(name)]]
                 [TITLE(data-area)]
                 [LIST(data-area)]
                 [OPCLASS(data-area)]
                 [REQID(name)]
                 [LDC(name)]   LUs only
                 [NLEOM]

     Exceptional   conditions: INVERRTERM,   INVLDC,   RTEFAIL, RTESOME

INTERVAL CONTROL

1. ASKTIME

    Updates EIBTIME and EIBDATE

2. DELAY   [INTERVAL(hhmmss) or INTERVAL(0) or TIME(hhmmss)]
                 [REQID(name)]

Exceptional conditions: EXPIRED, INVREQ

3. POST   [INTERVAL(hhmmss) or INTERVAL(0) or TIME(hhmmss)]
                 [SET(pointer-ref)]
                 [REQID(name)]

Exceptional conditions: INVREQ, EXPIRED

4. WAIT EVENT   ECADDR(pointer-value)

5. START   [INTERVAL(hhmmss) or INTERVAL(0) or TIME(hhmmss)]
                 TRANSID(name)
                 [REQID(name)]
                 [FROM(data-area) LENGTH(data-value)[FMH]]
                 [TERMID(name)]
                 [SYSID(name)]
                 [RTRANSID(name)]
                 [RTERMID(name)]
                 [QUEUE(data-area)]
                 [NOCHECK]
                 [PROTECT]

     Exceptional   conditions: IOERR,   INVREQ,   ISCINVREQ,   SYSIDERR, TERMIDERR, TRANSIDERR

6. RETRIEVE   INTO(data-area) or SET(pointer-ref)
                 LENGTH(data-area)
                 [RTRANSID(data-area)]
                 [RTERMID(data-area)]
                 [QUEUE(data-area)]
                 [WAIT]

     Exceptional   conditions: ENDDATA, ENVDEFERR, INVREQ, INVTS-REQ, IOERR, LENGERR, NOTFND

7. CANCEL   [REQID(name)[TRANSID(name)][SYSID(name)]]
     Exceptional conditions: INVREQ, ISCINVREQ, NOTFND, SYSIDERR

TASK CONTROL
1. SUSPEND
2. ENQ or DEQ   RESOURCE(data-area)
                      [LENGTH(data-value)]

    Exceptional conditions: ENQBUSY (ENQ only)

PROGRAM CONTROL
1. LINK   PROGRAM(name)
             [COMMAREA(data-area) LENGTH(data-value)]
    Exceptional conditions: PGMIDERR
2. XCTL   PROGRAM(name)
             [COMMAREA(data-area) LENGTH(data-value)]
    Exceptional conditions: PGMIDERR
3. RETURN   [TRANSID(name) [COMMAREA(data-area)
              LENGTH(data-value)]]
    Exceptional conditions: INVREQ
4. LOAD   PROGRAM(name)
             [SET(pointer-ref)]
             [LENGTH(data-area)]
             [ENTRY(pointer-ref)]
             [HOLD]
    Exceptional conditions: PGMIDERR
5. RELEASE   PROGRAM(name)
    Exceptional conditions: PGMIDERR

STORAGE CONTROL
1. GETMAIN   SET(pointer-ref)
              LENGTH(data-area)
              [INITIMG(data-value)]
              [SHARED]

    Exceptional conditions: NOSTG
2. FREEMAIN   DATA(data-area)

TRANSIENT DATA
1. WRITEQ TD   QUEUE(name)
               FROM(data-area)
               [LENGTH(data-value)]
               [SYSID(name)]
    Exceptional conditions: IOERR, ISCINVREQ, LENGERR, NOSPACE,
                             NOTOPEN,
                             QIDERR, SYSIDERR
2. READQ TD   QUEUE(name)
              SET(pointer-ref) or INTO (data-area)
              [LENGTH(data-area)]
              [SYSID(name)]

Exceptional conditions: IOERR, ISCINVREQ, LENGERR, NOTOPEN, QBUSY(CICS/OS/VS only), QIDERR, QZERO, SYSIDERR

3. DELETEQ TD   QUEUE(name)
                [SYSID(name)]

Exceptional conditions: ISCINVREQ, QIDERR, SYSIDERR

TEMPORARY STORAGE

1. WRITEQ TS   QUEUE(name)
                FROM(data-area)
                LENGTH(data-value)
                [ITEM(data-area) [REWRITE]]
                [SYSID(name)]
                [MAIN or AUXILIARY]

Exceptional conditions: INVREQ, IOERR, ISCINVREQ, ITEMERR, NOSPACE, QIDERR, SYSIDERR

2. READQ TS   QUEUE(name)
                SET(pointer-ref) or INTO(data-area)
                LENGTH(data-value)
                [ITEM(data-value) or NEXT]
                [SYSID(name)]

Exceptional conditions: IOERR, ISCINVREQ, ITEMERR, LENGERR, QIDERR, SYSIDERR

3. DELETEQ TS   QUEUE(name)
                [SYSID(name)]

Exceptional conditions: ISCINVREQ, QIDERR, SYSIDERR

ABNORMAL TERMINATION RECOVERY

1. HANDLE ABEND   PROGRAM(name) or LABEL(label) or CANCEL or RESET

Exceptional conditions: PGMIDERR (if PROGRAM is specified)

2. ABEND   [ABCODE(name)]
           [CANCEL]

TRACE CONTROL

1. ENTER   TRACEID(data-value)
           [FROM(data-area)]
           [ACCOUNT]
           [MONITOR]
           [PERFORM]

2. TRACE ON or OFF
[SYSTEM[BF][BM][DC][DI][FC][IC][IS][JC][KC][PC][SC][SP][TC][TD][TS][UE]]
           [EI]
           [USER]
           [SINGLE]

DUMP CONTROL

1. DUMP   DUMPCODE(name)
              [FROM(data-area)
              LENGTH(data-value)]
              [TASK]
              [STORAGE]
              [PROGRAM]
              [TERMINAL]
              [TABLES]
              [PCT][PPT][SIT][TCT][FCT][DCT]

JOURNAL CONTROL

1. JOURNAL   JFILEID(data-value)
              JTYPEID(data-value)
              FROM(data-area)
              LENGTH(data-value)
              [REQID(data-area)]
              [PREFIX(data-value) PFXLENG(data-value)]
              [STARTIO]
              [WAIT]

   Exceptional conditions: JIDERR, IOERR, LENGERR, NOJBUFSP, NOTOPEN

2. WAIT JOURNAL   JFILEID(data-value)
                    [REQID(data-value)]
                    [STARTIO]

   Exceptional conditions: JIDERR, INVREQ, IOERR, NOTOPEN

SYNC POINT CONTROL

1. SYNCPOINT   [ROLLBACK]

BUILT-IN FUNCTIONS

1. BIF   DEEDIT
          FIELD(data-area)
          LENGTH(data-value)

ANSWERS

Chapter 2 Transaction Flow

1. Describe the general layout of a CICS region and explain the function of each area.

   The CICS region consists of:

   The nucleus which contains the management modules and their respective tables, common system area and common work area. The resident area where resident application programs are kept.

   The dynamic storage area where tasks are processed.

2. Explain a transaction and what it comprises.

   A transaction is a collection of the necessary resources and programs to accomplish a unit of work.

3. A - Explain the function of the terminal control program. The TCP handles communications between the terminals and CICS.
B - What is the purpose of the terminal control table? The TCT consists of TCTTEs which exist for each terminal. The TCTTE contains information about the characteristics of each terminal.
C - State the teleprocessing access methods that are supported. VTAM, TCAM and BTAM.

4. A - Explain the function of the file control program. The FCP handles file requests.
B - State the file access methods that are supported. VSAM, BDAM, ISAM, and DL/I.

5. What is online processing? Online processing is the accepting of information from a terminal, manipulating that information and then sending a message back to the terminal.

Chapter 3 Transaction Processing

1. Indicate the differences between a transaction and task. A task is one iteration of a transaction and is unique by a task sequence number. CICS deals only with tasks. Users work with transactions.

2. A - Describe a reentrant program.
A reentrant program is one that does not modify itself.
B - Why must CICS programs be reentrant?
CICS programs must be reentrant because all tasks share only one copy of each program.

3. A - Explain the function of the task control program.
The KCP manages tasks.
B - What is the purpose of the program control table?
The PCT contains all the transactions known to this version of CICS along with the first program to be called by the transaction and the TWA size.

4. A - Explain the function of the program control program.
The PCP handles XCTLs, LINKs, and RETURNs as well as the loading and unloading of programs.
B - What is the purpose of the processing program table?
The PPT contains the names of all the load modules along with their memory or disk address.

5. Define multitasking.
The ability to process more than one task at a time.

6. What is the EIB?
The EIB contains information from various CICS control blocks saving the application program from referring to these control blocks.

Chapter 4 CICS Essentials

1. Why are resources shared in CICS?
Resources are shared among tasks to reduce storage requirements. This is done by having only one copy of the resource.

2. State the function of a CICS command.

A CICS command allows an application program to make a request of the operating system, an access method, or CICS.

3. What is a dsect?
   A dsect is a convenient way of assigning labels without reserving storage.

4. What is the difference between a HANDLE CONDITION and an IGNORE command?
   A HANDLE CONDITION command creates a go to environment. An IGNORE command does not create a go to environment but instead gives control back at the next sequential instruction following the command causing the condition.

5. Why is addressability important in CICS?
   Addressability is important because all tasks are processed in the DSA and it is very easy to have an invalid address and corrupt another task's storage area.

Chapter 5 Terminal Control

1. Describe the difference between an unformatted and formatted data stream.
   A formatted data stream contains a three-character control field preceding each data field whereas an unformatted data stream does not contain three-character control fields.

2. Why is it preferable not to use the HANDLE AID command?
   It generates additional unnecessary overhead and can cause invalid processing.

3. What is the difference between the INTO and SET options on the RECEIVE command?
   The INTO option moves the information in the TIOA into the reserved area specified and frees the TIOA.
   The SET option simply returns the address of the TIOA.

4. Why is it recommended not to transmit extra characters (i.e., spaces)?
   Transmitting extra characters takes longer and slows down response time.

Chapter 6 Program Control

1. Indicate the difference between a LINK and XCTL command.
   A LINK command creates an additional lower logical level and expects control back.
   A transfer control passes control to another program on the same logical level and does not expect control back.

2. Describe the COMMAREA option on the LINK, XCTL, and RETURN commands.
   The COMMAREA option allows information to be passed to another program or task. The COMMAREA option can pass any area to which it has addressability. The receiving program can only receive the information in the DFHCOMMAREA.

3. Why is pseudo-conversational programming better than conversational programming?
   Pseudo-conversational programming ties up less resources and does not require waiting for a human to respond.

4. State the purpose of the TRANSID option on the RETURN command.
The TRANSID option allows us to state the next transaction to be executed when the operator presses a function key.

5. What is the HANDLE ABEND command used for?
The HANDLE ABEND allows the establishing of an exit so cleanup processing can be done in the event of abnormal task termination.

Chapter 7 Basic Mapping Support

1. Define the function of basic mapping support.
BMS allows the program to be device independent and it translates formatted data streams which enables the program to reference data by symbolic labels.

2. Define a formatted data stream.
A formatted data stream must contain at least an attribute.

3. What is a map and how is it defined?
A map defines a terminal screen indicating the location of fields.
It is defined with the the the following macros: DFHMSD, DFHMDI, DFHMDF.

4. A - What is the difference between the MAPONLY and DATAONLY option of the SEND command?
MAPONLY indicates to send only the default data located in the physical map. DATAONLY indicates to send only the data residing in the application program.
B - What happens if neither is specified?
If MAPONLY and DATAONLY are not specified, the default data is merged with the data in the program and all of it is transmitted to the terminal.

5. What is the difference between the ERASEAUP option on the SEND MAP command and the terminal control command EXEC CICS ERASEAUP END-EXEC?
Both erase all the unprotected fields and sets them to low-values but the SEND MAP command allows attributes to be sent.

6. Describe what happens when the SEND MAP command is executed.
The SEND MAP command inserts the necessary control information and then requests the terminal control program to send the data to the terminal.

7. Describe what happens when the RECEIVE MAP command is executed.
When the RECEIVE MAP command is issued the data in the TIOA is interpreted by BMS and placed in the proper symbolic labels in the program.

8. In what table must mapset names be defined and why?
Mapset names are defined in the PPT because they are considered to be programs.

9. How can the modified data tag (MDT) be turned on and off?
MDT's can be set: at map definition, at task execution, and by the operator.

10. What is symbolic cursor positioning?
Symbolic cursor positioning allows the cursor to be placed in the field desired by simply moving a minus one to the length field.

11. Why is it a good practice to save data beyond task termination?
Saving data can reduce character transmission and help give better response time.

Chapter 8 File Control

1. What is the purpose of the file control table?
   The FCT contains all the characteristics about each dataset.

2. Explain the difference between VSAM exclusive control and CICS exclusive control when reading a record for update.
   VSAM exclusive control locks out a control interval while CICS exclusive control for protected resources locks out a single record.

3. After a record has been rewritten from the Linkage Section, why is it a good idea to move zeros to the BLL cell associated with the record description?
   The area containing the record is automatically freed. Zeroing the BLL cell helps to preserve integrity.

4. What is the function of an UNLOCK command?
   The UNLOCK command releases exclusive control and terminates a MAS-SINSERT operation.

5. Describe three different methods of deleting VSAM records. VSAM records can be deleted by:
   A - A READ/UPDATE command followed by a DELETE command.
   B - A DELETE command with no previous READ/UPDATE command.
   C - A DELETE command with the GENERIC/KEYLENGTH options.

6. Define browsing.
   Browsing is the act of going through a direct access file sequentially.

Chapter 9 Storage Control

1. Define the purpose of the storage control program.
   SCP manages the DSA.

2. Why is the idea of initializing acquired storage not a good idea?
   Initialization is time-consuming and usually once the storage has been acquired, the program moves data to the area.

3. After a FREEMAIN command has been executed, why should zeros be moved to the BLL cell associated with the area?
   Since the area has been freed, the address is no longer valid. This helps to maintain integrity.

Chapter 10 Temporary Storage

1. What is the function of the temporary storage program?
   TSP manages main and auxiliary temporary storage.

2. What is the purpose of the temporary storage table?
   The TST contains the names of the auxiliary queues which are to be recovered in the event of an abend.

3. Describe the difference between main and auxiliary temporary storage.
   Main temporary storage causes no I/O and is not recoverable while auxiliary temporary storage is recoverable but causes I/O.

4. What is a temporary storage queue?
   A queue can contain one or more temporary storage records and is identified by a 1-8 character name.

5. A - What is the function of the ITEM option when adding a temporary storage record?
   ITEM will contain the number of the record just added.
   B - What is the function of the ITEM option when rewriting a temporary storage record?
   It indicates the record to be replaced.
6. What is the difference between the NEXT and ITEM options when reading temporary storage records?
   The NEXT option indicates to read the next available record which may not be the one desired.
   The ITEM option always returns the record desired if it exists.

Chapter 11 Transient Data

1. What is the function of the transient data program?
   TDP handles extra and intrapartition transient data and automatic task initiation.
2. What is the purpose of the destination control table?
   The DCT contains the names of all queues and for automatic task initiation, the trigger level.
3. What is the difference between extrapartition and intrapartition transient data?
   Extrapartition is used to pass information into or out of CICS. Intrapartition is for use within the CICS region.
4. Describe automatic task initiation.
   ATI is the process of initiating a task with no human intervention based on the accumulation of records.
5. Explain the difference between a direct destination and an indirect (alias) destination.
   An indirect destination allows multiple applications to share the same device (i.e., printer).
6. Explain the difference between temporary storage and transient data.
   Temporary storage is for use only within CICS and can't initiate a task.
   Transient data can be used in or outside of CICS and can initiate a task.

Chapter 12 Interval Control

1. What is the function of the interval control program?
   ICP manages all time related functions.
2. What is the purpose of the START command?
   The START command allows the initiating of a task based on time.
3. Describe three ways to initiate a task.
   The operator, transient data, and interval control.
4. What is the function of a POST command?
   The POST command allows CICS to notify our task when a specified period of time has elapsed.
5. Describe a method of controlling response time.
   Through the use of the POST and WAIT commands.